MW00616171

C. S. Lewis on Politics and the Natural Law

Conventional wisdom holds that C. S. Lewis was uninterested in politics and public affairs. The conventional wisdom is wrong. As Justin Buckley Dyer and Micah J. Watson show in this groundbreaking work, Lewis was deeply interested in the fundamental truths and falsehoods about human nature and how these conceptions manifest themselves in the contested and turbulent public square. Ranging from the depths of Lewis' philosophical treatments of epistemology and moral pedagogy to practical considerations of morals legislation and responsible citizenship, this book explores the contours of Lewis' multi-faceted Christian engagement with political philosophy generally and the natural-law tradition in particular. Drawing from the full range of Lewis' corpus and situating his thought in relationship to seminal thinkers both ancient and modern, *C. S. Lewis on Politics and the Natural Law* offers an unprecedented look at politics and political thought from the perspective of one of the twentieth century's most influential writers.

JUSTIN BUCKLEY DYER is associate professor of political science and director of the Kinder Institute on Constitutional Democracy at the University of Missouri. He is the author of *Natural Law and the Antislavery Constitutional Tradition* and *Slavery, Abortion, and the Politics of Constitutional Meaning*. He earned a Ph.D. in government at the University of Texas at Austin and a B.A. and M.P.A. at the University of Oklahoma.

MICAH J. WATSON is 2015–16 William Spoelhof Teacher-Scholar Chair and associate professor of political science at Calvin College. He is the co-editor of *Natural Law and Evangelical Political Thought*. In 2010–11 he was the William E. Simon Fellow in Religion and Public Life at Princeton University. He earned a Ph.D. in politics at Princeton University, and M.A. in Church-State Studies at Baylor University.

C.S. Lewis on Politics and the Natural Law

JUSTIN BUCKLEY DYER

University of Missouri

MICAH J. WATSON

Calvin College

CAMBRIDGE
UNIVERSITY PRESS

CAMBRIDGE
UNIVERSITY PRESS

University Printing House, Cambridge CB2 8BS, United Kingdom

One Liberty Plaza, 20th Floor, New York, NY 10006, USA

477 Williamstown Road, Port Melbourne, VIC 3207, Australia

4843/24, 2nd Floor, Ansari Road, Daryaganj, Delhi - 110002, India

79 Anson Road, #06-04/06, Singapore 079906

Cambridge University Press is part of the University of Cambridge.

It furthers the University's mission by disseminating knowledge in the pursuit of education, learning and research at the highest international levels of excellence.

www.cambridge.org
Information on this title: www.cambridge.org/9781107518971

First published 2016
First paperback edition 2017

A catalogue record for this publication is available from the British Library

Library of Congress Cataloging in Publication data
Names: Dyer, Justin Buckley, 1983- author. | Watson, Micah Joel, 1973- author.
Title: C.S. Lewis on politics and the natural law / Justin Buckley Dyer,
University of Missouri, Columbia; Micah J. Watson,
Calvin College, Michigan.
Description: New York : Cambridge University Press, 2016.
Identifiers: LCCN 2016011207 | ISBN 9781107108240 (Hardback)
Subjects: LCSH: Lewis, C. S. (Clive Staples), 1898-1963–Political and social views. |
Natural law. | Values. | Human rights. | Common good. |
BISAC: POLITICAL SCIENCE / History & Theory.
Classification: LCC PR6023.E926 Z644 2016 |
DDC 823/.912–dc23 LC record available at
https://lccn.loc.gov/2016011207

ISBN 978-1-107-10824-0 Hardback
ISBN 978-1-107-51897-1 Paperback

For our parents

For, above all other spheres of human life, the Devil claims politics for his own, as almost the citadel of his power.
    – C.S. Lewis to Don Giovanni Calabria (August 10, 1953)

Contents

Acknowledgments

Lewis wrote that friendship could be a school of virtue or a school of vice, making good men better and bad men worse. We are grateful for the many friends who have made this book much better than it otherwise would have been. On the business side, we would like to thank Lew Bateman and his editorial team at Cambridge University Press for their working closely with us on this project. We also acknowledge helpful feedback from the anonymous reviewers at the Press. Chapter 2 grew out of an article previously published as "Lewis, Barth, and the Natural Law" in *Journal of Church and State* 57(1): 1–17, the original research for which was supported by a summer fellowship from the H.B. Earhart Foundation. Permission to republish portions of that essay here is gratefully acknowledged. As a co-authored project, we each took somewhat different paths to our joining forces to work on this book. Yet we did have the opportunity to present together various parts of the book, receiving very constructive comments from Paul DeHart and Kody Cooper at a 2014 meeting of the Southwestern Political Science Association and from members of a panel at the 2013 Symposium on Religion and Public Life at the Paul B. Henry Institute of Calvin College. Along the way we also have amassed our own individual debts of gratitude.

I (JBD) thank the many people who provided feedback and encouragement throughout this project. Foremost among them is my co-author for accepting an invitation to join me in this work and for seeing it through to the end. J. Budziszewski, Josh Hawley, Carson Holloway, Nathan Tiemeyer, and Mark Tungesvik each read through and commented on various parts of the manuscript. Several of my colleagues at the University of Missouri took an interest in the topic from the beginning, and I am grateful to Vanya Krieckhaus and John Petrocik for many serious discussions – and some friendly banter – about Lewis, natural law, and moral realism. During the 2014–2015 academic year, I had the privilege of teaching both an undergraduate tutorial and a general community seminar on Lewis' political thought. In different ways the enthusiasm and fresh insight from those two groups sharpened my thinking about the relevance of Lewis' writings to the world of politics. The University of Missouri has been a terrific place to pursue my intellectual interests, and I thank Cooper Drury, Chair of the Political Science Department, and Michael O'Brien, Dean of the College of Arts and Science, for their support.

My wife, Kyle, and our boys, Bennett and Pierce, have been steadfast in their love and encouragement. Kyle and I grew up together, and one of our favorite teachers, Mr. Lowe, first introduced us to Lewis when he made *The Lion, the Witch, and the Wardrobe* mandatory reading in his fifth-grade class. Years later, another of my favorite teachers, Mrs. Moore, gave the students in my high school English class a modest assignment: go to the library, pick out a book, and read it. As I scanned the musty and worn-out books on the shelf that day, the name "C.S. Lewis" on the spine of a book titled *Mere Christianity* caught my eye. I recognized Lewis' name from the Narnia stories and so I chose to read that book. The first chapter of *Mere Christianity*, which is a short meditation on the law of human nature, sparked a life-long intellectual interest in the perennial philosophy of natural law. I am grateful to have a career that allows me to indulge that interest and for the teachers who have guided me along the way. To my mom and dad – my first and best teachers – I dedicate this book.

I (MJW) am grateful to Baylor University's Barry Hankins, Scott Moore, and Ralph Wood, who oversaw my first foray into Lewis studies in an MA thesis in the late 1990s. Robert George and J. Budziszewski have been more than generous in providing feedback and guidance about the natural law and about Lewis. As this project straddled academic seasons at Union University and Calvin College, I'm grateful for the support and input of friends and colleagues at both places. Sean Evans was a particularly supportive Chair and friend. Mark Campbell, Bryan Carrier, Tim Ellsworth, Scott Huelin, Paul Jackson, and Ben Mitchell all encouraged me in various ways with this project. Justin Barnard read over the manuscript and in countless office visits and conversations has shaped my view of Lewis and so many other things. Jesse Covington and Bryan McGraw have been faithful friends in offering constructive criticism and suggestions. My new colleagues at Calvin have been nothing short of wonderful, and I am profoundly grateful to the Van Reken family for supporting the William Spoelhof Teacher-Scholar-in-Residence Chair. I would also be remiss if I did not thank my co-author for inviting me to join him in this endeavor.

While the life of this book project is only a couple of years, the presence of C.S. Lewis has lived with my family for much longer. I cannot quite apologize for that, but I do thank my wife Julie for all the reading, proofreading, and listening she has done, not to mention making possible our life together and the lives that we have been blessed to welcome: Abigail, Anastasia, Annika, Alexandra, and John. God uses you to remind me that there is more life and wonder to this season in the "Shadowlands" than I would have ever realized on my own. Finally, I express my love and gratitude to my mom and my dad, who first introduced me to an imaginary world with talking animals and a majestic Lion. Like Lewis, their greatness lies in their pointing me toward a reality beyond the one I can see, and it is to them that I dedicate this book.

The Apolitical and Political C.S. Lewis

I think especially of those young men of my father's generation who watched their own earlier ethical principles die along with the deaths of their friends in the trenches of the mass murder of Ypres and the Somme; and who returned determined that nothing was ever going to matter to them again and invented the aesthetic triviality of the nineteen-twenties.

– Alasdair MacIntyre, *After Virtue*[1]

Mathematics nearly ended the remarkable career of C.S. Lewis before it began. In April 1916, William Kirkpatrick wrote to Albert Lewis about the future prospects for his eighteen-year-old son. Kirkpatrick was Lewis' tutor and noted that the young Lewis had remarkable literary gifts. He lacked, however, any aptitude in science or math, and this might limit Lewis' options for university. Kirkpatrick suggested a legal career, which would have had Lewis following his father's path.[2]

Lewis nevertheless intended to pursue an academic career, although Kirkpatrick's caveat about mathematics would prove prescient. The future don had applied to one Oxford college, only to be turned down and accepted by another. But before he could commence his studies, Lewis also needed to pass an additional test required university-wide, known as "Responsions," which included an examination on basic mathematics. Despite another tutoring sojourn with Kirkpatrick, Lewis

---

[1] Alisdair MacIntyre, *After Virtue*, 2nd ed. (Notre Dame, IN: Notre Dame University Press, 1984 [1981]), 41.
[2] Alister McGrath, *C.S. Lewis – A Life: Eccentric Genius, Reluctant Prophet* (Carol Stream, IL: Tyndale House, 2013), 44.

realized he was singularly unsuited for algebra and trigonometry. This did not bode well for his future at Oxford.

In addition to Responsions, there was another motivation behind Lewis' cramming with the Great Knock, as Kirkpatrick was known. By 1917 it was inevitable that every eligible young man would be called up for the Great War. Lewis and his father reasoned that an artillery assignment some distance from the lines would be far preferable to an infantry deployment in the trenches. Once again math stood in the way. For understandable reasons, the British military expected their artillery officers to have a rather strong competence in mathematics. Second Lieutenant C.S. Lewis was soon commissioned in the Somerset Light Infantry, where he fought, was wounded, and lost friends in the trenches of northern France.

One consequence of Lewis' military service seems almost trivial amid the broader canvas of the war, but nevertheless was instrumental for Lewis' future career in the academy: After the war Oxford University waived the Responsions entrance requirement for returning soldiers. Lewis' weakness in math, which had threatened an academic career while also putting him at the front lines, would no longer stand in his way.[3] In retrospect, a man with Lewis' literary gifts would still have made a name for himself even without an elite university, yet it is difficult to think of C.S. Lewis without thinking also of Oxford. And there likely would have been no Oxford for Lewis without the war.

On his return to Oxford after his time in the trenches, Lewis wrote to his father about the experience of reconvening with his fellow students – many now veterans of a terrible war – in the Junior Common Room of University College in 1919, and reading the minutes from the last meeting, made some five years prior with nothing to record in the meantime. "I don't know of any little thing that has made me realize the absolute suspension and waste of these years more thoroughly," Lewis reflected.[4] The staggering waste and incomprehensible loss accompanying the Great War shaped the contours of subsequent world events and cast an immense shadow over the turn-of-the-century generation of Britons. This

---

[3] Writing of the exemption, Lewis' brother Warnie wrote, "In this he was fortunate, for I do not believe that at any stage in his career he could have passed an examination of any kind in elementary mathematics: a view with which he himself agreed, when I put it to him many years later." W.H. Lewis, "Memoir of C.S. Lewis," in Warren Lewis, ed., *Letters of C.S. Lewis*, rev. ed. (Orlando, FL: Harcourt, 2003 [1966]), 28.

[4] C.S. Lewis to Albert Lewis (January 27, 1919), in Walter Hooper, ed., *Collected Letters of C.S. Lewis*, vol. 1 (New York: HarperCollins, 2004), 428.

generation of course included Lewis, even as an Irishman, and the war affected his life in even more profound ways than allowing him to escape the clutches of math.

Napoleon observed that we gain insight into a man's psyche by noting what was happening in the world when he was twenty years old. In his recent biography of Lewis, Alistair McGrath comments that Lewis turned twenty only a few weeks after the Great War ended, and thus we might expect to find that his "world of thought and experience would have been irreparably and irreversibly shaped by war, trauma, and loss."[5] McGrath observes that this raises a puzzle for understanding Lewis, since Lewis always downplayed the effects of the war on his life, going so far as to rank their significance below his nightmarish experiences at English boarding schools prior to his happier tutelage under Kirkpatrick. Unlike many of his fellow soldiers – the young men of MacIntyre's father's generation – Lewis went on to become one of the foremost defenders of traditional ethical values and a lifelong critic of aesthetic triviality.[6]

McGrath treats this puzzle with a judicious mixture of historical biography and speculative but careful reconstruction of Lewis' mindset through use of his public and private writings. He concludes that Lewis' seeming dismissal of the importance of the war concealed a psychological strategy to protect himself from being overwhelmed. This distancing of himself from what he had been through was, as Lewis acknowledged in his autobiography, "a treaty with reality, the fixing of a frontier."[7] Still, Lewis' protestations of insignificance notwithstanding, the meaninglessness and carnage of the war played a crucial role in facilitating Lewis' transformation from failed poet to Oxford don, Christian apologist, and one of the most enduring and influential figures of the twentieth century.

As Lewis conceded, he never did fully reckon with his formative war years. Perhaps Lewis' concerted "treaty with reality" explains his conspicuous silence, in his autobiography and elsewhere, about what led to the Great War in the first place: politics. Before all the enlistments and training, the viscera and trauma of the fighting men in the trenches and the resulting physical and spiritual brokenness were political decisions

---

[5] McGrath, *C.S. Lewis – A Life*, 49.

[6] In contrast to the description MacIntyre offers in *After Virtue*, 41. Lewis parodied the malaise of the 1920s in his first postconversion book, *The Pilgrim's Regress: Wade Annotated Edition*, ed. David C. Downing (Grand Rapids, MI: Wm. B. Eerdmans, 2014 [1933]), 45.

[7] McGrath, *C.S. Lewis – A Life*, 51; C.S. Lewis, *Surprised by Joy: The Shape of My Early Life* (Orlando, FL: Harcourt, 1996 [1955]), 158.

and counterdecisions made by European politicians and their civil servants and military officers. All the elements of politics are present in any consideration of the First World War: power, authority, scarcity, (in)justice, (in)security, and a tragic failure to promote and protect a vision of the common good.

One might expect some mention of these elements, if only a sardonic line or two, from a profoundly reflective man who fought and was wounded in the war. But Lewis is quiet about the politics of the time even in his mature reflections, and if the conventional wisdom about Lewis' subsequent career is correct, he remained quiet about politics for the rest of his life.[8] We should not be surprised, then, given the conventional wisdom, that there is very little scholarly treatment of Lewis' political thought, despite an ever-growing literature on all things Lewis.[9]

Yet the conventional wisdom about Lewis and politics is mistaken, wrong in its understanding of Lewis and his works, and also in its reliance on a truncated view of what counts as genuinely "political." Not only was Lewis keenly interested in politics, but he also wrote a great deal about the subject. As we suggest in this book, students of Lewis and politics alike would do well to reconsider this towering twentieth-century figure from the unconventional disciplinary angle of political theory. In subsequent chapters we recover, historically situate, and describe Lewis' political thought and its application. The burden, at the outset, is to establish Lewis' credentials as a political thinker, even if an unconventional one, who is worthy of a volume dedicated to his political thought. This means first overturning the conventional wisdom that Lewis eschewed politics and political thinking.

THE APOLITICAL C.S. LEWIS?

Establishing Lewis' status as an interesting and insightful political thinker is something of a challenge, as it must overcome the testimony of some of Lewis' closest friends and even Lewis himself. The evidence for Lewis'

---

[8] Lewis remained quiet about politics, though not uninvolved, if this speculation from Harry Lee Poe is correct. Poe has uncovered evidence that suggests Lewis may have acted on behalf of the British government during World War II. See Harry Lee Poe, "C.S. Lewis Was a Secret Government Agent." Christianitytoday.com, Dec. 10, 2015, www.christianitytoday .com/ct/2015/december-web-only/cs-lewis-secret-agent.html (accessed Dec. 10, 2015).

[9] For a comprehensive overview of the secondary literature on Lewis as well as a critical analysis of the growing Lewis hagiography, see Samuel Joeckel, *The C.S. Lewis Phenomenon: Christianity and the Public Sphere* (Macon, GA: Mercer University Press, 2013).

disdain for and ignorance of day-to-day politics is not hard to come by. "Jack was not interested in politics," writes Lewis' stepson, Douglas Gresham.[10] Warnie Lewis, noting his brother's reputation for having "contempt for politics and politicians," explains that the household conversation in their childhood was dominated by a rather one-sided "torrent of grumble and vituperation" about Irish politics such that Lewis simply equated adult conversation with politics.

The Lewis brothers' early stories of Animal-land and Boxen were replete with talking animals and dealt with mundane political intrigues and maneuvers. The twelve-year-old Lewis even wrote two novels that "revolved entirely around politics." Warnie Lewis concluded that the early, stifling emphasis on politics in the Lewis home led to the "long-term result" of a "disgust and revulsion from the very idea of politics before he was out of his teens." In an earlier biography of Lewis, George Sayer noted that the subject matter of Boxen was "military and political, aspects of life in which the adult Lewis showed no interest whatsoever."[11] Lewis' friend Chad Walsh, author of *C.S. Lewis: Apostle to the Skeptics*, wrote in that first book about Lewis that despite Lewis' brilliance, "for a Christian social philosophy one turns to Maritain, Niebuhr, Berdyaev, George MacLeod and many others – not to C.S. Lewis."[12]

The evidence from Lewis himself is extensive, though three short examples will suffice. In a letter to Warnie, Lewis mentions an argument he had with Owen Barfield about the extent to which a Christian should feel concerned about far-off foreign affairs; in this case the subject was the Soviet incursion into Finland and the Mannerheim line.[13] Lewis' commentary captures both his awareness of political matters and his frustration with how politics (and economics) have changed: "[T]he world, as it is now becoming and has partly become, is simply *too much for* people of the old square-rigged type like you and me. I don't understand its economics, or its politics, or any dam' thing about it."

The claim about Lewis' hostility toward politicians is well grounded, though even Lewis recognized that his antipathy to politicians might have been overwrought. Sixteen years after his 1940 letter to Warnie, Lewis

---

[10] Douglas Gresham, *Jack's Life: The Life Story of C.S. Lewis* (Nashville, TN: B&H Books, 2005), 28.

[11] George Sayer, *Jack: A Life of C.S. Lewis* (Wheaton, IL: Crossway, 2005), 50.

[12] Chad Walsh, *C.S. Lewis: Apostle to the Skeptics* (New York: Macmillan, 1949), 160, cited in Gilbert Meilander, *The Social and Ethical Thought of C.S. Lewis* (Grand Rapids, MI: Eerdmans, 1947), 1.

[13] Lewis, *Collected Letters*, vol. 2, p. 350.

offered high praise to Chad Walsh's *Behold the Glory*, noting that the bit he needed most was Walsh's defense of politicians. Walsh had likened politicians to physicians, most of whom do the best they can given the materials they have. Some are stupid, others wicked, but this does not distinguish them as a class from any other class of human beings, and many do attempt to do some good in a limited, earthly way.[14] Lewis conceded it was a message he needed to hear.

A final example: Six days before he died in November 1963, Lewis responded to a Mrs. Frank Jones, noting that "Our papers at the moment are filled with nothing but politics, a subject in which I cannot take any interest." Immediately after declaring his indifference to politics, Lewis went on to lament the inevitability of a forthcoming and likely long-serving Labour government, though the "regimentation, austerity, and meddling" that accompany that party would be mitigated by the death of Sir Stafford Cripps, the "late nursery governess of England." In these snippets and anecdotes, Lewis proclaims both ignorance of and hostility toward politics, though as we shall see it is a paradoxically well-informed ignorance and a moth-drawn-to-the-flame hostility.

Other biographical details have become part of the conventional portrayal of the apolitical Lewis. In the early 1950s Lewis famously declined an invitation from Winston Churchill to become a Commander of the British Empire.[15] He once wrote to his brother than he "loathed great issues" and would prefer to see a "Stagnation party – which at General Elections would boast that during its term of office *no* event of the least importance had taken place."[16] Lewis famously claimed to avoid newspapers, and to the end of his life expressed skepticism and at times even despair about politics.[17] Several commentators insist on Lewis' "fatuous

---

[14] Lewis, *Collected Letters*, vol. 3, p. 713.

[15] Lewis, *Collected Letters*, vol. 3, p. 147. His reasoning here was that this award might give ammunition to those who would dismiss his work as merely political, and conservatively political at that.

[16] Lewis, *Collected Letters*, vol. 2, pp. 368–369.

[17] In a 1959 letter to the American newspaper editor Dan Tucker, Lewis wrote despondently, "A hundred years ago we all thought that Democracy was it. Neither you nor I probably think so now. It neither allows the ordinary man to control legislation nor qualifies him to do so. The real questions are settled in secret and the newspapers keep us occupied with largely imaginary issues. And this is all the easier because democracy always in the end destroys education. It did so for you sometime ago and is now doing so for us (see a speech of Screwtape's wh. will soon appear in the *Sat. Evening Post*). I am, you see, at my wit's end on such matters." Lewis, *Collected Letters*, vol. 3, p. 1105. A few years later, in 1962, Lewis wrote to the author and playwright J.B. Priestly: "I doubt if

ignorance of politics," citing for support Warnie's anecdote about how Lewis once mistook Yugoslavia's Marshall Tito for the King of Greece.[18]

Lewis himself, those close to him, and more distant observers seem to present several compelling reasons *not* to write a book on Lewis' political thought. There are several claims to be teased out here. One is that Lewis disliked politics. Another is that he was uninterested in politics and, therefore, third, that he was ignorant about political matters. One can conclude from these mixed claims what we have called the conventional wisdom about Lewis and politics, namely, that he doesn't have much to say and what he does say is not particularly interesting.

It is undeniable and unsurprising that Lewis held many politicians in disdain and was pessimistic about the potential for political solutions to live up to their advertising. Nevertheless, the conventional claims about the apolitical Lewis are overstated. We know from Lewis' personal letters, his education and teaching, and his published works that he was both very interested in and knowledgeable about politics and political thought. Of course, for our purposes, much depends on how one defines "politics." It is true that Lewis was not actively involved in partisan politics and took little interest in transitory policy questions. But politics in the fullest sense means more than parliamentary intrigue and debates about taxes and tariffs. In reality, Lewis did have much to say about the underlying foundations of a just political order. Though he may not have been interested in contemporaneous political maneuvering, he was, as John West notes, always interested in identifying the "permanent in the political."[19]

While we do not intend to provide a full biographical treatment of Lewis in this work, we have already offered some biographical evidence that Lewis was in fact deeply interested in political matters. The

---

I am a Tory. I am much more nearly a political sceptic." Lewis, *Collected Letters*, vol. 3, p. 1371.

[18] See, for example, Christopher Ricks, "Dabblers in Ink and Self-Admiration," *New York Times* (April 8, 1979), www.nytimes.com/books/01/02/11/specials/tolkien-carpenter .html, and Joseph Sobran, "The Prophetic C.S. Lewis," *The Imaginative Conservative* (May 13, 2012), www.theimaginativeconservative.org/2012/03/prophetic-cs-lewis.html. For Warnie's recollection, see Clyde Kilby and Marjorie Lamp Mead, eds., *Brothers and Friends: The Diaries of Major Warren Hamilton Lewis* (New York: Ballantine Books, 1988), 236.

[19] John G. West, "Finding the Permanent in the Political: C.S. Lewis as a Political Thinker," in Andrew A. Tadie and Michael H. Macdonald, eds., *Permanent Things: Toward the Recovery of a More Human Scale at the End of the Twentieth Century* (Grand Rapids, MI: Wm. B. Eerdmans, 1996). Available at www.discovery.org/a/457.

Great War couldn't help but have had an enormous influence on Lewis, and, as we have seen, his childhood in politically turbulent Ireland was dominated by the unceasing political interests of his father.[20] We also note that Lewis' interest in politics and an antipathy toward politics and politicians are not necessarily mutually exclusive, but more likely reinforcing.

Nor was Lewis as ignorant of even partisan or mundane political matters as he is sometimes made out to be. While he may have mistook Marshall Tito for the King of Greece, his personal letters include more informed references to British elections,[21] international summits,[22] various political figures,[23] racism and democracy,[24] unions,[25] communist advances in China and Hungary,[26] Joseph McCarthy and American party politics,[27] the Cuban Missile Crisis,[28] and capital punishment.[29] Lewis should not be mistaken for a policy wonk or an expert in the minutiae of elections or international relations, but neither was he ignorant or apathetic about politics, as he is often made out to be.

Lewis' education was also more deeply steeped in politics and political thought than is appreciated. His interest in literature, learning, and politics began at an early age. His father was a lawyer almost obsessed with political matters and his mother a teacher who encouraged him to study logic. Flora Lewis worried about his health and consequently – as we've noted – Lewis and his brother spent most of their days inside reading and creating mythical, and political, stories of fantastic lands and talking animals.[30] Lewis kept a diary as a child, and by the age of ten not only had he recorded his observations from his reading of *Paradise Lost* by John Milton, he had written an essay called "Home Rule" about the future relationship between Ireland and the British crown.[31] Prior to his

---

[20] Adam Barkman, *C.S. Lewis and Philosophy as a Way of Life* (Allentown, PA: Zossima Press, 2009), 419. And we have not even mentioned the role it played in introducing Lewis to the Moore family, a set of relationships that would bear heavily in Lewis' life until the passing of Mrs. Moore in 1951.

[21] Lewis, *Collected Letters*, vol. 3, p. 62.   [22] Ibid., 382.

[23] The index to Lewis' *Collected Letters* contains several entries for major contemporaneous political figures such as Queen Elizabeth II, General Douglas MacArthur, Winston Churchill, and Dwight Eisenhower.

[24] Lewis, *Collected Letters*, vol. 3, p. 618.   [25] Ibid., 1314.

[26] Ibid., 183 and 806, respectively.   [27] Ibid., 528–529 and 219, respectively.

[28] Ibid., 1392–1393.   [29] Ibid., 246–247 and 1299–1300.   [30] Sayer, *Jack*, 46–52.

[31] Barkman, *C.S. Lewis and Philosophy*, 444; Lewis, "Home Rule," in *The Lewis Papers: Memories of the Lewis Family, 1850–1930*, vol. 6, ed. Warren Lewis, 112–113.

entrance to University College of Oxford, Lewis had read the classics of English literature and mastered French, Italian, and Greek.[32]

Although by any account Lewis possessed an impressive intellect, his early education that continued under Kirkpatrick and culminated at Oxford gave him a unique knowledge base from which to consider a host of academic subjects, including political thought. While at Oxford, Lewis earned three first-class honors degrees. Honor Moderations concentrated on the Greek and Latin classics. "Greats" included Roman History, translation of Plato and Aristotle, ancient history, Greek and Latin prose, logic, and moral and political philosophy. Lewis earned his third degree in a relatively new subject at the time, English, which included Anglo-Saxon. Both Cambridge and Oxford award their degrees by class: first, second, and third. Though first-class degrees were (and are) rare, Lewis earned three first-class degrees in Honors Moderations, Greats, and English.[33] This suited him very well for both philosophy and literature, and his first university position was as a lecturer in philosophy.

As a student and a teacher, Lewis read, wrote, and taught about many of the great political philosophers in the Western canon. As Adam Barkman points out in a note about Lewis' early essay "On Bolshevism," we know that Lewis was teaching his political science students about Lenin as late as 1939 and that even as a literary scholar Lewis continued to teach his students in history, English, and political science the canon of Western political thought beginning with Plato.[34] "While teaching English literature at Magdalen," A.J.P. Taylor wrote, "Lewis helped in the history school by teaching political theory. He took the history students. His lectures covered Rousseau and Aristotle, et al. He loved doing this."[35]

Lewis was steeped in the classics of the Western tradition. With an education hard to imagine today, Lewis could appreciate the intellectual

---

[32] Sayer, *Jack*, 94. Lewis confessed to his friend George Sayer that he often found himself "thinking" in Greek.

[33] Jeffrey D. Schultz and John G. West Jr., *The C.S. Lewis Readers' Encyclopedia* (Grand Rapids, MI: Zondervan Publishing House, 1998), 33–34.

[34] Barkman, *C.S. Lewis and Philosophy*, 158.

[35] Ibid., 447, citing A.J.P Taylor, "The Fun of the Thing," in *In Search of C.S. Lewis*, ed. Stephen Schofield, 117–122 (South Plainfield, NJ: Bridge, 1983), 118. See also Barkman's valuable discussion of Lewis's two sets of lectures, "The Good – Its Place among the Values" and "The Moral Good – Its Place among the Values." See Barkman, *C.S. Lewis and Philosophy*, 329–348. Lewis' notes on Locke, Hume, Berkeley, and other figures are extant, many of which are housed at the Marion E. Wade Center at Wheaton College or the rare books collection at the Davis Library at the University of North Carolina – Chapel Hill.

and philosophical transitions that had transpired from Plato to Locke to the contemporary theorists of his own day in the mid-twentieth century. With his background in the ancient Greeks as well as the Scholastics and early modern thinkers, Lewis was well versed in philosophy and ethics and political thought, including natural-law theory, virtue ethics, and consequentialism. His interests in world mythologies also gave him a breadth of perspective that transcended a purely Western or parochial focus.[36]

Lewis not only appreciated the classical and medieval authors in a sense that might well be impossible today, but he also saw himself as uniquely qualified to translate older thought for modern use. In his inaugural address after his appointment to Cambridge University, Lewis compared himself to a dinosaur because he was one of the last of a dying breed of students of the classics who could read them as a native.[37] Yet Lewis was also a product of the modern age, perhaps more so than he recognized. As we demonstrate in subsequent chapters, he ultimately subscribed to a Lockean form of social contract democracy, tempered by Millian concerns about social conformity, just one example of Lewis' affinity with modernity.[38] Lewis straddled the fault lines between modernity and antiquity in such a way as to allow him to comment intelligibly on both.

We are left with a puzzle at this point. Lewis' brother, his stepson, Lewis himself, and several friends and former students tell us that he both despised politics and had little interest or knowledge of the subject. Yet his letters, his education, and his teaching tell a different story. In assessing these claims about Lewis' supposed ignorance of political matters, much depends on what we mean by "politics." If we accept the definition of politics as the negative domain of sausage-making legislative deals, bureaucratic and institutional power structures, and the seemingly constant state of electoral campaigning, then we will not find much political thought from Lewis. We grant that Lewis disdained

---

[36] See, for example, the appendix to *Abolition of Man*.

[37] C.S. Lewis "*De Descriptione Temporum*," in *Selected Literary Essays* (Cambridge: Cambridge University Press, 1969), 13–14.

[38] Lewis' self-identification with democracy is found in his essay "Equality," in *Present Concerns* (San Diego, CA: Harcourt Brace Jovanovich, 1986), 17–20. His simple description of what the social contract should mean is found in his essay "Delinquents in the Snow," in Walter Hooper, ed., *God in the Dock* (Grand Rapids, MI: Wm. B. Eerdmans, 1970), 306–310.

this side of politics, at one point referring to government in a private letter as "at best a necessary evil."[39]

There are good reasons, however, to think of politics as more than the merely instrumental hurly-burly maelstrom of self-interest and cynicism we see on the news and blogs. The word "politics" comes to us from the Greeks, whom, as we have seen, Lewis knew and read intimately. In the Aristotelian sense, politics refers to the business of the *polis*, the almost-untranslatable Greek word describing a comprehensive community, which combined spheres and identities we moderns tend to keep separate: religion, government, family, school, and business. The *polis*, Aristotle tells us, is established and maintained with a view to some good.[40] As a result, political life implicates perennial questions that pertain to human beings *as* human beings. What is the good life? How should we live together? What things are so good as to be required, by force if necessary, and what things are so evil as to be prohibited, by force if necessary? Do human beings have a deeper purpose than mere survival or pleasure? Conceived of in this way, politics is inextricably tied to the most fundamental questions about human nature and purpose.[41]

Lewis spent his life wrestling with those fundamental questions, and drew on his considerable gifts and his faith in attempting to provide answers to them. When we think of politics in a more comprehensive way, we see that Lewis' writings brim with political themes. Screwtape delivers an address on politics and democratic education.[42] The Chronicles of Narnia describe an original state of nature and the founding of a new polity, not to mention the adventures and misadventures of several monarchs and tyrants, all of whom exercise power for good or ill. Lewis' favorite of his own books, *Till We Have Faces*, is told entirely from the first-person perspective of Orual, a queen responsible for the well-being of her people.[43] *Mere Christianity*, first as a radio address over the BBC and then later as the best-selling book, includes a chapter on social morality.[44]

---

[39] C.S. Lewis to Mrs. Edward A. Allen (February 1, 1958), in Lewis, ed., *Letters of C.S. Lewis*, 473.

[40] Aristotle, *Politics*, 1252a.

[41] See Strauss' "What Is Political Philosophy?," in Leo Strauss, *What Is Political Philosophy? And Other Studies* (Chicago, IL: University of Chicago Press, 1988).

[42] "Screwtape Proposes a Toast," in *C.S. Lewis: Essay Collection and Other Short Pieces*, ed. Lesley Walmsley (London: HarperCollins, 2000).

[43] Lewis, *Collected Letters*, vol. 3, p. 1148. We are grateful to John G. West for the observation about Orual's political standing to a young graduate student (Watson) in a personal email in the late 1990s.

[44] Lewis, *Mere Christianity* (New York: HarperCollins, 2001 [1952]), 82–87.

Lewis' *The Four Loves* opens with a discussion of patriotism, and his massive volume on English literature in the sixteenth century includes several passages offering sophisticated treatments of various political thinkers and themes.[45] Lewis' *Abolition of Man*, about which we have much to say in Chapter 3, deals explicitly with education and natural law.[46] *Abolition*'s themes are then presented in fictional form in the third of Lewis' Space Trilogy, *That Hideous Strength*.[47] This short and incomplete listing does not even include the scores of essays and newspaper articles[48] that address such topics as equality,[49] criminal justice,[50] capital punishment,[51] pacifism,[52] nuclear war,[53] unalienable rights,[54] social contract theory,[55] Christian political parties,[56] and the welfare state.[57] The conventional wisdom about Lewis' interest in and aptitude for politics and political thinking, in a broad sense, is simply mistaken.[58]

---

[45] C.S. Lewis, *The Four Loves*, in *C.S. Lewis: The Inspirational Writings* (New York: Inspirational Press, 1994), 224–228; C.S. Lewis, *English Literature in the Sixteenth Century, Excluding Drama: The Completion of the Clark Lectures* (Oxford: Clarendon Press, 1954).

[46] C.S. Lewis, *The Abolition of Man* (New York: HarperCollins, 2001 [1944]).

[47] C.S. Lewis, *That Hideous Strength: A Modern Fairy-tale for Grown Ups* (New York: Scribner, 2003 [1945]).

[48] C.S. Lewis, *Present Concerns* (San Diego, CA: Harcourt Brace Jovanovich, 1986.)

[49] Lewis, "Equality," in ibid., 17–20.

[50] C.S. Lewis, "The Humanitarian Theory of Punishment," in *God in the Dock*, 287–300.

[51] Lewis, "Capital Punishment and Death Penalty," in ibid., 339–340; Lewis, *Collected Letters*, vol. 3, pp. 246–247.

[52] Lewis, "Why I Am Not a Pacifist," in *The Weight of Glory: And Other Addresses*, ed. Walter Hooper (New York: Harper Collins, 2001).

[53] Lewis, "On Living in an Atomic Age," in *Present Concerns*, 73–80.

[54] Lewis, "We Have No Right to Happiness," in *God in the Dock*, 317–322.

[55] Lewis, "Delinquents in the Snow," in *God in the Dock*, 306–310.

[56] Lewis, "Meditation on the Third Commandment," in *God in the Dock*, 196–199.

[57] Lewis, "Is Progress Possible?," in *God in the Dock*, 311–316.

[58] We agree, then, with several scholars who have made treated Lewis' political thought as worthy of attention. See, for example, John G. West, "Finding the Permanent in the Political: C.S. Lewis as a Political Thinker," in *Permanent Things: Toward the Recovery of a More Human Scale at the End of the Twentieth Century*, ed. Andrew Tadie and Michael Macdonald (Grand Rapids, MI: Eerdmans, 1995), 137–50; Judith Wolf, "On Power," in *The Cambridge Companion to C.S. Lewis*, eds. Robert MacSwain and Michael Ward (Cambridge: Cambridge University Press, 2010), 174–188; Stanley Hauerwas, "On Violence," in *The Cambridge Companion to C.S. Lewis*, 189–202; Gilbert Meilander, *The Taste for the Other: The Social and Ethical Thought of C.S. Lewis* (Grand Rapids, MI: Eerdmans, 1980); David J. Theroux "C.S. Lewis on Mere Liberty and the Evils of Statism." Independent.org, August 23, 2010. www.independent.org/newsroom/article.asp?id=2846 (accessed November 22, 2015); and Adam Barkman, *C.S. Lewis and Philosophy*, 417–495.

Nevertheless, illustrating that the conventional wisdom falls short does not provide a positive case for why we should consider what Lewis had to say about politics. In one sense, of course, making that case is the burden of the chapters that follow. We have suggested that Lewis' fluency in ancient, medieval, and modern thinking is reason enough to warrant a study of his political thought in its own right. As Barkman insists, Lewis is a "valuable voice for the enduring relevance of Old Western Culture, and as such ought to be given more consideration by socio-political philosophers."[59] An additional motive for studying Lewis' political thought is found in his enduring popularity and influence, particularly among American evangelical Christians. In a 1973 article commemorating the tenth anniversary of Lewis' death, the evangelical writer Calvin Linton acknowledged: "Lewis has altered our sensibility, the *way* we think about things; he has given us words and phrases by which we grasp vital ideas; he has given us a pattern of feeling within which we better comprehend artistic and Christian truths."[60]

Today Lewis retains a devoted readership, and C.S. Lewis scholarship shows no sign of abating. It is arguable that C.S. Lewis has had a greater impact on Christians in the last hundred years than any other writer. In the introduction to the *C.S. Lewis Readers' Encyclopedia*, first published in 1998, Christopher W. Mitchell, of the Marion E. Wade Center at Wheaton College, writes of Lewis:

Thirty-five years after his death, C.S. Lewis remains one of the most enduring and often-quoted writers in England and America, and one of the very few writers of his time who has never gone out of print. Lewis was already a best-selling author by 1942 and in 1947 was heralded as "one of the most influential spokesmen for Christianity in the English-speaking world" by *Time* magazine, which featured his picture on the front cover. In 1963, the year of Lewis' death, distinguished poet and teacher Chad Walsh measured the impact of Lewis on American religious thinking as something rarely, if ever, "equaled by any other modern writer."[61]

Dubbed the "apostle to the skeptics" by Chad Walsh, Lewis first broke into the public eye with *The Screwtape Letters* in 1943. By 1947 Lewis had sold over one million copies of his books, spoken on twenty-nine

---

[59] Barkman, *C.S. Lewis and Philosophy*, 418.

[60] Calvin Linton, "C.S. Lewis Ten Years Later," *Christianity Today* (November 9, 1973) **28** (3): 4. Given the surge in evangelical political participation beginning in the 1970s, Lewis' influence on evangelicals is all the more politically significant. On evangelical participation in American politics generally, see Jon A. Shields, *The Democratic Virtues of the Christian Right* (Princeton, NJ: Princeton University Press, 2009).

[61] Schultz and West, *C.S. Lewis Readers' Encyclopedia*, 7.

radio broadcasts to audiences averaging 600,000 listeners, and appeared on the cover of *Time* magazine. *Mere Christianity* still ranks in the top ten of religious books sold each year, and in a 1990s poll conducted by evangelical mainstay *Christianity Today* readers voted it the "most influential book" (other than the Bible). Votes for *Mere Christianity* doubled the number of votes for such classics as *Pilgrim's Progress, My Utmost for His Highest,* and *The Cost of Discipleship.*[62] In 2000 *Mere Christianity* topped the magazine's Books of the Century list, and in 2006 the editors compiled the fifty most influential books for evangelical Christians, ranking Lewis' *Mere Christianity* third.[63] The annual sales of his books continue to number several hundred thousand, if not more.[64] Certainly Lewis' contributions in diverse literary genres account for some of his following, in addition to his ability to communicate to the everyday reader.

The student of politics and of society generally, then, should be interested in Lewis if for no other reason than that Lewis has had an enormous impact on the thinking of hundreds of thousands of people in several countries and across the several decades since his death. It is impossible, in particular, to fully understand evangelicals and evangelical thought without understanding C.S. Lewis. Ultimately, however, we think Lewis worth studying because he incisively identified and winsomely addressed eternal realities and lasting earthly concerns. In the chapters that follow, we elucidate the major themes of Lewis' approach to political philosophy and connect them back to what Lewis called the "permanent things."

In Chapter 2 we describe the underlying philosophical commitments that ground Lewis' thought. Walter Hooper described Lewis as the "most thoroughly converted man" he had ever met. Lewis' commitment to a

---

[62] Scott Burson and Jeffrey L. Walls, *C.S. Lewis and Francis Shaeffer: Lessons for a New Century from the Most Influential Apologists of Our Time* (Downers Grove, IL: Intervarsity Press, 1998), 13.

[63] "The Top 50 Books That Have Shaped Evangelicals," *Christianity Today* (October 6, 2006), www.christianitytoday.com/ct/2006/october/23.51.html. *Mere Christianity* was beat out by Donald McGavran's *Understanding Church Growth* and Rosalind Rinker's *Prayer: Conversing with God.* This ordering suggests a slight difference between *Christianity Today*'s editors and its readership.

[64] It is hard to precisely estimate Lewis' annual book sales, given several different publishers. See Sarah Pulliam Bailey, "C.S. Lewis Still Inspires 50 Years after His Death," Religion News Service (November 22, 2013), reprinted at www.huffingtonpost.com/2013/11/22/cs-lewis-50-year-death_n_4325358.html. As one indication of Lewis' enduring popularity, Bailey notes that HarperOne has sold close to 10 million copies of Lewis' non-Narnia books in its C.S. Lewis Signature Classics series since 2001.

rigorous and uncompromising Christianity was the common thread that united Lewis' world and the remarkable variety of literary works that he produced. Among Lewis' core beliefs were certain commitments about the sort of world we find ourselves in. Following long-standing tenets of Christian theology and tradition, Lewis believed in a *created* world that nevertheless had *fallen*. Sparring with rival descriptions that reject the intelligibility of creation and sin, Lewis insisted on the superiority of the Christian approach and defended the role of reason as a legitimate means of pursuing truth about ourselves and the world. Lewis' conception of human reason provides the foundation for his strong commitment to natural law, what he referred to as the Tao, and this natural-law thinking had profound consequences for his political thought.

Whereas creation and the fall are standard Christian doctrines, the efficacy of human reason has been and remains hotly contested. In Chapter 3 we contrast two very different responses to Nazi ideology and the challenge of the Second World War. Swiss theologian Karl Barth vociferously attacked natural theology and natural law, finding in these notions an almost blasphemous rejection of the one true revelation of God in the specific person and testimony of Jesus Christ. Christian proponents of natural law, Barth averred, crossed over into heresy, not only inviting theological and political monstrosities such as Nazi Germany, but also aligning themselves with the anti-Christ. Lewis disagreed, to say the least, and he polemically attacked what he understood to be the consequences of a "Barthianism" that would collapse any understanding of morality into power-worship. Both thinkers saw natural law as integral to understanding modernity and its liabilities, though their views of natural law's role in God's creation were (and are) irreconcilable.

Making a case for natural law's practical importance is not, however, the same as laying out a historical understanding of the claims of the natural-law tradition and its modern critics. In Chapter 4 we describe Lewis' treatment of the sixteenth-century origins of modernity and, in particular, the antiteleological revolution precipitated by Machiavelli, Hobbes, and Bacon, furthered by Rousseau and Hegel, and applied to the practical education of young British schoolchildren by the emotivism of modern language theorists. Lewis was alarmed by the prospect that these theories would work their way into the schools and broader culture, vitiating the moral training necessary for the cultivation of good men and women. Contrary to the heirs of Hobbes, Lewis believed in an objective moral reality, discoverable by human reason and applicable to human character and behavior. Lewis' straightforward apologetic defense of natural law, *The Abolition of Man*, and his fictional portrayal of the same arguments in the capstone of his Space Trilogy, *That Hideous Strength*, offer a trenchant and creative critique of how this stream of modern thought will obliterate humanity's notion of the good and the very concept of what it means to be human.

In Chapters 5 and 6 we turn from Lewis' critiques to a portrayal of Lewis' more practical and positive political thought. Given Lewis' affinity for natural-law theory and ancient Greek philosophy, why didn't Lewis advocate for a return to a more traditional and hierarchical conception of politics? We argue that while Lewis stoutly rejected the Hobbes–Rousseau–Hegel trajectory, his politics nevertheless reflect a close affinity with the thought of English philosopher and fellow Oxonian John Locke. Lewis affirmed something like Locke's social contract theory, and he shared Locke's aversion to theocracy and his commitment to a theistically grounded natural law and a limited government. Perhaps surprisingly for some of his devoted followers, however, Lewis' distrust of government's ability to promote virtue led him to some counterintuitive conclusions about the inefficacy and impropriety of some "morals" legislation. In Chapter 6 we describe Lewis' reliance on a version of John Stuart Mill's harm principle as it applies to matters of sex, marriage, and religion in society. We conclude that chapter by describing how Lewis thought Christians should arrive at their moral and political beliefs, and what they might do to responsibly advocate for those positions in the public sphere.

In the conclusion we return to Lewis's *Abolition of Man* as the lynchpin for understanding all of his work, and in particular his political thought. We assess the legacy of his straightforward rational approach to defending the moral law by detailing the imaginative portrayal he left us in his Space Trilogy and the Chronicles of Narnia. The former series depicts in vivid and at times horrifying detail the consequences for human beings rejecting the truth about what sort of creatures they are and what they are meant to be. The Chronicles are Lewis' contribution to the all-important task of moral education, providing positive examples through children's literature of the enduring norms that make human flourishing possible.

For Lewis, the stakes could not be higher. All political communities aim at a good, as Aristotle tells us in the beginning of his *Politics*, and despite initial appearances Lewis cared a great deal about political life precisely because of the role it plays in helping or hindering human beings in realizing their telos, or their good. We have suggested that politics is at root about a conception of the good life and how we are to live together with our neighbors. "It is a serious thing," Lewis wrote in a sermon,

to live in a society of possible gods and goddesses ... to remember that the dullest and most uninteresting person you can talk to may one day be a creature which, if you saw it now, you would be strongly tempted to worship, or else a horror and a corruption such as you now meet, if at all, only in a nightmare. All day long we are, in some degree, helping each other to one or the other of these destinations. It is in the light of these overwhelming possibilities, it is with the awe and the circumspection proper to them, that we should conduct all our dealings with one another, all friendships, all loves, all play, all politics.[65]

We begin our dealings with Lewis' politics, then, by delving into the bedrock of Lewis' philosophical and theological convictions regarding the foundational doctrines of creation and the fall, and the viability and limits of human reason.

---

[65] C.S. Lewis, "The Weight of Glory," in *The Weight of Glory*, 45–46.

2

Creation, Fall, and Human Nature

> Those who refuse to accept design do so because they think the world-story
> at least as intelligible without it as with it. This opinion is very commonly
> associated with a conception of the universe according to which the laws of
> matter and energy are sufficient to explain, not only all that is, but all that
> has been or that will be. If we thus know the sort of explanation which is
> sufficient to cover the facts, why (it is asked) should we travel further afield
> into the misty realms of theology or metaphysics?
> – Lord Arthur James Balfour, *Theism and Humanism* (1915)

In the early twentieth century, the *Times of London* invited several
prominent authors and social commentators to personally diagnose what
is wrong with the world. In response, the English journalist and Catholic
convert G.K. Chesterton is rumored to have written, simply, "I am."
Although the story may very well be apocryphal, it highlights a serious
answer to a serious question: *We* are what is wrong with the world.
According to the traditional Christian teaching, rooted in the doctrines
of creation and fall, humanity was created good, but human nature has
since become marred and corrupted. Everything Lewis wrote about ethics
and politics rested on his understanding of these two first acts of the
biblical drama, which cut against the underlying assumptions of post-
Darwinian political thought and some critical aspects of ancient Greek
political philosophy.

On a certain account of evolutionary theory, as well as a certain
account of Greek philosophy, the idea of creation is foolishness. The
answer to the question what is wrong with the world (if the question
yields an intelligible answer at all) is therefore much different on rival
premises. For Lewis, however, the revealed truth of our created-yet-fallen

human nature was the starting point for any social inquiry. "According to that doctrine," Lewis explained, "man is now a horror to God and to himself and a creature ill-adapted to the universe not because God made him so but because he has made himself so by the abuse of his free will."[1] Packed densely in Lewis' brief summary of the doctrine of man's fall are several propositions: (1) the Creator is distinct from his creation; (2) God created humanity with free will; (3) through the abuse of free will humanity rebelled against God; and (4) by that rebellion human nature has become marred by corruption and is now a shadow of what it was designed to be.

On what grounds are these propositions contested? For post-Darwinian thought, the answer is easy. A full-throated materialistic account of the origins of life on earth leaves little room for a doctrine of creation or any notion of intelligent design or divine purpose in nature. If the laws of chemistry and physics explain the origins of the universe, including the rise and development of life on earth, then supernatural creation is superfluous. On this account, the whole of reality can be reduced to physical matter, obedient to fixed laws or principles, discoverable by human reason. The universe uncovered by modern scientists is therefore ultimately without meaning or rational causation, a universe without design.[2] To be fair, reductive materialism was a creed on the market long before Darwin's *Origin of Species* was published in 1859. The Epicurean poet Lucretius reduced the whole of reality to eternally existent matter in *De Rerum Natura*, dated 54 BC, and materialism has had adherents across the centuries. Darwin's theory, however, seemed to offer for the first time a plausible mechanical explanation for how life evolved on earth without any divine agency or supernatural cause.[3] As

---

[1] C.S. Lewis, *The Problem of Pain* (New York: HarperCollins, 1996 [1940]), 63.

[2] See, e.g., the popularly influential and widely read book by Richard Dawkins, *The Blind Watchmaker: Why the Evidence of Evolution Reveals a Universe without Design* (New York: Norton, 1996 [1986]).

[3] Darwin's theory is more ambiguous on the question whether evolution is without purpose. In *On the Origin of Species*, Darwin repeatedly refers to natural selection as a process oriented to "perfection," which seems to imply some degree of natural purpose conforming to a normative standard of perfection or goodness. See, e.g., Charles Darwin, *On the Origin of Species*, rev. ed. (New York: D. Appleton, 1864), 425. "And as natural selection works solely by and for the good of each being," Darwin concludes, "all corporeal and mental endowments will tend to progress toward perfection." For a detailed treatment of evolutionary theory and philosophical defense of natural purposes, see Étienne Gilson, *From Aristotle to Darwin and Back Again: A Journey in Final Causality, Species, and Evolution* (Notre Dame, IN: University of Notre Dame Press, 1984).

Richard Dawkins has famously maintained, to anyone who will listen, Darwinism "provides the only satisfying explanation for why we all exist, why we are the way that we are."[4]

Greek philosophy's challenge to the supernatural creation of nature is different from the challenge of materialism, and it predates Darwinism. The tradition of philosophy inaugurated by Socrates allows for, and even privileges, ideas and metaphysical realities. All is not matter. Yet like Darwinism, the Greek philosophical tradition – or at least one account of that tradition[5] – insists on the ability of human reason to uncover truths about a world intelligible apart from any doctrine of creation. As the eminent Straussian political theorist Thomas Pangle maintains, Socratic philosophy entails "the deeply gratifying, progressive discovery of the unfaltering and unalterable attributes and causal relations that define the beings that make up our perceived world." The biblical account of creation, according to Pangle, however, denies "the very possibility of what philosophic science means by knowledge." If God created the cosmos, Pangle suggests, then everything in existence is the result of "an unfathomable and totally autonomous will" inscrutable to human reason, and it would be a fool's errand to attempt to acquire knowledge of a will inscrutable to us.[6]

Pangle's interpretation of Socratic philosophy as committed to philosophic naturalism is, of course, highly contested, and his assertion that the God of Abraham is a voluntaristic and capricious deity is at odds with the traditional view of orthodox Judaism and Christianity. Nonetheless, Pangle's accounts of atheistic philosophic naturalism and theological voluntarism both provide useful foils for understanding why Lewis thought the doctrine of creation was so important. Pangle makes two large claims that Lewis and the broader Christian natural-law tradition emphatically reject. First, Pangle asserts that philosophic knowledge results from inquiry into the causal relationships of beings that make up

---

[4] Dawkins, *The Blind Watchmaker*, x. Dawkins famously claimed that Darwin's theory of evolution made it possible to be "an intellectually fulfilled atheist" (10).

[5] The thesis that Socratic philosophy is committed to naturalism is controversial, and many scholars would offer an account of the Socratic tradition different from the account given by Strauss and Pangle (discussed in this chapter). See, e.g., David D. Corey, "Socratic Citizenship: Delphic Oracle and Divine Sign," *Review of Politics* (2005) 67(2): 201–228. See also Nicholas Smith and Paul Woodruff, *Reason and Religion in Socratic Philosophy* (Oxford University Press, 2000).

[6] Thomas L. Pangle, *Political Philosophy and the God of Abraham* (Baltimore, MD: Johns Hopkins University Press, 2003), 29.

our *perceived* world, which by definition makes it impossible to engage in a philosophic inquiry into the cause of the world itself. Second, Pangle insists that the doctrine of creation entails a voluntaristic deity whose arbitrary will is unfathomable to human beings. In Pangle's hands, rational inquiry thus stands as a rival to biblical revelation, and he insists the universe presupposed by philosophy is uncreated and eternal (since a created universe ostensibly makes philosophy impossible). Although Pangle's conception of nature as an eternal and uncreated order does not rely on the reductive materialism of Darwinism or ancient Epicureanism, it does rule out, from the start, the existence of a creator independent of nature.

The arguments against creation from evolutionary theory and classical philosophy are not new, and Lewis responded to contemporaneous versions of them in his writings. The fatal conceit of a fully materialistic evolutionary theory, according to Lewis, was that it unwittingly vitiated and rendered unreliable human reason. Yet human reason is the means by which the original scientific discovery was purportedly made. In the jargon of contemporary analytic philosophy, the theory is therefore epistemologically self-defeating. To accept the theory requires a belief in the soundness of human reason, but the theory, once accepted, undermines confidence in our cognitive faculties. There are enormous difficulties, as Lewis noted, with a materialistic account of the development of reason.

Classical philosophy, as Pangle understands it, on the other hand, assumes the eternal validity of reason, but it rules out from the start the possibility that reason could be the product of supernatural mind. Lewis refers to this aspect of classical philosophy as "philosophic naturalism" to distinguish it from Darwinian materialism. Although on this account reality cannot be reduced to matter, nature is still a causally closed system. As Lewis put it, philosophic naturalism posits a "vast process of time and space which is *going on of its own accord*" as the "ultimate Fact, the thing you can't go behind."[7] Lewis argued that the main alternatives to the biblical creation narrative – materialistic Darwinism and philosophic naturalism – put us in the untenable position of either reasoning to the self-contradictory conclusion that reason is untrustworthy or relying on a worldview that cannot account for the existence and reliability of reason.

---

[7] C.S. Lewis, *Miracles: A Preliminary Study*, rev. ed. (New York: HarperCollins, 1996 [1947]), 7–8 (emphasis in original).

DARWINISM AND THE ARGUMENT FROM REASON

Darwin himself raised doubts about the reliability of reason from the premises of his own theory. "With me the horrid doubt always arises," Darwin wrote in a letter to a friend, "whether the convictions of man's mind, which has been developed from the mind of the lower animals, are of any value or at all trustworthy."[8] The analytic philosopher Alvin Plantinga dubs this horrid thought "Darwin's doubt," and Plantinga has constructed a formal argument against materialism based on its failure to account for the reliability of our cognitive faculties.[9] Plantinga's formulation is the most fully developed version of the so-called argument from reason, but, as he acknowledges, Lewis put together the first early prototype of the argument in his 1947 book *Miracles*.[10]

Lewis noted that scientists involved in empirical investigation assume the reliability of human reason, but he argued that materialism could not account for this reliability. Despite the pretensions of popular scientists, Lewis insisted that science and naturalism are therefore deeply at odds. "Unless human reasoning is valid no science can be true," Lewis maintained,

It follows that no account of the universe can be true unless that account leaves it possible for our thinking to be a real insight. A theory which explained everything else in the whole universe but which made it impossible to believe that our

---

[8] Charles Darwin, Letter to William Graham (July 3, 1881) in *The Life and Letters of Charles Darwin Including an Autobiographical Chapter*, ed. Francis Darwin (London: John Murray, 1887), vol. 1, pp. 315–316.

[9] Alvin Plantinga, *Where the Conflict Really Lies: Science, Religion, and Naturalism* (New York: Oxford University Press, 2011), 316–350. See also Alvin Plantinga, *Warrant and Proper Function* (New York: Oxford University Press, 1993). On p. 238, n. 28, Plantinga acknowledges his debt to Lewis' argument in *Miracles*.

[10] See ibid., 310 n. 4. For a full treatment and defense of Lewis' argument, see Victor Reppert, *C.S. Lewis' Dangerous Idea: In Defense of the Argument from Reason* (IVP Academic, 2003). Lewis famously revised his argument in *Miracles* for a subsequent edition in response to criticism he received from the philosopher Elisabeth Anscombe. For an overview of Anscombe's criticism of Lewis' initial argument and Lewis' subsequent revision of the argument, see Victor Reppert, "*Miracles*: C.S. Lewis' Critique of Naturalism," in Bruce L. Edwards, ed., *C.S. Lewis: Life, Works, and Legacy*, 4 vols. (Praeger, 2007), vol. 3, pp. 153–181. According to private correspondence we have had with Joseph Boyle, Elizabeth Anscombe told Boyle she thought Lewis was a genius and respected him for acknowledging her point and revising his argument accordingly in subsequent editions. In print, Anscombe similarly insisted that Lewis' revision of the argument against naturalism demonstrated his "honesty and seriousness." *The Collected Philosophical Papers of G.E.M. Anscombe*, vol. 2: *Metaphysics and the Philosophy of Mind* (Oxford: Blackwell, 1981), x.

thinking was valid, would be utterly out of court. For that theory would itself be reached by thinking and if thinking is not valid that theory would, of course, be itself demolished. It would have destroyed its own credentials. It would be an argument which proved that no argument was sound – a proof that there are no such things as proofs – which is nonsense.[11]

Why can't materialism account for the validity, or logical cogency, of human reason? The basic argument, as Lewis put it elsewhere, is that according to reductive materialism, reason is merely the "epiphenomenon which accompanies chemical or electrical events in a cortex which is itself the by-product of a blind evolutionary process." If this is the case, "there is no reason for supposing it yields truth." Yet the scientific enterprise demands that we do suppose reason yields truth. "The scientist," Lewis maintained, "has to assume the validity of his own logic (in the stout old fashion of Plato or Spinoza) even in order to prove that it merely subjective, and therefore he can only flirt with subjectivism."[12]

Lewis' thinking along these lines had a noble lineage, and he was influenced by a similar argument the scholar and former Prime Minister Lord Arthur Balfour offered in his 1914 Gifford Lectures at the University of Glasgow. Subsequently published as *Theism and Humanism*, Balfour's Gifford Lectures argued that the world depicted by Darwinian evolution – a "strictly determined physical system, depending on the laws of matter and energy alone" – left no room "for psychical states at all." In other words, matter by itself could not explain the existence of reason, minds, or consciousness in the universe. "They are novelties," Balfour maintained, "whose intrusion into the material world cannot be denied, but whose presence and behavior cannot be explained by the laws which that world obeys."[13] To think rationally, we must take the existence of the mind as a datum and simply assume reason's ability to uncover propositions that are true. Reductive materialism denies the existence of minds in a metaphysical sense and, absurdly, gives us reason to doubt the reliability of reason. In a 1962 issue of *Christian Century*, Lewis listed Balfour's

---

[11] Lewis, *Miracles*, 21–22.

[12] Lewis, "The Poison of Subjectivism," in Walter Hooper, ed., *The Seeing Eye: And Other Selected Essays from Christian Reflections* (New York: Ballantine Books, 1967), 100.

[13] Balfour, *Theism and Humanism: Being the Gifford Lectures Delivered at the University of Glasgow, 1914* (London: Hodder & Stoughton, 1914), 54. Our attention was first drawn to the connection between Balfour and Lewis by reading John G. West's excellent review of *Mind and Cosmos* in the Spring 2013 issue of the *Claremont Review of Books*. See John G. West, "Dissent of Man," *Claremont Review of Books* (2013) 13(2), www.claremont.org/article/dissent-of-man/.

Theism and Humanism among the top ten books that influenced his thought, and the marks of Balfour's argument can be seen throughout *Miracles*.[14]

Far from a merely theoretical debate, Balfour asserted, "all we think best in human culture" was at stake in the controversy over mind and matter, reason and evolution.[15] Beauty, goodness, knowledge, and ultimately the self are possible as objective realities only if reason is a metaphysical intrusion into our physical world. If we insist that all thoughts are simply chemical or physical phenomena, and conclude that reason is therefore unlikely to yield true beliefs, we will saw off the branch of the tree we are sitting on.[16] It is a self-defeating venture: if the argument is successful, then we destroy the very foundation of argumentation. If we are to function as sane human beings, reason must be our starting point. "There can be no question either of attacking or defending it," Lewis insisted.[17] To mount either an attack or a defense of reason is to presume we can analyze reason from the outside without simultaneously relying on the laws of logic and inference, that is, without reasoning. But doing so is an impossible task, something akin to pulling out our eyes to have a look at them.[18] Attacking and defending reason are both self-defeating enterprises, since we cannot do either one without starting from the premise that reason is trustworthy. So understood, reason neither needs nor permits a rational defense.

Although not admitting of analysis from the outside, reason (if simply taken as a datum) does provide evidence about the character of our universe and the inadequacy of Darwinian evolution to fully account for that universe. To be clear, Lewis saw no conflict between reason and a biological theory that explains the progressive development of life on earth by means of natural selection. That theory, he allowed, may be

---

[14] In his essay "Is Theology Poetry?," Lewis also insisted that Balfour's *Theism and Humanism* was "a book too little read." See C.S. Lewis, "Is Theology Poetry?," in *The Weight of Glory: And Other Addresses*, ed. Walter Hooper, rev. (New York: Harper-Collins, 2001 [1949]), 121.

[15] Ibid., 248.

[16] For an example of this argument depicted in fiction, see C.S. Lewis, *That Hideous Strength: A Modern Fairy-tale for Grown Ups* (New York: Scribner, 2003 [1945]), 355. Lewis uses this metaphor of a tree branch in a slightly different context in *Mere Christianity*, rev. ed. (New York: HarperCollins, 2001 [1952]), 48. "When you are arguing against [God] you are arguing against the very power that makes you able to argue at all: it is like cutting off the branch you are sitting on."

[17] Lewis, *Miracles*, 33.

[18] See Lewis' use of this metaphor in "The Poison of Subjectivism," 99.

proved more or less accurate by successive discoveries.[19] His argument about the inadequacies of Darwinism always applied to what he called the "Myth of Evolutionism," a "work of the folk imagination" that took a biological theorem and fashioned from it a metanarrative that fulfilled the "imaginative and emotional needs" of modern human beings by providing a materialistic explanation for everything.[20] It was significant, Lewis thought, that what he called "Evolutionism" was an appealing and emotionally fulfilling doctrine, not a grim victory of reason over imagination. To borrow a line from the distinguished philosopher of mind, Thomas Nagel, materialistic Darwinism was (and is) a "heroic triumph of ideological theory over common sense."[21]

ATHEISTIC RATIONALISM AND THE ARGUMENT FROM REASON

In a comment on Evolutionism's emotional appeal, Lewis acknowledged his own deeply felt desire, early in life, for God *not* to exist, and he conceded that the myth appealed to every part of him except his reason. Lewis thus took it as his "painful duty to wake the world from an enchantment" made possible by the general ethos of modern times.[22] In many educated quarters today the same felt desire for God not to exist remains strong. "I don't want there to be a God," Nagel famously confessed. "I don't want the universe to be like that." Nagel attributes "much of the scientism and reductionism of our time" to the widespread and deeply felt desire *not* to live in a universe created by a supernatural authority. Yet the "cosmic authority problem" is the horse, Nagel insists, Evolutionism the cart.[23] And, like Lewis, Nagel's reason has prevented him from accepting the myth as a true account of the universe. Nagel, however, also discounts the plausibility of creation or the supernatural, for he professes to "lack the *sensus divinitatis* that enables – indeed compels – so many people to see in the world the expression of divine purpose."[24] A self-described "objective idealist in the tradition of Plato," Nagel (like Pangle but in a different vein) represents a contemporary atheistic alternative to Darwinism rooted in the tradition of Greek

---

[19] Lewis, "Funeral of a Great Myth," in *The Seeing Eye*, 117.   [20] Ibid., 114.
[21] Thomas Nagel, *Mind and Cosmos: Why the Materialist Neo-Darwinian Conception of Nature Is Almost Certainly False* (New York: Oxford University Press, 2012), 128.
[22] Lewis, "Funeral of a Great Myth," 128.
[23] Thomas Nagel, *The Last Word* (New York: Oxford University Press, 1997), 130–131.
[24] Nagel, *Mind and Cosmos*, 12.

philosophy.[25] Rational intelligibility, on Nagel's hypothesis, is simply a fundamental part of nature, and nature is an eternal and uncreated whole.

Lewis' argument from reason was not simply an argument against materialism, however; it was also an argument for the plausibility of theism and creation. It cut against blind, purposeless materialism *and* teleological, rational naturalism. Lewis endeavored to show that materialism was self-refuting, but he also maintained that

Naturalism, even if it is not purely materialistic, seems to me to involve the same difficulty, though in a somewhat less obvious form. It discredits our processes of reasoning or at least reduces their credit to such a humble level that it can no longer support Naturalism itself.[26]

As he indicated, Lewis posed the argument from reason as a challenge to both materialism *and* atheistic rationalism. Lewis conceded, however, that his challenge to atheistic rationalism was less obvious. One could agree with Lewis' critique of materialism without believing in a divine reason that stands outside nature. What did Lewis have to say to a philosophic naturalist who might insist that reason is simply an attribute of nature?

Lewis argued that mind and matter are different kinds of things that exist in our world. On this point, Lewis and the philosophic naturalist together oppose the materialist who insists that all is matter. The question, then, is how these two different things – mind and matter – relate to one another. The philosophic naturalist insists that each is an attribute of nature, and nature is an eternal whole. Lewis, following the Christian tradition, maintained that a rational God created all of material nature. Material nature is thus contingent on an eternal reason, and every instance of rational thought in our world is in some sense a participation in that eternal reason. Thus far, Lewis articulated the orthodox Christian teaching on creation.

The basic argument Lewis marshaled to criticize the alternative hypothesis (that reason is simply part of nature) rested on several key inferences. First, Lewis insisted that nature is rationally intelligible. But in order to be rationally intelligible, he argued, nature must either possess a mind or result from a mind. Lewis then concluded that the first alternative (that nature possesses a mind) is untenable, so that we are left only with the second alternative (that nature results from a mind). The key premise

---

[25] Ibid., 17. Admittedly, Nagel and Pangle might not agree on much else.
[26] Lewis, *Miracles*, 22.

that led Lewis to dismiss the first alternative was that on the naturalist account matter predates mind chronologically. "It is agreed on all hands that reason, and even sentience, and life itself are late comers in Nature," Lewis insisted. And if "there is nothing but Nature, therefore, reason must have come into existence by a historical process."[27] The philosophic naturalist thus must provide a plausible explanation for how reason could develop from nonrational matter. Although this doesn't exactly put the philosophic naturalist in the same boat as the materialist, Lewis did think the philosophic naturalist's position required a critical jump from unreason to reason that was utterly implausible.

The rational creation of nature, Lewis maintained, provided a better explanation of reality than the alternatives posed by varieties of naturalism. Rationality, Lewis suggested, "is the little tell-tale rift in Nature which shows that there is something beyond or behind her."[28] Reason, in other words, is a fundamental and irreducible agency in the world that ruptures any strictly deterministic model of reality (as the materialists hold) *and* cannot be adequately explained as something that developed from within nature itself (as atheistic rationalists hold). As a kind of inference to the best explanation, Lewis concluded that theism better explains the relationship between reason and matter than naturalism. It is, of course, possible to believe in God *and* naturalism if we are willing to posit a cosmic consciousness indistinct from nature, an eternal mind that is simply part of the natural whole. But this would not do, Lewis thought. That cosmic mind would

not be the product of the total system, but the basic, original, self-existent Fact which exists in its own right. But to admit *that* sort of cosmic mind is to admit a God outside of Nature, a transcendent and supernatural God.[29]

A satisfactory account of the reliability of reason, on which the scientific enterprise rests and which we cannot refute without falling into contradiction, Lewis maintained, depends on the existence of a self-sufficient and uncaused reason.

Without supposing the need for a creator, someone like Nagel might simply suggest that there must be a "cosmic predisposition to the formation of life, consciousness, and the value that is inseparable from them."[30] For Lewis, that alternative would not do. It would be absurd, he insisted, to "believe that Nature produced God, or even the human mind."[31] The

---

[27] Ibid., 27–28.   [28] Ibid., 45.   [29] Ibid., 46–47.
[30] Nagel, *Mind and Cosmos*, 123.   [31] Ibid., 49.

apparent absurdity of nonreason developing into reason without a rational cause is the chief difficulty Lewis saw in philosophic naturalism. But is there not a third option, in addition to naturalism and creation? Could reason and nature not both eternally coexist without one creating the other? In other words, why the need for a doctrine of the supernatural creation of the natural universe?

The explanatory need for a doctrine of creation, according to Lewis, arises because the independent and eternal self-existence of nature and reason is an unintelligible concept. "If there can be such a thing as sheer 'otherness,'" Lewis admitted, "if things can co-exist and no more, it is at any rate a conception which my mind cannot form."[32] Either reason created nature, or nature created reason. But to say that the two things eternally exist independent of each other is to say they are wholly other and separate, not part of the same system or existing within a common medium, including even our thoughts. If whole otherness is possible, Lewis insisted, we will never know, since the very moment we think of two things together they cease to be wholly other.

Such speculation about the possibility of eternal coexistence is at any rate beside the point, since the fact remains that reason and nature are not wholly other. They are related and meet at the frontier called mind. There, at the frontier, reason has broken into nature; it has invaded nature to conquer and colonize. Reason is in the world, but not of the world. And the world, on its own, cannot account for the existence of reason. Rational thought, understood on these terms, is a metaphysical intrusion into the physical world. It is the point at which reason and nature meet. Yet reason is not simply part of nature, and nature could never have produced reason. All of these considerations, for Lewis, lent credence to the theist's argument:

For him, reason – the reason of God – is older than Nature, and from it the orderliness of Nature, which alone enables us to know her, is derived. For him, the human mind in the act of knowing is illuminated by the Divine reason. It is set free, in the measure required, from the huge nexus of non-rational causation; free from this to be determined by the truth known. And the preliminary processes within Nature which led up to this liberation, if there were any, were designed to do so.[33]

Theism and the doctrine of creation *ex nihilo* thus account for the orderliness and predictability of nature and the fitness between our

---

[32] Lewis, *Miracles*, 47.   [33] Ibid., 34–35.

rational capacities and the natural world. If the world seems as if it was designed with an order that is discoverable by human reason, it is precisely because it was.

On this account, there is deep concord, rather than conflict, between creation and modern science. As the analytical philosopher Robert Koons notes,

the truly remarkable thing about the explosive growth of modern science is that it happened in Christian Europe in the later medieval and early modern period, rather than at other times and places, with societies that were richer, more populous and better organized (such as Rome, China, India, central America, or the Islamic empire). Many historians have concluded that the impetus of Christian theism provides the answer to this puzzle.[34]

Contrary to Pangle's claim that the biblical doctrine of creation denies the possibility of scientific knowledge, many historians of science hold the doctrine of creation to be the *sine qua non* of the modern scientific enterprise.[35] The theistic worldview and the doctrine of creation *ex nihilo* together engender belief in the intelligibility of nature and the fitness of the human mind to undertake scientific investigation.[36] The only other alternative is to posit that reason is inexplicably and irreducibly a fundamental part of nature.[37] Lewis thought there were at least rational grounds on which to question the plausibility of that alternative. "All the evidence we have points" to creation, Lewis maintained, "and difficulties spring up on every side if we try to believe otherwise."[38]

CREATION, REASON, AND THE NATURAL LAW

According to the doctrine of creation, as Lewis understood that doctrine, the reason of God is the self-existent principle by which the natural world was created. Reason is thus the rightful ruler of nature, and God gave

---

[34] Robert Koons, "Science and Theism: Concord, Not Conflict," in *The Rationality of Theism*, ed. Paul K. Moser and Paul Copan (London: Routledge, 2003), 81-2.

[35] See, in particular, the early essay by M.B. Foster, "The Christian Doctrine of Creation and the Rise of Modern Natural Science," *Mind* (1934), 43(172): 446–468.

[36] See Koons, "Science and Theism," 82. Koons identifies seven elements of Western theism. The first is "belief in the intelligibility and mathematical exactitude of the universe, as the artifact of a perfect Mind, working with suitable material that it has created *ex nihilo*, and the closely connected Hebraic conception of God as a law-giver."

[37] This is the alternative put forward by Nagel. Candidly, he concedes the hypothesis is put forward because of his "ungrounded assumption" that a supernatural being did not create the universe. See Nagel, *Mind and Cosmos*, 12.

[38] Lewis, *Miracles*, 51.

human beings the choice and the duty to rationally rule their nonrational appetites and passions. But in actual human experience appetite and passion meet reason as a rebel against a lawful sovereign.[39] Reason does not rule, and the human soul is internally disordered. Reason itself is not what it was supposed to be. Now the reason of each man is "not only a weak king over its own nature, but a bad one." Human reason is disfigured and out of harmony with the natural world it was designed to rule.[40]

Human imperfection is the fact of which the doctrine of the fall takes account. With Chesterton, Lewis would agree that *we* are what is wrong with the world, but both would add that what is wrong with us is that our reason does not rule as it ought. The doctrines of creation and fall, understood in this way, guard against two philosophical errors: reductive materialism, by which the whole of reality is reducible to matter, and philosophic naturalism, by which mind is presumed to be merely and reducibly part of the natural world. "No philosophical theory which I have yet come across," Lewis declared, "is a radical improvement on the words of Genesis, that 'In the beginning God made Heaven and Earth.'"[41] In the biblical creation narrative, however, we are also introduced to the problem of evil. If God created this world, why is there so much pain, misery, and evil in it? The question makes no sense until the existence of a divine creator is presumed. If there is no creator, if the natural whole is eternal – and, more problematically, if all reality is mindless matter – then there is no ultimate standard of good and there is nothing wrong with the world. The world just is, eternally.

But if the narratives of creation and fall are truly descriptive of the human condition, how do the doctrines go together? Why, in short, did creation fall? The question about how to reconcile the existence of a divine creator with the existence of evil cuts to the heart of the relationship between God, goodness, and reason. As Lewis noted, "It has sometimes been asked whether God commands certain things because they are right, or whether certain things are right because God commands them."[42] The question has its origins in Plato's *Euthyphro* and has been refined over the years in light of Trinitarian Christian theology.[43] When God, as the omnipotent Creator, acts, does he do so according to any pattern of reason or goodness? One alternative (to borrow lines from the cofounder of the English rock band Pink Floyd) is simply to insist that *what God wants/God gets* and then conclude that *God wants good/God*

---

[39] Ibid., 49.   [40] Lewis, *The Problem of Pain*, 78–79.   [41] Lewis, *Miracles*, 51.
[42] Lewis, *The Problem of Pain*, 99.   [43] See Plato, *Euthyphro* 10e.

wants bad.[44] In other words, a possible explanation for why evil exists is that God's actions transcend our categories of goodness and reason and therefore appear utterly arbitrary to us. God is powerful; he gets what he wants. Judging by the world we have, he wants bad and good, suffering and health, cruelty and kindness.

Against this claim (of which much more will be said in the next chapter), Lewis followed the dominant stream in Christianity by insisting "God's will is determined by His wisdom which always perceives, and His goodness which always embraces, the intrinsically good."[45] Lewis came around to this position late in life. A younger Lewis, still an atheist and an aspiring postwar poet, published a collection of poems under the pseudonym Clive Hamilton (a moniker that combined his first name and his mother's maiden name). The 1919 book, *Spirits in Bondage*, was an extended moral critique of the universe, a nihilistic jeremiad that the power behind the universe is beyond good and evil. In one poem titled "Ode for New Year's Day," Lewis lamented:

> For Nature will not pity, nor the red God lend an ear.
> Yet I too have been mad in the hour of bitter paining
> And lifted up my voice to God, thinking that he could hear
> The curse wherewith I cursed Him because the Good was dead.
> But lo! I am grown wiser, knowing that our own hearts
> Have made a phantom called the Good, while a few years have sped
> Over a little planet. And what should the great Lord know of it
> Who tosses the dust of chaos and gives the suns their parts?[46]

Even after his conversion to Christianity, Lewis retained sympathy for what he referred to as the Heroic Pessimism "magnificently summed up in Housman's line 'Whatever brute and blackguard made the world.'"[47]

The problem with Housman's claim, Lewis came to realize, is that if "a Brute and Blackguard made the world, then he also made our minds. If he made our minds, he also made that very standard in them whereby we judge him to be a Brute and Blackguard."[48] If our sense that something is wrong with the world sheds light on reality, then we have to have a rational standard of goodness against which to judge the things that have gone wrong. A moral critique of the universe, to be more than an

---

[44] Roger Waters, "What God Wants, Part 1" (song lyrics) from the album *Amused to Death* (Columbia Records, 1992).
[45] Lewis, *The Problem of Pain*, 99.
[46] Clive Hamilton, *Spirits in Bondage: A Cycle of Lyrics* (London: William Heinemann, 1919), 25.
[47] Lewis, "De Futilitate," in *The Seeing Eye*, 89.   [48] Ibid., 90.

expression of an arbitrary personal distaste for the universe as it is, must appeal to a real standard of morality or goodness. That standard, Lewis believed, was ultimately God, from whom all instances of rationality and goodness flow. "Heroic anti-theism thus has a contradiction in its centre," Lewis concluded.[49] It cuts off, from the start, the only thing that makes the moral critique of the universe remotely tenable.

Of course, there remains a mystery in the lived human experience, and evil poses serious theoretical challenges. Something *is* wrong with the world, and things are not as they ought to be. The biblical tradition, beginning in the book of Genesis, pairs the story of creation with the story of the fall precisely to account for this fact. As the narrative of creation exists to guard against error, Lewis suggested, so too does the narrative of the fall. The story's "sole function" is to meet and contradict

two sub-Christian theories of the origin of evil – Monism, according to which God Himself, being "above good and evil," produces impartially the effects to which we give two names, and Dualism, according to which God produces good, while some equal and independent Power produces evil. Against both these views Christianity asserts that God is good; that He made all things good and for the sake of their goodness; that one of the good things He made, namely, the free will of rational creatures, by its very nature included the possibility of evil; and that creatures, availing themselves of this possibility, have become evil.[50]

In other words, the doctrine of the fall reconciles God's goodness with the existence of evil and reasserts the self-existence and eternality of God the creator.

REASON AND THE FALL

At first glance, the doctrine of the fall gives us reason to question the reliability of our reason, ironically putting the Christian in the same boat as the reductive materialist. If man's reason is "not only a weak king over its own nature, but a bad one," why should we trust it all? This speculative theological question has enormous practical import, and Lewis' answer to the charge of reason's unreliability is foundational to the rest of his political thought. To the materialist, Lewis replied simply that we must assume the reliability of reason to make any argument, including an argument against reason. The radical Christian critic of reason comes at it from a different angle, however. For him, reason is created good but is

---

[49] Ibid., 90.   [50] Lewis, *The Problem of Pain*, 63.

now utterly and totally depraved, marred so much as to be worthless. Lewis' response to the Christian critic of reason is similar to his response to the materialist – he points out that without first assuming the reliability of reason the Christian could not come to any conclusions at all, including conclusions about the extent of the human mind's corruption. If "our depravity were total we would not know ourselves to be depraved," Lewis maintained in a simple but profound observation.[51]

Across his various writings, Lewis often was responding to something that might be caricatured as the Calvinist position, though it is a later exaggeration even of Calvin, who insisted that charging "the intellect with perpetual blindness, so as to leave it no intelligence of any description whatever, is repugnant not only to the Word of God, but to common human experience."[52] Both Lewis and Calvin agree that we have real knowledge of our corruption. We know on some level, Lewis claimed, that we "actually are, at present, creatures whose character must be, in some respects, a horror to God."[53] We therefore *know* that our condition is that of beings in open rebellion against a good God, and this knowledge of our condition is presupposed by any intelligible offer of divine clemency. Reason, even after the fall, does yield true insights into our world. In "regard to the constitution of the present life," Calvin maintained, "no man is devoid of the light of reason."[54] Far more damaged in the fall, according to Lewis and Calvin alike, was the human will. Citing the seventh chapter of Paul's epistle to the Romans, Lewis insisted "the general tenor of scripture does not encourage us to believe that our knowledge of the Law has been depraved in the same degree as our power to fulfill it." Although our will is in a worse state than even our mind, neither is *totally* depraved; there remains a necessary distinction, Lewis reminds us, "between imperfect sight and blindness."[55]

---

[51] Ibid., 61.

[52] John Calvin, *Institutes of the Christian Religion* (1509–1564), trans. Henry Beveridge (Edinburgh, UK: Calvin Translation Society, 1846), vol. 1, book 2, chapter 2, section 12, pp. 314–315.

[53] Lewis, *The Problem of Pain*, 62.

[54] Calvin, *Institutes of the Christian Religion*, vol. 1, book 2, chapter 2, section 13, p. 317.

[55] "The Poison of Subjectivism," 108. There are two senses in which the doctrine of total depravity might be understood. The first is that we are totally depraved in the sense that no part of us is left unaffected by the fall, so that our depravity is pervasive. The second is that we are totally depraved in the sense that our nature has no element of goodness left. When he criticizes the doctrine of total depravity, Lewis criticizes the second sense of total depravity.

Lewis' emphasis on the fallen state of the human will, more so than the fallen state of the human mind, is evident in his account of the indispensability of courage among the virtues. The classical tradition, going back to Aristotle, held prudence to be the most important virtue for the moral life because it guided the other virtues; but Lewis insisted that courage is the central moral virtue.[56] Why? Because sin has so affected the will, the strength of every other virtue – including the theological virtues of faith, hope, and love – relies on courage when tested. In his autobiography, Lewis approvingly recalled Samuel Johnson's observation that "where courage is not, no other virtue can survive except by accident."[57] In the *Screwtape Letters*, the more experienced demon-tempter, Screwtape, explains to his nephew why "the Enemy" (i.e., God) allows his "patients" to live in a dangerous world. Speaking of courage, Screwtape writes:

This, indeed, is probably one of the Enemy's motives for creating a dangerous world – a world in which moral issues really come to the point. He sees as well as you do that courage is not simply *one* of the virtues, but the form of every virtue at the testing point, which means, at the point of highest reality. A chastity or honesty or mercy which yields to danger will be chaste or honest or merciful only on conditions. Pilate was merciful till it became risky.[58]

In his reading of Romans 7, Lewis emphasized the defect in our will over the defect in our reason. "In that very chapter" where St. Paul "asserts most strongly our inability to keep the moral law," Lewis observes, "he also asserts most confidently that we perceive the Law's goodness and rejoice in it according to the inward man."[59] We often know what we ought to do, and yet we do not do it. A wayward and weak will is a much deeper problem in the human condition than a depraved mind. Even after the fall, goodness and truth do shine through into our reason, yet we willfully turn from God into ourselves. As George MacDonald wrote, in a line often paraphrased by Lewis, the "one principle of Hell is – 'I am my own!'"[60]

---

[56] On this point, Lewis is arguably departing from the classical Christian teaching that prudence is the cardinal virtue. See, e.g., Thomas Aquinas, *Summa Theologiae*, trans. Fathers of the English Dominican Province (London: R. & T. Washbourne, 1914-1938), II-II, Q. 123, A .12.

[57] C.S. Lewis, *Surprised by Joy: The Shape of My Early Life* (London: Harcourt, 1955), 89.

[58] Lewis, *Screwtape Letters* (New York: Macmillan, 1961), 137–138 (emphasis in original).

[59] Lewis, "The Poison of Subjectivism," 108.

[60] *George MacDonald: An Anthology*, ed. C.S. Lewis (New York: Touchstone, 1996), 88.

One consequence of Lewis' understanding of the relationship between will and reason after the fall is that it rescues the broad tradition of intellectual inquiry, both moral and speculative, from the charge of being hopelessly lost without access to divine revelation in Scripture. Of course, Lewis did concede a legitimate challenge from within Christianity to a form of rationalism divorced from the claims of theology, but he always thought the dichotomy between reason and revelation was a red herring. For Lewis, reason was itself a form of revelation, and honest Christianity, he claimed, served only to sharpen the intellect.[61] "I believe in Christianity as I believe that the sun has risen; not only because I see it," Lewis later confessed, "but because by it I see everything else."[62] There was nothing in existence for which Lewis thought the claims of Christianity were simply irrelevant. The core Christian claims about nature – that it was created good, has since become corrupt, and will one day be restored – could be true or false, but never simply irrelevant.

Like Darwin, some Christians continue to raise the horrid doubt whether the convictions of our minds are of any value at all. Lewis' theology answered this doubt. Against Darwin, he claimed that reason was trustworthy because by it man participated (albeit imperfectly) in the divine reason, the rational principle by which nature was created. Against the Christian critic of reason, Lewis appealed to Scripture and the lived human experience to claim that human reason was damaged but not destroyed in the fall. This was consistent with the dominant Christian tradition, both before and after the Reformation, including within the original expression of Calvinism. In "matters of policy and economy, all mechanical arts and liberal studies," Calvin maintained, man's unregenerate mind can and does labor and make progress; people of different faiths across temporal and spatial boundaries can therefore reason together about earthly matters, including political organization.[63]

To insist that pagans and Christians can reason together about policy, economics, and the liberal arts is not to say that these things somehow fall outside the gambit of revelation, however. It is not the case that we reason about politics or economics while taking theological claims by dint of revelation. Rather, it is that we reason about both policy and theology, and in both we use data that have been disclosed to us. Nature itself is a record of revelation, and even without Scripture the pagan mind can be illuminated by God's revelation in nature. Following Richard Hooker,

---

[61] Lewis, *Mere Christianity*, 75.   [62] Lewis, "Is Theology Poetry?," 92.
[63] Calvin, *Institutes of the Christian Religion*, vol. 1, book 2, chapter 2, section 12, p. 316.

who was following Aquinas, Lewis insisted that it is therefore false to neatly divide the intellectual world into competing camps of Christians (who have access to revelation) and pagans (who do not). In his introduction to Hooker in *English Literature in the Sixteenth Century*, Lewis offered comments that could be read as autobiographical:

He [i.e., Hooker] is writing to defend the freedom of Man from what he believes to be a false conception of supernatural authority. He feels as his deepest enemy what I have called the "Barthianism" of the puritans, the theology which set a God of inscrutable will "over against" the "accursed nature of Man" with all its arts, sciences, traditions, learning, and merely human virtues. In the light of that ruthless antithesis there was only one question to be asked about any institution. Is it "of God?"; then fall down and worship: is it "of Man?"; then destroy it. Hooker is always insisting that the real universe is much more complex than that. "All things which are in the Church ought to be of God. But they may be two ways accounted such." For, often, "the same thing which is of men may be also justly and truly said to be of God." . . . For explicit divine injunction, embodied in scripture, is but "a part of that rule" which we were created to live by. There is another part, no less God-given, which Hooker calls "nature," "law rational," which men commonly use to call the Law of Nature," "the light of Reason." The most permanent value of Hooker's work lies in his defence of that light.[64]

Lewis, as well, took as his deepest antithesis the "Barthianism" of the Puritans, a term he coined in reference to the ideas of the twentieth-century Swiss Reformed theologian Karl Barth.

In the midst of the moral and theological crises of the twentieth century, particularly the rise of Nazism in postwar Germany, Barth came to reject any pretensions to the reliability of human reason in matters theological, political, or moral. On this score, Barth rejected even what Calvin and the Reformers accepted, and he made claims about the consequences of sin and human depravity that were even "more pointed" than the claims of the Reformers.[65] One practical consequence of Barth's theology was an explicit rejection of the natural-law tradition in ethics and politics, the very defense of which Lewis took to be the "most permanent value of Hooker's work." It was the natural law, for Lewis, that brought together goodness and reason, and any attack on the natural-law tradition threatened to tear the two asunder. To think and

---

[64] C.S Lewis, *English Literature in the Sixteenth Century* (Oxford: Clarendon Press, 1954), 453–454.
[65] Karl Barth, "No! An Answer to Emil Brunner," in Emil Brunner and Karl Barth, *Natural Theology*, trans. Peter Fraenkel (Geoffrey Bles: The Centenary Press, 1946; reprint, Eugene, OR: Wipf & Stock, 2002), 101.

argue intelligibly about moral reality, Lewis insisted, reason and goodness had to be united – and this he took to be the work of the natural law.

THE LAW OF HUMAN NATURE

Lewis was a trenchant moral realist but a reluctant natural-law theorist. On the one hand, he acknowledged in a posthumously published essay that the aim of his public writings was never "to reintroduce in its full Stoical or medieval rigour the doctrine of Natural Law."[66] Lewis' insistence that he did not intend to reintroduce natural law in its full medieval rigor, however, was not a denial that great ancient or medieval natural-law thinkers such as Cicero or Aquinas heavily influenced his own ethical thought; each clearly did.[67] Rather, Lewis was signaling that in his public vocation as a spokesman for Christianity, his aims were much less ambitious. As Lewis insisted throughout his writings, he considered a belief in a moral law known through the exercise of reason to be one of the pillars of "all clear thinking about the universe we live in." The other pillar was an awareness that we each fail to keep the known moral law.[68] In this way, Lewis drew attention to the natural law primarily as preparation for the work of the Gospel. As an apologist for Christianity in the modern world, Lewis endeavored to make claims about moral reality without associating those claims directly with a particular moral or ethical system.

For good reason, then, Lewis offered no final worked-out ethical theory. His aim was lower. He offered a defense of moral reality itself. But in his defense of moral realism, Lewis asserted two things that put him squarely in the natural-law camp: (1) the foundational principles of morality are obligatory rational principles, that is, they are known through reason and morally obligatory for us to follow; and (2) the highest aspect of human nature, our reason, ought to rule our appetites and passions. To these broad Platonic claims, Lewis connected the core Christian doctrines of creation and fall. Given the fall, Lewis claimed, the purpose of the moral law is not simply individual human flourishing. Rather, the paramount end of the moral law is to bring us into a harmonious relationship with God, a relationship that had been severed by the fall. Because we are unable to keep the moral law, however, we cannot

---

[66] Lewis, "On Ethics," in *The Seeing Eye*, 74.
[67] Though Lewis downplayed any original influence that Aquinas had on his thinking. See Chapter 6, section on "Teleology, Perfectionism, and the Harm Principle."
[68] Lewis, *Mere Christianity*, 8.

work our way back to God. Virtue by itself will not solve our deepest problem. Enmity to and separation from God are aspects of the human condition presupposed by the Christian message of repentance and forgiveness, and this is precisely why Lewis thought the claims of the natural-law tradition were foundational to clear thinking about the universe we inhabit. The moral law is a reality we meet in human experience. It can be denied but not evaded, and it must be confronted before Christianity can gain a hearing.

As in Fyodor Dostoevsky's account of the young university student Raskolnikov, moral reality meets us in the world as a fact and as a sign of contradiction.[69] Dostoevsky's *Crime and Punishment* follows the downward spiral of a brilliant but poor university student, Raskolnikov. Caught in a bind, he believes himself to be an extraordinary thinker who has the potential to alter the entire course of human history, yet he is held back by poverty and difficult circumstances. In an attempt to better his situation, he murders a cantankerous old woman and her half-sister in order to steal the old woman's valuables. As the wily police detective investigates Raskolnikov, it becomes clear that he acted in accordance with a theory he had written about as a student. Porfiry, the police detective, offers this summary of Raskolnikov's theory:

> The point is that in [Raskolnikov's] article people are divided into two classes, the "ordinary" and the "'extraordinary." The ordinary ones must live in submission and have no right to transgress the laws, because, you see, they are ordinary. And the extraordinary have the right to commit any crime and break every kind of law just because they are extraordinary.[70]

Raskolnikov does in practice what he allows for in theory, and at times he seems quite comfortable with his consistency.[71] But as the story progresses, he is increasingly burdened by a guilty conscience.

In the end, Raskolnikov chooses confession and repentance, and he finds redemption in a chastened conscience healed through the ministrations of human and divine love. In a private letter, Dostoevsky later explained the transformation and healing in the character of Raskolnikov:

---

[69] For a recent, clear elaboration of this idea, see J. Budziszewski, *The Line Through the Heart: Natural Law as Fact, Theory, and Sign of Contradiction* (Wilmington, DE: ISI Books, 2009).

[70] Fyodor Dostoevsky, *Crime and Punishment*, ed. George Gibian, trans. Jessie Coulson (New York: W.W. Norton, 1964), 248–249.

[71] There is a version of Raskolnikov in the characters of Jadis and Uncle Albert in Lewis' *The Magician's Nephew* (New York: Harpers Trophy, 1983), 20–21, 71.

Insoluble problems arise for the murderer; unsuspected and unexpected feelings torment his heart. The truth of God and the law of the earth take their toll, and he ends up being forced to denounce himself, forced, even if he should perish in jail, to rejoin people. The feelings of isolation and separation from mankind which he felt as soon as he committed the crime wore him down. The law of truth and human nature took its toll, . . . the criminal himself decides to accept the torments in order to redeem his act. But it is difficult for me to clarify fully my idea. Besides this, my story makes allusion to the idea that the punishment meted out by the law to the criminal deters the criminal far less than the lawgivers think, because he himself requires it morally.[72]

For Dostoevsky, like Lewis, the ingrained moral law is an integral part of the human experience, and it is the very thing that demonstrates to us our wretched condition. Lewis, like Dostoevsky, insists there is a further point to the law beyond virtue that culminates in redemption.

At the end of *Crime and Punishment*, Raskolnikov discovers in his prison cell the New Testament given to him by the woman who loves him, and he recalls the story of Lazarus she had read to him earlier. "But that is the beginning of a new story," Dostoevsky tells us, "the story of the gradual renewal of a man, of his gradual regeneration, of his slow progress from one world to another, of how he learned to know a hitherto undreamed-of reality."[73] For Lewis, as well, the end of the moral law is our redemption. Right relationship with God is the ultimate telos, or purpose, of human life; but the fall introduced sin into the world and obscured humanity's knowledge of God and damaged the human will to obey Him.

This had of course been true across the centuries, but Lewis perceived something unique in the modern situation. Somehow, in the modern era, men and women had come to approach the very question of sin and our relationship with God from a different angle. "The ancient man approached God (or even the gods) as the accused person approaches his judge," Lewis observed:

For the modern man the roles are reversed. He is the judge: God is in the dock. He is quite a kindly judge: if God should have a reasonable defence for being the god who permits war, poverty, and disease, he is ready to listen to it. The trial may even end in God's acquittal. But the important thing is that Man is on the Bench and God is in the Dock.[74]

---

[72] *Crime and Punishment*, 539.   [73] Ibid., 527.
[74] C.S. Lewis, "God in the Dock," in *God in the Dock: Essays on Theology and Ethics*, ed. Walter Hooper (Grand Rapids, MI: William B. Eerdmans, 1970), 244.

Lewis' strategy for presenting Christianity to modern audiences was to first make them see themselves as the one in the dock over whom God presides as judge.

Following St. Paul's example in the Mars Hill oration, Lewis addressed his audience in terms they would be familiar with. In the fifth chapter of *Mere Christianity*, Lewis explained why he chose to get at his "real subject" (Christianity) in a "roundabout way" (a discussion of natural law). "It is after you have realized that there is a Moral Law, and a Power behind the law, and that you have broken that law and put yourself wrong with that Power," Lewis asserted, " – it is after all this, and not a moment sooner, that Christianity begins to talk."[75] Getting Christianity to talk to modern ears – or, perhaps more accurately, getting modern ears to listen to Christianity – was Lewis' mission as a public intellectual. Yet not all Christians agreed that natural-law theory could or should serve Christian ends. Standing against the tradition Lewis represented was the general theological outlook Lewis polemically dubbed "Barthianism" – a rival within Christianity that denied the plausibility of natural-law philosophy and positively denounced it as contrary to the Gospel of Christ. Karl Barth – perhaps the most influential Protestant theologian of Lewis' day – took to task the entire natural-law tradition as an illegitimate and incongruent invasion of philosophy into the realm of theology. Lewis' response to Barth, which we treat in detail in the next chapter, thus clarifies and draws out Lewis' natural-law theory and sets natural law as the cornerstone of his political thought.

[75] Lewis, *Mere Christianity*, 38–39.

3

Divine Commands, Natural Law, and Modern Politics

Goodness is seen with the eye of the understanding. And the light of that eye, is reason.

– Richard Hooker, *Laws of Ecclesiastical Polity* (1593)

"Fortified by strong coffee and one or two Brasil cigars,"[1] Karl Barth spent an afternoon in May 1934 drafting the Barmen Declaration, a statement of faith meant to reaffirm the distinctive theology of the Reformation in the midst of the German Church crisis of the 1930s. As Barth later recalled, the German Church, at that moment, was confronted by the "demand to recognize in the political events of the year 1933, and especially in the form of the God-sent Adolf Hitler, a source of specific new revelation of God, which, demanding obedience and trust, took its place beside the revelation attested in Holy Scripture."[2] After Hitler's rise to power, the official German Evangelical Church had largely adopted the political and cultural program of the Nazi regime. "The swastika and the cross were to be welded together," Clifford Green notes, "*Mein Kampf* and the Bible placed on the same altar – and in that order." The head of the Church, Ludwig Müller, gave himself the title of Reich's Bishop (*Reichsbischof*), and Jews and non-Aryans were prohibited from taking up leadership positions in the Church.

"Jesus Christ, as he is attested to us in Holy Scripture," the Declaration affirms, "is the one Word of God whom we have to hear, and whom we

---

[1] Eberhard Busch, *Karl Barth: His Life from Letters and Autobiographical Texts*, trans. John Bowden (Philadelphia: Fortress Press, 1976), 245.
[2] Karl Barth, *Church Dogmatics* (New York: Charles Scribner's Sons, 1957), II.1, 172–178.

have to trust and obey in life and in death. We reject the false doctrine that the church could and should recognize as a source of its proclamation, beyond and besides this one Word of God, yet other events, powers, historic figures, and truths as God's revelation."[3] In the context of the Nazi challenge, Barth's reference to "events, powers, historic figures, and truths" was a clear allusion to Hitler's political project, with its toxic mix of racist nationalism, socialism, and militarism. Still, Barth's challenge was not limited specifically to the German crisis, and throughout his life he remained antagonistic to *any* claimed source of theological knowledge outside of God's revelation in the person of Jesus Christ, including any claim that God had revealed truths "in reason, in conscience, in the emotions, in history, in nature, and in culture and its achievements and developments."[4] In the Barmen Declaration, Barth traced the errors of the "German Christian" movement – and especially the syncretism of Nazism and Christianity – to the church's acceptance of "natural theology." In this Barth stood against modern liberal theology, which left its gates open to the Trojan horse of anti-Christian philosophy and culture by questioning the historicity of the Gospel narratives and affirming God's ongoing progressive revelation in human history.[5] But he also stood against the centuries-old theological tradition of natural law, which had long been embraced by Catholics and Protestants alike, including such theological giants as Augustine, Aquinas, Luther, and Calvin.

Barth acknowledged that Luther and Calvin had indeed affirmed the validity of natural theology during the era of the Reformation and that it was in the "church in all lands for a long time" thought to be "admissible and right and perhaps even orthodox to combine the knowability of God in Jesus Christ with his knowability in nature, reason, and history."[6] Yet he could not perceive the limiting principle in this theology. Who is to judge what use of nature, reason, and history is rightful and true? And why could the Germans not legitimately make use of their distinctive history, culture, and philosophy when developing a natural

---

[3] *Barmen Declaration* (May 31, 1943). Reprinted in Clifford Green, ed., *Karl Barth: Theologian of Freedom* (Minneapolis, MN: Fortress Press, 1991), 149. On the historical context of the Barmen Declaration, rooted in the Nazi crisis, see Timothy Gorringe, *Karl Barth: Against Hegemony* (Oxford University Press, 1999), 129–138.

[4] Barth, *Church Dogmatics*, II.1, 172–178.

[5] One of the principal targets of Barth's criticism was the German Protestant theologian Friedrich Schleiermacher (1768–1834), who is often remembered as the "father" of modern liberal theology.

[6] Barth, *Church Dogmatics*, II.1, 174.

theology to stand beside the truths revealed in Scripture? Although Barth did not go so far as to deny the *possibility* of theological knowledge outside of God's revelation in Christ, he did "deny and designate as a false doctrine the assertion that all these things can be the source of church proclamation, a second source alongside and apart from the one Word of God."[7]

A few years after the Barmen Declaration, Pope Pius XI made such an appeal to natural theology in his encyclical *Mit Brennender Sorge* ("With Burning Concern"), a papal letter penned in German and read in Catholic parishes on Passion Sunday 1937. At first sounding chords in harmony with Barmen, the letter asserted that God's revelation in "the Gospel of Christ is final and permanent" and "admits of no substitutes or arbitrary alternatives such as certain leaders pretend to draw from the so-called myth of race and blood."[8] But Pius XI also affirmed the natural law tradition and appealed to the "eternal principles of an objective morality" written on the "tablet of the human heart" and knowable through the exercise of "reason unblinded by sin and passion."[9] Barth had no patience for such affirmations. As he later wrote in a letter to British Christians, he considered it futile "to make any impression on the evil genius of the new Germany by seeking to refute it on the ground of Natural Law." All "Janus-headed" arguments based on human nature, Barth claimed provocatively, lead "to the misty twilight in which all cats become grey. They lead to – Munich."[10]

LEWIS' RESPONSE TO THE NAZI CHALLENGE

In August 1941 Barth's letter to Britain was published as a pamphlet titled *This Christian Cause.*[11] The influential theologian's message for the Anglo-Christian community was simple: They must resist Hitler "unequivocally in the name of peculiarly Christian truth, unequivocally in the name of Jesus

---

[7] Ibid.   [8] Pius XI, *Mit Brennender Sorge* (1937), para. 17.
[9] Ibid., paras. 29–30. Pius XI was alluding to Romans 2:14, which declares that Gentiles who "do by nature things contained in the law" show "the work of the law written in their hearts." For Barth's commentary on this passage (in which he does not directly take up the question of natural law), see Karl Barth, *The Epistle to the Romans*, 6th ed., trans. Edwyn C. Hoskyns (Oxford University Press, 1963 [1933]), pp. 67–68.
[10] Karl Barth, "A Letter to Great Britain from Switzerland" (April 1941), in Karl Barth, *This Christian Cause* (New York: Macmillan, 1941).
[11] See Carys Moseley, *Nations and Nationalism in the Theology of Karl Barth* (Oxford University Press, 2013), 147.

Christ."[12] As the press turned out copies of Barth's pamphlet, C.S. Lewis took to the airwaves with a different message. On August 6 the Oxford don and lay theologian delivered the first of his celebrated BBC broadcast talks, which would later be compiled and published as *Mere Christianity*. A producer for the BBC had invited Lewis to give a series of talks explaining the foundational beliefs of Christianity to a war-weary nation, and in his first fifteen-minute segment Lewis introduced the British public to the idea of natural law.

"This law," Lewis explained, "was called the Law of Nature because people thought that every one knew it by nature and did not need to be taught it." "And," he added,

I believe they were right. If they were not, then all the things we said about the war were nonsense. What was the sense in saying the enemy were in the wrong unless Right is a real thing which the Nazis at bottom knew as well as we did and ought to have practised? If they had had no notion of what we mean by right, then, though we might still have had to fight them, we could not more have blamed them for that than for the colour of their hair.[13]

Lewis used the confrontation with the evil of Nazism to highlight the reality of the moral law in a dramatic way. "If your moral ideas can be true," he argued, "and those of the Nazis less true, there must be something – some Real Morality – for them to be true about."[14] The reality of basic moral principles, known on some level to everyone, was foundational to Lewis' understanding of the Christian message. The first, basic point of his lecture therefore was that "human beings, all over the earth, have this curious idea that they ought to behave in a certain way, and cannot really get rid of it." An essential second claim was that "they do not in fact behave in that way." Contrary to Barth, Lewis maintained that these two claims – there is a natural moral law and we fail to keep it – "are the foundation of all clear thinking about ourselves and the universe we live in."[15]

A defense of objective moral principles, universal in application and knowable by reason, would become a central theme in nearly all of Lewis' writings. In an essay written just after his first BBC talk, but left unpublished until his death, Lewis offered a fuller explanation of his approach to ethics and distanced himself from those who would claim "the world must return to Christian ethics in order to preserve

---

[12] Barth, "A Letter to Great Britain from Switzerland."
[13] C.S. Lewis, *Mere Christianity* (New York: HarperCollins, 2001), 5.   [14] Ibid., 13.
[15] Ibid., 8.

civilization, or even in order to save the human species from destruction."[16] The truth of the matter, according to Lewis, was the reverse. Instead of returning to Christian ethics, the world must simply return to a belief in real, objective morality; only then would it be able to return to Christianity. For "Christianity is not the promulgation of a moral discovery. It is addressed only to penitents, only to those who admit their disobedience to the known moral law. It offers forgiveness for having broken, and supernatural help towards keeping, that law, and by so doing re-affirms it."[17]

The challenge faced by the modern world is that many people deny that morality has any objective basis at all. Morality, on various modern accounts, is merely a social construct that exists to serve the interests of its creators. That idea, Lewis thought, was "the disease that will certainly end our species (and, in my view, damn our souls) if it is not crushed."[18] Again Lewis drew on the Nazi experience to support his point. "Everyone is indignant when he hears the Germans define justice as that which is to the interest of the Third Reich," he noted.

But it is not always remembered that this indignation is perfectly groundless if we ourselves regard morality as a subjective sentiment to be altered at will. Unless there is some objective standard of good, overarching Germans, Japanese, and ourselves alike whether any of us obey it or not, then of course the Germans are as competent to create their ideology as we are to create ours. If "good" and "better" are terms deriving their sole meaning from the ideology of each people, then of course ideologies themselves cannot be better or worse than one another. Unless the measuring rod is independent of the things measured, we can do no measuring. For the same reason it is useless to compare the moral ideas of one age with those of another: progress and decadence are alike meaningless words.

With this assessment, Barth no doubt would have agreed. For the twentieth century's most influential Reformed theologian, however, the only true measuring rod was the revelation of God in the person of Jesus Christ; all ethics, all philosophy, all worldly wisdom was vanity in light of the one, true Word of God.

---

[16] C.S. Lewis, "On Ethics," in Walter Hooper, ed., *The Seeing Eye: And Other Selected Essays from Christian Reflections* (New York: Ballantine Books, 1967), 59. On the dating of the essay, see Hooper's introduction to *The Seeing Eye*, xv.

[17] Lewis, "On Ethics," 63.

[18] C.S. Lewis, "The Poison of Subjectivism" in Walter Hooper, ed., *Christian Reflections* (Grand Rapids, MI: William B. Eerdmans, 1995), 73.

NATURAL LAW AND TWENTIETH-CENTURY PROTESTANTISM

Lewis was preaching fidelity to the old moral law, revealed in nature and known by reason, at a time when the idea of natural law was under serious attack by prominent Protestant theologians as well as secular philosophers, scientists, and social planners. Indeed, Lewis chose to begin his apologetic for Christianity on the BBC radio program by appealing to the "law of human nature." His goal for the talks, he later explained, was to "defend the belief that has been common to nearly all Christians at all times."[19] But many Protestants had already sundered the natural-law tradition from their theologies by the time Lewis endeavored to defend what had been held in common by Christians throughout the centuries. Karl Barth's theological leadership in the midst of the German church crisis at least made the separation of natural law and Protestant theology explicit. Two events that cast natural law to the wayside of twentieth-century Protestant theology were the 1934 Barmen Declaration and a highly publicized debate the same year between Barth and the Swiss Reformed theologian Emil Brunner. After the Barth–Brunner debate in 1934 and until the end of the Cold War, Stephen Grabill notes, it was "nearly impossible" to find "English-language monographs written by Protestants on natural law."[20]

Prodded by the frequent suggestion that he "write a polemical treatise against Karl Barth," Brunner penned a pamphlet titled "Nature and Grace" in the early months of 1934.[21] Brunner's central claim against Barth was that God has revealed himself in creation, so that the natural world contains a "self-communication of God" to human beings.[22] Our innate theological and moral knowledge, Brunner further claimed, was attested to in Scripture and presupposed by the biblical concepts of sin and responsibility. "The reason why men are without excuse," he claimed in an allusion to St. Paul's epistle to the Romans, "is that they will not

---

[19] Lewis, *Mere Christianity*, viii.

[20] Stephen J. Grabill, *Rediscovering the Natural Law in Reformed Theological Ethics* (Grand Rapids, MI: William B. Eerdmans, 2006), 4. One significant exception to this claim about the dearth of Protestant interest in natural law is John T. McNeil's 1946 article "Natural Law in the Teaching of the Reformers," *Journal of Religion* (1946) 26(3): 168–182. For a broader overview of the relationship between twentieth-century Protestantism and natural law, see Jordan J. Ballor, "Natural Law and Protestantism: A Review Essay," *Christian Scholar's Review* (2012) 41(2): 193–209.

[21] Emil Brunner, "Nature and Grace" (1934), in Emil Brunner and Karl Barth, *Natural Theology* (Eugene, OR: Wipf and Stock Publishers, 2002), 15.

[22] Ibid., 25.

know the God who so clearly manifests himself to them."[23] Like Lewis, Brunner thought the Gospel presumed man's knowledge of the very moral law he stood accused of breaking. Without some real knowledge of God and his Law, man could not be morally responsible for his actions.

Of course for Brunner, as for Lewis, the fullness of God's revelation was found only in Jesus Christ, but Brunner nonetheless understood the traditional Christian teaching, affirmed in the Bible, to be that God also reveals himself in his creation. *Preserving grace* was the phrase Brunner used to describe "the manner in which God is present to his fallen creature," and Brunner's doctrine of preserving grace carried a distinctively Calvinist heritage.[24] "Within the sphere of this preserving grace," Brunner taught, "belong above all those 'ordinances' which are the constant factors of historical and social life, and which therefore form a basic part of all ethical problems."[25] These "creation ordinances" function as a kind of law by which God graciously preserves his fallen creatures by directing them toward their own good. Following Calvin, Brunner called these collective ordinances the *lex naturae*.[26] The theological task for a generation that denied and evaded the law of nature, Brunner concluded, was "to find the way back to a true *theologia naturalis*."[27]

Barth's response to Brunner's polemic, which he considered to be an "alarm signal," was swift and uncompromising.[28] Rather than joining Brunner in his call for a true natural theology, Barth categorically rejected any kind of theology whose "subject differs fundamentally from the revelation in Jesus Christ and whose method therefore differs equally from the exposition of Holy Scripture."[29] Natural theology was, for Barth, a dangerous excursion away from the Gospel and a possible abyss into which the modern church might fall. Holding fast to what he took to be the principles of the Reformation, Barth unflinchingly branded Brunner a heretic for embracing a theology that he found indistinguishable from that of a "Thomist" (i.e., Roman Catholic) or a "Neo-Protestant" (i.e., liberal Protestant).[30] As a corollary to his complete rejection of natural theology, Barth further cast doubt on those "moral and sociological axioms" that had long been taken to be the foundation of civil life by theologians and philosophers within the natural-law tradition. "But

---

[23] Ibid., 25.   [24] Ibid., 28.   [25] Ibid., 29.
[26] Cf. John Calvin, *Institutes of the Christian Religion* (1536), II.8.
[27] Brunner, "Nature and Grace," 59.
[28] Karl Barth, "No! Answer to Emil Brunner" (1934), in *Natural Theology*, 69.
[29] Ibid., 75.   [30] Ibid., 90.

what are these axioms?" Barth asked. "Or who – among us, who are 'sinners through and through'! – decides what they are?"[31] Would attributing to these axioms a true validity and a divine origin "be anything other than the rebellious establishment of some very private *Weltanschauung* as a kind of papacy?"[32] Moving forward, Barth maintained that evangelical theology and practical ethics (including politics) must be based solely on the commandments of God revealed in his Word. The task of modern Protestant theology was to make the claims of Luther and Calvin on this score even "more pointed than they themselves did."[33]

THE DIVIDED SOUL OF PROTESTANTISM

The Barth–Brunner debate opened a chasm between the older natural-law tradition and the new Protestant theology. In his concluding remarks to Brunner, Barth declared natural theology to be of profit only to the "church of the antichrist" (i.e., Rome).[34] Lewis, for his part, equated Barth's theology with something "not unlike devil worship."[35] In his academic masterwork, *English Literature in the Sixteenth Century*, Lewis coined the term "Barthianism" to describe the modern Calvinist penchant for flattening "all things into common insignificance before the inscrutable Creator."[36] This general flattening was the product of a "theology which set a God of inscrutable will 'over against' the 'accursed nature of Man.'"[37] The "wholly other" God of Barthianism (at least in Lewis' rendering) was to be worshiped on account of power rather than goodness, and it was the idea of worshipping power divorced from goodness that Lewis found so unpalatable that he equated it with devil worship.

For Lewis, Barth's theological voluntarism was one opposite and rival error characteristic of the twentieth century. The other was nihilism. The devil "always sends errors into the world in pairs – pairs of opposites," Lewis counseled the listeners of one of his broadcast talks. "He relies on your extra dislike of one to draw you gradually into the opposite one."[38] As an intellectual and literary historian, Lewis traced the roots of the two great modern errors of theological voluntarism and philosophical nihilism

---

[31] Ibid., 87.   [32] Ibid., 87.   [33] Ibid., 101.   [34] Ibid., 128.

[35] C.S. Lewis, *English Literature in the Sixteenth Century Excluding Drama* (Oxford University Press, 1954), 33. See also C.S. Lewis, *The Problem of Pain* (New York: HarperCollins, 1996 [1940]), 29: "The doctrine of Total Depravity – when the consequence is drawn that, since we are totally depraved, our idea of good is worth simply nothing – may thus turn Christianity into a form of devil-worship."

[36] Lewis, *English Literature*, 449.   [37] Ibid., 453.   [38] Lewis, *Mere Christianity*, 186.

to the ideas and experiences of the sixteenth century. That century gave us Luther and Calvin's theology, Machiavelli's politics, and Bacon's natural science and dreams of power. In the sixteenth century the modern world was born, and by its constellation of ideas the natural-law tradition was fatally undercut in the modern mind.

"Theologically," Lewis wrote, "Protestantism [in the sixteenth century] was either a recovery, or a development, or an exaggeration" of "Pauline theology."[39] But in the "mind of St. Paul himself," Lewis maintained, "this theology was by no means an intellectual construction made in the interests of speculative thought."[40] It was, first and foremost, an affirmation of a specific religious experience. Lewis spoke of this religious experience both as a Protestant and as a Christian convert, and he therefore spoke of what he knew:

The experience is that of catastrophic conversion. The man who has passed through it feels like one who has waked from nightmare into ecstasy. Like an accepted lover, he feels that he has done nothing, and never could have done anything, to deserve such astonishing happiness. Never again can he "crow from the dung-hill of desert." All the initiative has been on God's side; all has been free, unbounded grace. And all will continue to be free, unbounded grace. His own puny and ridiculous efforts would be as helpless to retain the joy as they would have been to achieve it in the first place. Fortunately they need not. Bliss is not for sale, cannot be earned. "Works" have no "merit," though of course faith, inevitably, even unconsciously, flows out into the works of love because he is saved. He is not saved because he does works of love: he does works of love because he is saved. It is faith alone that has saved him: faith bestowed by sheer gift. From this buoyant humility, this farewell to the self with all its good resolutions, anxiety, scruples, and motive-scratchings, all the Protestant doctrines originally sprang.[41]

Within this experience of "catastrophic conversion" there is joy and hope, undergirded by a sense of helplessness and self-abnegation.

But what of people who do not experience this conversion, people whom God apparently did not elect to receive grace as an unmerited gift? "Inside the original experience," Lewis maintains, "no such question arises. There are no generalizations. We are not building a system. When we begin to do so, very troublesome problems and very dark solutions appear."[42] In his systematic theology, John Calvin was the man who first moved on "from the original Protestant experience to build a system, to extrapolate, to raise all the dark questions and give without flinching the dark answers."[43] Among the dark answers to the dark questions were

---

[39] Lewis, *English Literature*, 33.   [40] Ibid., 33.   [41] Ibid., 33.   [42] Ibid., 34.
[43] Ibid., 43.

suggestions that man's innate sense of goodness is utterly worthless and
unreliable and that God's free and arbitrary decree is the sole criterion of
goodness – a "view that comes near to saying that omnipotence must be
worshipped even if it is evil, that power is venerable when stripped of all
good."[44] In his *Institutes of the Christian Religion*, Calvin taught, for
example, that man was "devoid of all uprightness" and had "no ability in
himself for the study of righteousness." In man's fall from grace "human
virtue was totally overthrown." Fallen man, who had "no remaining
good in himself" was dependent on God alone for his salvation.[45] God
initiates and completes this salvation in some men but not others. The
conclusion must be that by the "mere pleasure of God" salvation is
"spontaneously offered to some, while others have no access to it."[46]
We are dead men all, objects of divine wrath. For reasons impenetrable to
the human mind God chooses to execute judgment on some and forgive
others.

Calvin's *Institutes*, Lewis remarked, was "a master-piece of literary
form; and we may suspect that those who read it with most approval were
troubled by the fate of predestined vessels of wrath just about as much as
young Marxists in our own age are troubled by the approaching liquidation
of the *bourgeoisie*."[47] That is to say, they were not troubled at all. In
other places, Lewis drew similar parallels between Calvinism and Marxism.
The connection, for Lewis, was what he considered to be the amoralism
and fatal determinism of each. When taken to their logical conclusions,
neither system left room for free will or reasoned moral inquiry.
Although Calvin did explicitly appeal to the natural law, many of
Calvin's followers, as J. Budziszewski notes, think "considering what
he believed about sin, he shouldn't have."[48] With respect to modern
theology, Lewis identified Barth with this strain of modern Calvinism.
Christians at Oxford University, Lewis wrote in a letter to his brother
Warren near the beginning of the war,

[44] Ibid., 50.
[45] Calvin, *Institutes*, 2.2.1. As we note in the last chapter, Calvin maintained that "in regard
to the present life, no man is devoid of the light of reason." See ibid., 1.2.2. In Calvin's
soteriology, however, the light of reason in the present life counts for naught, and as
Calvin talks about salvation he reaches some of the conclusions he previously avoided
(e.g., that human reason is perpetually blind and reason tells us nothing about goodness).
[46] Ibid., 3.21.1.   [47] Lewis, *English Literature*, 43.
[48] J. Budziszewski, "More Than a Passing Fancy? The Evangelical Engagement with Natural Law," in Jesse Covington, Bryan McGraw, and Micah Watson, eds., *Natural Law
and Evangelical Political Thought* (Lanham, MD: Lexington Books, 2013), 255.

have all been reading a dreadful man called Karl Barth, who seems the right opposite to Karl Marx. They [i.e., the Oxford Barthians] all talk like Covenanters or Old Testament Prophets. They don't think human reason or human conscience of any value at all: They maintain, as stoutly as Calvin, that there's no reason why God's dealings should appear just (let alone, merciful) to us: and they maintain the doctrine that all our righteousness is filthy rags with a fierceness and sincerity which is like a blow in the face.[49]

Although the results were at times "refreshing," Lewis thought the "total effect" of the Barthian ascendency at Oxford was "withering."[50] Despite his effort to be ecumenical in his BBC talks and popular apologetics, Lewis often treated Calvinism (or, at least, a caricatured version of Calvinism) as a theological *bête noir*, which, within the intellectual and cultural milieu of the sixteenth century, plunged "the unregenerate man as deep as the astrologers" and exalted "the elect as highly as the magicians."[51] Astrologers assumed that human events were preordered, the inevitable outcome of material causes that turned men into tennis balls batted around by celestial racquets. Magicians sought to control human events and transcend the laws of physics, to accumulate power and conquer nature. In this way, Lewis suggests, astrology minimizes while magic exaggerates the "power and dignity of man." In an intriguing connection between trends in theology and politics, Lewis suggests that the new polities that emerge in this period, built on the new religion, "embody limitless power and freedom in the prince, and make the subjects his (as they were the stars') tennis balls."[52]

By contrast, Lewis cast his own lot with the sixteenth-century Anglican theologian and priest Richard Hooker, a man with whom "the medieval conception of Natural Law" had "reached its fullest and most beautiful expression."[53] In his *Laws of Ecclesiastical Polity*, Hooker taught that the works "even of God himself" proceed by an eternal law.[54] "They err

---

[49] C.S. Lewis to Warren Lewis (February 18, 1940), in Walter Hooper, ed., *Collected Letters of C.S. Lewis*, vol. 2 (New York: HarperCollins, 2004), 351.

[50] Ibid. Interestingly, Lewis concludes: "I have no doubt the young gentlemen are substantially right: this is the goods. We ought to have expected that if the real thing came it would make one sit up (you remember Chesterton 'Never invoke the gods unless you want them to appear. It annoys them very much')." In a comment on an early draft of this chapter, J. Budziszewski suggested Lewis thought the Oxford Barthians had "the goods" in the sense that they represented "a certain permanent intellectual possibility, in its pure, shocking form." Of course, it doesn't follow that Lewis thought the Oxford Barthians represented "*Christianity* in its pure, shocking form." In light of the criticism Lewis continued to level against Barth, we think this is an accurate interpretation.

[51] Lewis, *English Literature in the Sixteenth Century*, 49–50.   [52] Ibid., 50.

[53] Ibid., 50.   [54] Hooker, *Of the Laws of Ecclesiastical Polity* (1593), 1.2.1.

therefore who think that the will of God to do this or that there is no reason besides his will."[55] In a comment on Hooker's theology, Lewis explained: "God does nothing except in pursuance of that 'constant Order and Law' of goodness which He has appointed to Himself. Nowhere outside the minds of devils and bad men is there is there a *sic volo, sic jubeo.* The universe itself is a constitutional monarchy."[56] But if the King of Heaven is bound by a constitution of goodness and reason, it is a constitution voluntarily adopted. According to Hooker, "the freedom of the will of God" was not in any way "abated, let, or hindered" by its submission to an eternal law, for "the imposition of this law upon himself is his own free and voluntary act."[57]

Lewis and the older natural-law tradition did not deny that God is free.[58] But, then again, neither did Calvin or Barth deny that God is good. The real disagreement was about (1) whether human beings have *any* knowledge of goodness apart from God's revelation in Jesus Christ and (2) how goodness relates to God's will. On the first, Lewis clearly disagreed with Barth's claim that the "starting-point of every ethical question and answer" is the "command of God" revealed in the person of Jesus Christ.[59] In ethical inquiry the starting point, according to Lewis, was simply the "primary platitudes of practical reason," which are epistemologically prior to God's divine self-disclosure and offer of redeeming grace.[60] Lewis claimed biblical warrant for this contention. In an essay for a 1943 issue of *Religion in Life,* he insisted:

He would be a brave man who claimed to realize the fallen condition of man more clearly than St. Paul. In that very chapter (Romans 7) where he asserts most strongly our inability to keep the moral law he also asserts most confidently that

---

[55] Ibid., 1.2.5.   [56] Lewis, *English Literature,* 50.

[57] Hooker, *Ecclesiastical Polity,* 1.2.6.

[58] For a discussion of the place of God's freedom in classical natural law theory, see Paul DeHart, "Reason and Will in Natural Law," in Covington et al., *Natural Law and Evangelical Political Thought.*

[59] Barth, *Church Dogmatics,* II.2, sec. 36. As John Webster explains, "Barth believed that human action is generated, shaped, and judged by 'that which is,' and that 'that which is' is a Christological, not a pre-Christological, category." See John Webster, *Barth's Ethics of Reconciliation* (Cambridge University Press, 1995), 214–215.

[60] C.S. Lewis, "The Poison of Subjectivism," 78. Lewis' claim is consistent with what theologians working within the Thomist tradition generally hold to be an accurate description of the relationship between nature and grace. As the Catholic theologian Hans Urs von Balthasar maintained in a friendly engagement with Barth, "there is a real natural and rational order that is relatively independent of the order of grace and that it has a real, albeit relative priority over it." See Hans Urs von Balthasar, *The Theology of Karl Barth,* trans. John Drury (New York: Holt, Rinehart and Winston, 1971), 287.

we perceive the Law's goodness and rejoice in it according to the inward man. Our righteousness may be filthy and ragged, but Christianity gives us no ground for holding that our perceptions of right are in the same condition. They may, no doubt, be impaired, but there is a difference between imperfect sight and blindness. A theology which goes about to represent our practical reason as radically unsound is heading for disaster.

Repeating a provocative claim he made elsewhere, Lewis then concluded: "If we once admit that what God means by 'goodness' is sheerly different from what we judge to be good, there is no difference left between pure religion and devil worship."[61]

Yet if we do admit that our intuited yet imperfect knowledge of goodness is real, then we are confronted with the second question about "the relation between God and the moral law." "To say that the moral law is God's law," Lewis asserted, "is no final solution."[62] Alluding to an old question in the history of philosophy, Lewis asked, "Are these things right because God commands them or does God command them because they are right?"[63] If the first, then goodness is an empty appellation, a mere synonym for the inscrutable will of God. If the second, then goodness seems to exist apart from and above God himself. Neither is tenable. The solution, for the Christian, is to remember that in God is "such that in Him a trinity of persons is consistent with a unity of Deity." In our merely human categories, we conceive of a law and a lawgiver as separate things. The simplicity of the divine nature makes it possible, at least, to admit that our categories are inadequate and to

lay down two negations: that God neither obeys nor creates the moral law. The good is uncreated; it never could have been otherwise; it has in it no shadow of contingency; it lies, as Plato said, on the other side of existence ... But we, favoured beyond the wisest pagans, know what lies beyond existence, what admits no contingency, what lends divinity to all else, what is the ground of all existence, is not simply a law but also a begetting love, a love begotten, and the love which, being these two, is also imminent in all those who are caught up to share the unity of their self-caused life. God is not merely good, but goodness; goodness is not merely divine, but God.[64]

In its full explication, Lewis' natural-law theory rested on an ontological claim about the divine nature, a claim that was inseparable from Christian revelation.

---

[61] Ibid., 79.   [62] Ibid., 79.

[63] See Plato, *Euthyphro*, 10e. In the previous chapter we discuss this question in the context of the Christian doctrines of creation and fall. See Chapter 2, section on "Creation, Reason, and the Natural Law."

[64] Lewis, "The Poison of Subjectivism," 80.

COMMON GROUND AND POINTS OF DEPARTURE

Despite the real tensions that exist between Lewis and Barth, there was therefore, at the end of the day, a deep agreement that the Triune God whose nature is revealed to us in the person of Jesus Christ is the ultimate ontological foundation of ethics and the ultimate source of our practical reason. Along these same lines, Barth's affirmation of divine freedom was tempered by his appreciation for the way in which the commands of God flow from the relational love of the Trinity.[65] Human actions done in submission to the command of God are good, Barth tells us, "because the divine address which is an eternal and temporal event in Jesus Christ is good, because God Himself is good."[66] At least one interpretation of the import of Barth's theological ethics, Jesse Couenhoeven notes, is that "the divine life itself, in its relational perfection, is the standard of goodness that inspires and defines the divine command. Divine commands, then, are never simply arbitrary. Rather, they are shaped by and express the logic of the Triune life that God is."[67]

Beyond this deep ontological agreement, however, Lewis and Barth remained at odds over the practical consequences of embracing the natural-law tradition in ethics and politics, let alone theology. Barth considered natural law to be the work of the antichrist; Lewis deemed it the foundation for all clear thinking about the universe we inhabit. Each traced the foundational cracks in the modern worldview to different and rival sources. What are we to make of this? Barth and Lewis both championed systems of ethics that were ultimately rooted in Trinitarian Christian theology. Yet Barth rejected natural law as pagan and antichristian, and Lewis attributed to Barth a theology that was indistinguishable from devil worship. Barth, it is true, was "mainly attacking" the "modern rationalist conception of natural law, to which traditional Christian natural law is and has always been opposed."[68] It is also true that those working in the classical Christian natural-law tradition, such as Lewis, have long understood the natural law in light of and as part of salvation history.[69]

---

[65] See generally Barth, *Church Dogmatics*, II.2, secs. 36–39.

[66] Barth, *Church Dogmatics*, II.2, sec. 37.

[67] Jesse Couenhoven, "Karl Barth's Eschatological (Rejection of) Natural Law: An Eschatological Natural Law Theory of Divine Command," in Covington et al., *Natural Law and Evangelical Political Thought*, 37.

[68] J. Budziszewski, "More Than a Passing Fancy?," 256.

[69] See ibid., 256, and the appendix on pp. 273–76.

Still, it would not do justice to either thinker to say that they simply spoke past each other. Their disagreements about natural law were real and deep. According to Barth, the modern world was mired in ethical confusion, and clarity would come only from adherence to the divine command revealed in the Word of God. For Lewis, however, the modern crisis was a direct consequence of the sundering of the classical natural-law tradition in the early modern period. Far from being a "matter of merely speculative importance," Lewis concluded that the modern philosophical and theological critiques of natural law, which reached an apex in his lifetime, were of dire practical import. "Many a 'popular planner' on a democratic platform, many a mild-eyed scientist in a democratic laboratory means, in the last resort, just what the Fascist means. He believes that 'good' means whatever men are conditioned to approve."[70] No matter how pure the motives, the price of abandoning the natural-law tradition, Lewis feared, was practical nihilism.[71]

BARTHIANISM AND LEWIS' IMAGINATIVE TURN

Lewis' response to what he pejoratively called "Barthianism" was to offer a robust defense of reason and to make the case for the validity of foundational moral axioms. By the late 1930s, however, Lewis indicated that he had grown skeptical of the power of reasoned arguments to impact a generation that had ceased to believe in reason. In *Out of the Silent Planet* (1938) – the first book in his Space Trilogy – Lewis wrote himself into the novel as a minor character. In the concluding chapter, the fictional Lewis spends a weekend with the protagonist Elwin Ransom, discussing how Lewis can best communicate the important knowledge Ransom has gained about the nature of the cosmos. "A systematic report of these facts," Lewis tells us, "might, of course, be given to a civilized world," but today such a report "would almost certainly result in universal incredulity and in a libel action." The solution, Ransom suggests, is to communicate in fiction truths modern audiences would not take seriously as fact. "It was Dr. Ransom," the fictional Lewis says in the book,

---

[70] C.S. Lewis, "The Poison of Subjectivism," 81.
[71] Balthasaar reached a similar conclusion in his otherwise sympathetic study of Barth's theology. "If there is no philosophy," he wrote in a statement with which Lewis certainly would have agreed, "then there are no absolute truths and values any more. Man is left within the things that confront him in this temporal world, and no theology can save us from positivism." Balthasaar, *The Theology of Karl Barth*, 297.

who first saw that our only chance was to publish in the form of *fiction* what would certainly not be listened to as fact. He even thought – greatly overrating my literary powers – that this might have the incidental advantage of reaching a wider public ... To my objection that if accepted as fiction it would for that very reason be regarded as false, he replied that there would be indications enough in the narrative for the few readers – the very few – who at *present* were prepared to go further into the matter.[72]

Lewis, at this early stage of his literary career, was already laying the groundwork for his later emphasis on imaginative fiction over rational argumentation and apologetics.

The ability of the imagination to communicate truth is something Lewis felt deeply as early as March 1916, when he began reading George MacDonald's *Phantastes: A Fairie Romance*. It is difficult to overestimate the impact MacDonald – a prolific nineteenth-century Scottish Presbyterian minister and author – had on Lewis. In his autobiography *Surprised by Joy*, Lewis described the experience of reading *Phantastes* as "holiness," "as though the voice which had called to me from the world's end were now speaking at my side." The voice he heard was "joy," a technical term Lewis used throughout his life to describe a deep longing that is pleasurable to experience but has no real object of satisfaction in this world. Reading *Phantastes* thrust Lewis into the insatiable throes of joy so powerfully that his imagination, he later recalled, "was, in a certain sense, baptized; the rest of me, not unnaturally, took longer. I had not the faintest notion what I had let myself in for by buying *Phantastes*."[73]

What Lewis had let himself in for was a lifelong quest and longing for truth, beauty, and goodness as expressed and communicated in forms including, but not limited to, imaginative fiction. Philosopher Peter Kreeft notes that Lewis "found time to produce some sixty first-quality works of literary history, literary criticism, theology, philosophy, autobiography, Biblical studies, historical philology, fantasy, science fiction, letters, poems, formal and informal essays, a historical novel, a spiritual diary, religious allegory, short stories, and children's novels." Lewis, Kreeft

[72] C.S. Lewis, *Out of the Silent Planet* (New York: Scribner, 2003 [1938]), 151–152.

[73] C.S. Lewis, *Surprised by Joy*, 99–100. In the preface to *George MacDonald: An Anthology*, Lewis wrote that his "own debt" to MacDonald's *Unspoken Sermons* was "almost as great as one man can owe to another ..." Lewis continued: "I have never concealed the fact that I regarded him as my master; indeed I fancy I have never written a book in which I did not quote from him." See *George MacDonald: An Anthology*, ed. C.S. Lewis (New York: HarperCollins, 2001 [1946]), xxiv and xxxvii.

concludes, "was not a man: he was a world."[74] The common thread in each of Lewis' diverse works is an uncompromising, rigorous commitment to the pursuit of truth. That is to say, Lewis did not compartmentalize his thinking or the subjects he tackled in various literary genres. As Lewis' one-time private secretary and now the literary advisor of the Lewis estate, Walter Hooper, observes, Lewis' "whole vision of life was such that the natural world and the supernatural seemed inseparably combined."[75]

Lewis' commitment to maintaining a logically consistent and holistic worldview delayed his conversion to Christianity until his early thirties. Recognizing the philosophical and practical changes that Christianity would demand of him, he converted with full knowledge of what conversion meant intellectually and practically. Writing of his conversion, Lewis recalled that in the "Trinity term of 1929" he finally "gave in, and admitted that God was God, and knelt and prayed." He was "perhaps, that night, the most dejected and reluctant convert in all England."[76] After his conversion, Lewis used his literary and intellectual talents to communicate the Christian doctrines he now embraced. Over the next three decades, Lewis engaged in theological and philosophical disputes, made significant contributions to the world of literary criticism, held the attention of the nation in a series of BBC broadcast talks on the basic tenets of Christianity, and created fictional worlds that still evoke wonder generations later.

Yet many of Lewis' biographers have highlighted a significant and dramatic (and now controversial) debate between Lewis and the brilliant Oxford philosopher Elizabeth Anscombe, which supposedly led Lewis to abandon philosophy and turn instead to the genres of fiction and children's literature. Anscombe was the most significant student of the philosopher Ludwig Wittgenstein, and she went on to a remarkable career in academic philosophy. An eccentric character by Oxford standards, Anscombe was a Roman Catholic convert who had seven children, smoked cigars, and eschewed dresses for pants as a young female philosophy don. During a meeting of the Oxford Socratic Club in 1948,

---

[74] Peter Kreeft, *C.S. Lewis: A Critical Essay* (Grand Rapids, MI: Eerdmans, 1969), 4.

[75] C.S. Lewis, *The Seeing Eye*, ed. Walter Hooper (New York: Ballantine Books, 1992), inside cover.

[76] Lewis, *Surprised by Joy*, 125. Alister McGrath has recently argued persuasively that Lewis actually got the dating of his own conversion wrong. See McGrath, *C.S. Lewis – A Life*, 141–145. McGrath puts Lewis' conversion in 1930.

Anscombe disputed Lewis' contention, published in his book *Miracles*, that naturalism was logically self-refuting. Much has been made of the debate, but, an often overlooked point, as Anscombe herself has noted, is that Lewis conceded her point and revised a subsequent edition of *Miracles* to meet the objection.[77]

After the 1948 incident with Anscombe, Lewis did not again publish a work of philosophy or rational apologetics, and some of his biographers have suggested that Anscombe's criticism was so humiliating that Lewis lost faith in the power of reasoned argument or at least, perhaps, his own ability to argue and reason. A.N. Wilson goes so far as to say that Lewis was so embittered by the debate that he created the character of Jadis, the White Witch in the Chronicles of Narnia, as a manifestation of Anscombe herself. Another critic, John Beversluis, claims that the Lewis–Anscombe debate, combined with his grief over the death of his wife in 1960, transformed the once-robust rational thinker into a confused, sad, and broken man who barely hung on to his faith toward the end of his life. Describing Lewis after his wife's death as a "picture of human collapse," Beversluis concluded that the "Apostle to the Skeptics had himself become a skeptic – if not about the existence of God, at least about his [i.e., God's] nature."[78]

As Victor Reppert has demonstrated, the claim that Lewis lost his faith or retreated into skepticism after the Anscombe affair is a "pernicious falsehood about C.S. Lewis that richly deserves to be put to rest completely and permanently."[79] It is simply not true. Critics such as Belversluis, however, have rightly observed that toward the end of his life Lewis did not engage in the spirited apologetics or rational arguments that had made him famous in his early career. He never again wrote a book-length work of Christian apologetics or philosophy such as *The Problem of Pain* (1940) or the *Abolition of Man* (1943). Why? It is not, as some have suggested, because Lewis lost faith in reason or was otherwise broken by

[77] See the introduction to *The Collected Philosophical Papers of G.E.M. Anscombe*, vol. 2: *Metaphysics and the Philosophy of Mind* (Oxford: Blackwell, 1981), x. See also Anscombe's original essay, "A Reply to Mr. C. S. Lewis' Argument That 'Naturalism' Is Self-Refuting," in ibid., 224–232.

[78] John Beversluis, *C.S. Lewis and the Search for Rational Religion* (Grand Rapids, MI: Eerdmans, 1985),158. See also A.N. Wilson, *C.S. Lewis: A Biography* (W.W. Norton, 2002).

[79] Victor Reppert, "Understanding C.S. Lewis' Defense of Christianity," in Bruce Edwards, ed., *C.S. Lewis: Life, Works, and Legacy*, 4 vols. (Westport, CT: Praeger, 2007), vol. 3, p. 6.

the debate with Anscombe. Rather, he lost faith in the ability of rational arguments to penetrate the defenses modern society had erected against reason itself. By the late 1930s, in fact, Lewis was already contemplating whether imaginative fiction is a better medium to communicate truth to a postmodern audience. The change in Lewis' approach was a change in tactics or strategy, not substance. As Gilbert Meilander observes, "Much of [Lewis'] writing can be understood as an attempt to provide compelling Christian images which might shape and mold men's thinking about the kind of life they live and the kind they ought to live."[80]

The best example of Lewis' new strategy is found in *That Hideous Strength* (1945), the third installment of the Space Trilogy that began with *Out of the Silent Planet* (1938). Written well before the debate with Anscombe, Lewis tells the reader in the preface to *That Hideous Strength* that he is following the "traditional fairy tale" but nonetheless behind it all is a "serious 'point'" which he already "tried to make" in *Abolition of Man*.[81] The reason he tried to make serious points under the guise of fairy tales, Lewis later acknowledged, is because he supposed that "by casting these things into an imaginary world, stripping them of their stained-glass and Sunday School associations, one could make them for the first time appear in their real potency." Fairy tales, Lewis suggested, might "steal past those watchful dragons" modern society had trained to guard against rational arguments.[82]

The moral truths Lewis argued for in *Abolition of Man* – and which he attempted to steal past society's watchful dragons in *That Hideous Strength* – have decidedly political implications. In each book pernicious political trends in the modern world are related, ultimately, to a philosophical rejection of the natural-law tradition. In different ways, each book offers the same diagnosis of the modern predicament and each offers the same cure. The cure, significantly, is *not* primarily to win debates but is rather to shape emotional dispositions through moral education. Philosophical and theological ideas born in the early modern period, however, threatened to cripple and destroy the transmission of Western civilization's moral inheritance from one generation to the next.

---

[80] Gilber Meilander, *The Taste for the Other: The Social and Ethical Thought of C.S. Lewis* (Grand Rapids, MI: Wm. B. Eerdmans, 1978), 54.

[81] Lewis, *That Hideous Strength*, 8.

[82] C.S. Lewis, "Sometimes Fairy Stories May Say Best What's to Be Said," in *Other Stories and Other Essays on Literature*, ed. Walter Hooper (New York: Harcourt Brace Jovanovich, 1982), 42.

The modern rejection of natural law – the axioms of which were once embedded in and transmitted through cultural and educational institutions – would, Lewis warned, create a generation of "men without chests" who reject reason and are enslaved to their passions. Ultimately, there would arise an elite class of social conditioners who shape those passions – and thus enslave – at will. Political and moral freedom, as distinctive attributes of man, according to Lewis, depended on natural law for a foundation. Across his writings Lewis traced the pernicious trends in modern politics to the events and ideas of the sixteenth century, a century, he claimed, that began by abolishing eternal verities and ended by abolishing man himself.

4

The Early Modern Turn and the Abolition of Man

Thus the traditional wisdom of China finds at the basis of all things a divine principle or law – Tao [the way] – closely akin to what the Stoics described as Nature, to which all things in heaven and earth must conform, and to which human nature is akin; so that for man the highest knowledge is to know the Tao and the highest wisdom is to live by it.

– Charles Gore, *The Philosophy of the Good Life* (1930)

Ideas afoot in the sixteenth century, Lewis noted across his many and various writings, had in the modern world laid the axe to the root of traditional notions of justice, sovereignty, and rightful political rule. In Lewis' day, the modern philosophical rejection of an objective morality rooted in human nature had led to widespread moral nihilism. One practical outworking of this collective moral nihilism was the turn to totalitarian government (Nazism, Fascism, and Communism) in the mid-twentieth century. In the Western world the principal rival to these forms of totalitarianism had been liberal democracy, but Lewis often noted that liberal democracy was itself threatened by the same denial of objective moral principles. In a liberal democratic regime, moral nihilism tends toward a different form of totalitarianism: a benevolent scientific bureaucracy, which destroys or damages mediating institutions such as the church and the family, and makes genuine freedom (understood as a virtuous life built on economic, cultural, and ecclesiastical independence) difficult to achieve.

The best life, or at least the richest and happiest life, Lewis thought, was one that cultivated a "freeborn mind," a certain disposition of soul that was made possible by leisured wealth. Such a life is "no natural endowment of the animal Man," but rather has always been the "fine flower of the privileged class."[1] In modern times we have tried, and succeeded to a large degree, to make some limited amount of leisure and wealth available to all. This was, for Lewis, a good thing. Standards of living are higher, people live longer, eat better, work less, and travel more than any other generation in history. But there is a danger. We are not content with simply increasing standards of living across the board. In our democratic and scientific age we also want to equalize resources and rid the world of sickness, death, and hunger. Of course, as a Christian and a decent man, Lewis was in favor of healing sickness and fighting hunger, but he also recognized that the promise of doing so through the institutions of government rested on a claimed ability of the government to regulate and rationally plan various aspects of an increasingly complex international economy. Few, if any, have the requisite knowledge to do so, and, Lewis maintained, "the new oligarchy must more and more base its claim to plan on its claim to knowledge."[2] In order to apply this knowledge, government officials demand more and more discretion and power, but the kind of technical knowledge claimed by those who would plan our economic and political orders offers no special insight into the enduring questions of government: what is "the good of man, and justice, and what things are worth having at what price."[3] In the end, Lewis insisted, liberal democratic governments will be thrust back against the reality of human nature. The new leaders, invested with untrammeled power, will "take charge of the destiny of others," but they will "be simply men; none perfect; some greedy, cruel and dishonest."[4]

This is the central problem of modern government, as Lewis saw it. We have enormous material resources and technical knowledge, but we have not (because we cannot) overcome the problems and limitations of human nature. Lewis' warning was that technical knowledge gives no unique insight into the enduring questions of justice and the good life. As we noted in the introduction, Lewis was not merely an amateur when it came to these essentially theoretical topics. His first love, McGrath notes, was philosophy, and Lewis' first academic post was as a replacement lecturer for the Oxford philosopher Edgar F. Carritt, who had been a tutor and mentor to the young Lewis.[5] When Lewis did land a permanent academic

---

[1] Letter to Warfield M. Firor (December 3, 1950), *Collected Letters* 3:18.
[2] C.S. Lewis, "Willing Slaves of the Welfare State," *The Observer* (July 20, 1958).
[3] Ibid.   [4] Ibid.
[5] McGrath, *Intellectual World of C.S. Lewis* (Oxford: Wiley-Blackwell, 2013), 33.

position in English literature, he proceeded to study texts and periods with a particular attention to ideas. In approaching his academic work, Lewis explained, he was always less interested in the details of an author's life than the ideas the author was trying to communicate. "The poet is not a man who asks me to look at him," Lewis noted; "he is a man who says 'look at that' and points; the more I follow the pointing of his finger the less I can possibly see of him."[6]

In the same way, we have approached Lewis as an author who pointed and said, "look." In his scholarly research on English literature, as well as in his popular and more overtly political works such as *The Abolition of Man* and *That Hideous Strength*, Lewis' finger pointed to a crisis in political theory that began in the sixteenth century and culminated in the self-defeating modern attempt to conquer human nature. As we shall see, Lewis was particularly concerned with the modern educational pedagogy found in English-language textbooks, and he detected dire implications in the very way in which we use and understand language. "Our intellectuals," Lewis complained, "have surrendered first to the slave-philosophy of Hegel, then to Marx, finally to the linguistic analysts."[7] Lewis often drew connections between changes in early modern political thought and trends in educational psychology and the philosophy of language. These interconnected areas of philosophy – politics, education, and language – were greatly affected by the sundering of classical metaphysics in the early modern period.

THE EARLY MODERN TURN

Magic and astrology, Lewis explained in *Studies in Medieval and Renaissance Literature*, were two opposite but related preoccupations in the sixteenth century. Magicians "sought power over nature" through incantations and spells. Astrologers "proclaimed nature's power over man" and looked to the heavens to discern man's fate.[8] Each rejected the medieval Christian doctrine of man, which "had guaranteed him, on his own rung of the hierarchical ladder, his own limited freedom and efficacy: now, both the limit and the guarantee become uncertain – perhaps Man can do everything,

---

[6] C.S. Lewis, "The Personal Heresy in Criticism," *Essays and Studies* (1934) 19: 15.

[7] Lewis, "Is Progress Possible?," in Walter Hooper, ed., *God in the Dock* (Grand Rapids, MI: Wm. B. Eerdmans), 313–314.

[8] Lewis, *Studies in Medieval and Renaissance Literature* (Cambridge: Cambridge University Press, 1966), 52.

perhaps he can do nothing."[9] These opposite and rival ideas have ruled the modern age, and they continue to move science, philosophy, and religion. The modern applied scientist is the magician's surviving twin, the philosophical materialist the astrologer's. Often, aspects of each are combined in the same person, such as Lewis' fictional sociologist Mark Studdock, a man who is "theoretically a materialist" but who has "all his life believed quite inconsistently, and even carelessly, in the freedom of his own will."[10] In *That Hideous Strength*, Studdock insists that material nature is the impetus for all human action, yet he also chooses (or thinks he is choosing) to take part in a large-scale scientific program to conquer nature through the exertion of human will. What each of the seemingly contradictory notions embodied in the character of Studdock have in common is a rejection of the classical view of man as "a composite creature, animal rationale," in whom is a "choice to be governed by his reason or his animality."[11] On the older model, man is neither a beast nor a god. Modern men like Studdock treat man as though he were both a beast and a god.

In England the rejection of the older view of man in science and philosophy was precipitated by the work of fellow travelers Francis Bacon and Thomas Hobbes. The Aristotelian metaphysics of high medieval scholasticism proceeded on the assumption that to truly understand something, one needed to know not just what it is but why it is. An "inquiry into nature," Plato's Socrates taught, was a search for "the causes of each thing; why each thing comes into existence, why it goes out of existence, why it exists."[12] Aristotle further divided these causes into four categories: material, efficient, formal, and final. The material cause of something is the matter out of which it is made. A bronze sculpture is made of bronze, a man mainly of hydrogen, oxygen, and carbon. But neither Aristotle nor his medieval successors thought things or men could be reduced simply to matter. Classical metaphysics was also concerned with something's efficient cause (what brings it into being or maintains it in being), formal cause (what form or pattern makes it what it is rather than something else), and final cause (what purpose it is designed to serve).[13]

[9] Lewis, *English Literature in the Sixteenth Century Excluding Drama* (Oxford: Oxford University Press, 1954), 13–14.
[10] Lewis, *That Hideous Strength: A Modern Fairy-tale for Grown Ups* (New York: Scribner, 2003 [1945]), 266.
[11] Lewis, *English Literature*, 12.   [12] Plato, *Phaedo*, 96a 6–10.
[13] See Aristotle, *Physics* II.3 and *Metaphysics* V.2. See also J. Budziszewski's discussion in *The Line through the Heart: Natural Law as Fact, Theory, and Sign of Contradiction* (Wilmington, DE: ISI Press, 2009), 145–146.

The efficient cause of a sculpture is the craft of sculpting; its formal cause is the form or shape its matter takes; and its final cause is the purpose for which the sculptor created it. Yet Bacon and others argued that empirical observation told us nothing about final causes. Simply observing a sculpture did not tell us what it was for; neither could observing objects in nature tell us their function. "It is a correct position that 'true knowledge is knowledge by causes,'" Bacon wrote in a methodological response to Aristotle. And these causes

are not improperly distributed into four kinds; the material, the formal, the efficient, and the final. But of these the final cause rather corrupts than advances the sciences, except such as have to do with human action.[14]

Bacon left room for inquiry into the final cause of human action, since we can presumably know the purposes *we* bring to the table, but he dismissed as futile inquiry into any other final cause. Final causes, according to Bacon, were purposes that exist in the mind of God, something of which we have no knowledge outside of divine revelation in Scripture. "If any man shall think by view of an inquiry into these sensible and material things, to attain to any light for the revealing of the nature or will of God," Bacon warned, "he shall dangerously abuse himself."[15] This jettisoning of final causes from empirical analysis inaugurated a subtle but profound shift in ethics. Simply put, ethics and empirical science were concerned with vastly different things, and the "intermingling and tempering of the one with the other" had "filled the one full of heresies, and the other full of speculative fictions and vanities."[16]

From this starting point it was possible to go in different directions. One might suggest that all ethical statements are purely subjective (since empirical observation tells us nothing about ethics) *or* that all valid ethical commands are based on the empirically inscrutable will of God (since final causes exist only in the mind of God, the Creator). Thomas Hobbes would go in both of these directions at once as he applied the new Baconian science to the world of statecraft. Hobbes, who served for a time as Bacon's amanuensis, imitated the methods of Bacon's natural science and attempted to construct a theory of politics and human nature without reference to final causes.[17] Since matter is all that exists, Hobbes

---

[14] Francis Bacon, *Novum Organum* 2.2.
[15] Francis Bacon, *Valerius Terminus: Of the Interpretation of Nature*, chap. 1, para. 5.
[16] Ibid., chap. 1, para. 6.
[17] On Hobbes' service as an assistant to Bacon, see R.E.R. Bunce, *Thomas Hobbes* (New York: Continuum, 2009), 3.

reasoned, ostensibly metaphysical concepts – such as good and evil – had to be understood solely in terms of material processes. The words "good" and "evil," Hobbes maintained accordingly, "are ever used with relation to the person that useth them."[18] The same could be said for any other qualitative or value-laden statement. All such statements are ultimately about ourselves, Hobbes insisted; they describe only our own appetites and aversions, which can be explained by material causes.

UPROOTING THE CLASSICAL AND MEDIEVAL MODELS

Hobbes' metaphysics uprooted the classical understanding of a well-ordered soul as one in which reason rules the passions through well-trained emotions. According to Hobbes, reason is the handmaiden of the passions, and thoughts serve desire "as scouts and spies to range abroad and find the way to the things desired."[19] But if this is so – if moral statements are merely statements about individual appetites and aversions – then it is nonsense to say that what one man happens to fancy is normatively prescriptive for another – unless, perhaps, one man can physically force another man to do his bidding. The problem is that none of us, individually, is powerful enough to bend all others to our will. Only God can do that. As A.P. Martinich notes, the "root of obligation," for Hobbes, "is God's omnipotence, because irresistible power directed to an object literally binds, ties or constrains that object to a certain course of action."[20] Human beings, roughly equal to each other in terms of power, are not naturally obliged to obey anyone other than God. Individuals can, however, come together to create a human sovereign who is vested with near-irresistible power. Once created, the state – that "mortal god to which we owe, under the immortal God, our peace and defence" – imposes real obligations on people.[21]

For Hobbes, might makes right, in both religion and politics. But if we take God out of the picture, as many of Hobbes' contemporaries accused him of doing, then the ultimate source of right is the sovereign state.[22] If God is retained, as he is on the surface of Hobbes' teaching, the medieval

---

[18] Hobbes, *Leviathan*, chapter 6.   [19] Ibid., chapter 8.

[20] A.P. Martinich, *The Two Gods of Leviathan: Thomas Hobbes on Religion and Politics* (Cambridge: Cambridge University Press, 2003), 100.

[21] Hobbes, *Leviathan*, Chapter 17.

[22] In 1666 Parliament investigated *Leviathan* for its alleged atheism. See generally Samuel I. Mintz, *The Hunting of Leviathan: Seventeenth-Century Reactions to the Materialism and Moral Philosophy of Thomas Hobbes* (Cambridge University Press, 1962), and Philip

conceptions of goodness, obligation, and political sovereignty are still radically transformed. Against the Hobbesian understanding of sovereignty as mere power, Lewis offered a defense of the classical view of sovereignty as power bounded by goodness. "God, as we know from Scripture (Rom. I, 15)," Lewis wrote in a summary of the traditional Christian view, "has written the law of just and reasonable behaviour in the human heart."[23] A just civil law is simply a particular application of the principles of natural law to the political life of a community. Human life is good and should be protected, but whether this means prohibiting this or that act, or setting a penalty at this or that level, are questions to be determined by legitimate public authority, taking into consideration a variety of factors. Legislating is not an exact science. Still, if the civil law "contains anything contrary to Natural Law," Lewis wrote, summarizing the teaching of Aquinas and Augustine, "then it is unjust and we are not, in principle, obliged to obey it."[24]

On the classical view of sovereignty, this all means that political rule as such is limited to that which is right. Of course, we owe allegiance to public authority, but a tyrant – one who rules in his own interest rather than for the public good – is illegitimate.[25] As an unjust law is no law at all, an unjust ruler is no ruler at all.

Thus for Aquinas, as for Bracton, political power (whether assigned to king, barons, or the people) is never free and never originates. Its business is to enforce something that is already there, something given in the divine reason or in the existing custom. By its fidelity in reproducing that model it is to be judged. If it tries to be original, to produce new wrongs and rights in independence of the archetype, it becomes unjust and forfeits its claim to obedience.[26]

As the medieval conception of natural law waned, it was replaced with a new model of political sovereignty. God, by His mere will and power, lays down a law for man. So the prince does for his subjects. The new theory of sovereignty, exemplified by the work of Hobbes, "makes political power something inventive, creative. Its seat is transferred from the reason which humbly and patiently discerns what is right to the will which decrees what shall be right."[27] The theoretical change is subtle, but its effects are far-reaching and evident even in the colloquial way we

---

Milton, "Hobbes, Heresy and Lord Arlington," *History of Political Thought* (1993) 14: 501–546.

[23] Lewis, *English Literature*, 48.   [24] Ibid., 48. Cf. Aquinas *S.T.* I–II, Q. 95, A. 2.
[25] Lewis, *English Literature*, 48. Cf. Aquinas *S.T.* I–II, Q. 96, A. 4.
[26] Lewis, *English Literature*, 48.   [27] Ibid., 50.

talk about our government officials as creative leaders rather than insight-ful or wise rulers. As man began to see himself as the creator of what is right, Lewis noted, rulers ceased being *rulers* and instead became *leaders*.[28]

The "repudiation of medieval principles," Lewis noted, went furthest in Machiavelli's *The Prince* (1513), a book that predated Hobbes by over a century and enjoyed the "success of scandal" for pointing where the new theory of politics would tend.[29] The state, Machiavelli taught, was no natural community but was instead held together by the will and power of the prince.[30] Although states are founded by violence and maintained by cunning and fraud, princes are judged by the result of their actions, which, when successful, is to "win and maintain the state."[31] When speaking of the good, Machiavelli gives a preeminent place to glory. When speaking of virtue, Machiavelli dispenses with justice and temperance and focuses on prudence and courage, the respective qualities of the fox and the lion. Justice does not enter into Machiavelli's calculus about how the state can be won. The goal is glory achieved through power, and Machiavelli simply offers advice about how to obtain it. If not an "evil teacher of evil," as Leo Strauss famously suggested – perhaps with tongue in cheek – Machiavelli was at a minimum a man who took a "realist" approach to political analysis that dispensed with traditional notions of justice and goodness.[32]

Something like Machiavelli's methodological approach has become explicit in much of modern social science. The medieval tradition invoked concepts such as natural law and the common good to distinguish ana-lytically between political rule and tyranny. But such concepts become unintelligible or hopelessly subjective when detached from the worldview that gave them birth. All that is left after objective goods are abandoned are subjective values, and all that is left after justice is abandoned is power. Consider the eminent twentieth-century sociologist Max Weber's definition of the state as the "human community that (successfully) claims the monopoly of the legitimate use of physical force within a given territory." "Everywhere," Weber observed at the end of the Great War, "the development of the modern state is initiated through the action of the

---

[28] Ibid., 50. Cf. Lewis, "The Poison of Subjectivism," in *The Seeing Eye*, ed. Walter Hooper (New York: Ballantine Books, 1967).
[29] Lewis, *English Literature*, 50.
[30] See, e.g., Machiavelli, *The Prince* (1513), chapter 3.   [31] Ibid., chapter 18.
[32] Leo Strauss, *Thoughts on Machiavelli* (Chicago, 1978 [1958]), 10.

prince."[33] Weber's was a typically modern (and Machiavellian) view of political leadership and a view from which Lewis recoiled. But, then, everyone else recoiled when Machiavelli first made his case in *The Prince.* "For that very reason," Lewis insisted, "Machiavelli was not very important. He went too far. Everyone answered him; everyone disagreed with him."[34]

EUROPE'S HIDDEN "HATRED OF PERSONAL FREEDOM"

Despite enjoying a success of scandal, Lewis maintained, Machiavelli was on the vanguard of a change in political theory that would lay the foundation for twentieth-century totalitarianism. According to the new theory, there was no sovereign authority higher than the state. "And this means," Lewis observed,

that we are already heading, via Rousseau, Hegel, and his twin offspring on the Left and the Right, for the view that each society is totally free to create its own "ideology" and that its members, receiving all their moral standards from it, can of course assert no moral claim against it.[35]

Elsewhere, Lewis credited (or discredited) Rousseau for being the man who "first revealed" the "deep hatred of personal freedom" that was "hidden in the heart" of modern European civilization. "In his perfect democracy," Lewis' senior devil Screwtape says in a toast to the graduating class of the Tempters Training College,

only the state religion is permitted, slavery is restored, and the individual is told that he has really willed (though he didn't know it) whatever the Government tells him to do. From that starting point, via Hegel (another indispensable propagandist on our side) we easily contrived both the Nazi and the Communist state.[36]

Modern totalitarian theories of political sovereignty, Lewis suggested in this densely packed line, sprung forth from the ideas found in Rousseau.

In the discourses that made him famous, Rousseau asserted that without an adequate understanding of natural man all past philosophers had found it impossible to "agree on a good definition of natural law."[37] The

---

[33] Max Weber, "Politics as Vocation," in H.H. Gerth and C. Wright Mills, ed. and trans., *From Max Weber: Essays in Sociology* (New York: Oxford University Press, 1946), 78, 82.

[34] Lewis, *English Literature*, 51.   [35] Ibid., 50.

[36] C.S. Lewis, *The Screwtape Letters* (New York: HarperCollins, 1996 [1942]), 196.

[37] Jean-Jacques Rousseau, *The First and Second Discourses*, ed. Roger D. Masters, trans. Roger D. and Judith R. Masters (Boston: St. Martin's Press, 1964), 95.

inscription on the temple of the oracle at Delphi – "Know thyself" – contained a "precept more important and more difficult than all the thick volumes of the moralists." Yet modern man did not know himself.[38] Like the statue of Glaucus, he was disfigured. A true doctrine of natural law, Rousseau insisted, had to speak to the unchanging part of human nature that was yet unmarred by modernity, and it had to offer prescriptions that were known directly by nature's voice. For Rousseau, these were prerational sentiments such as pity and self-love. By privileging sentiment over reason, the eighteenth-century philosopher rejected the classical tradition's emphasis on "the inherently rational character of the natural law that defined man's secular, moral and social duties," and he severed whatever connection between reason and natural law remained in Hobbes.[39] Rousseau also often used the word "nature" in a way that was foreign to the classical tradition. Classical natural lawyers use "nature" to refer to our created design, but Rousseau wrote of "nature" as if it meant only what was primitive or unmodified or spontaneous.

Rousseau's philosophical project was to discover the true basis of man's primitive nature through a study of man's history. That history, Rousseau suggested, shows that men are naturally free and that society perverts the order of nature and creates slavery and inequality among men. "Man was born free, and everywhere he is in chains," Rousseau provocatively claimed.[40] It was civilization and the rule of law that destroyed man's natural freedom and created inequality.[41] From this starting point, Rousseau came up with this novel solution: If each individual would simply join his voice with the "general will" and submit to its authority, choosing to see his own will subsumed in the collective, then the rule of law would cease being the enemy of equality and freedom. The goal, as Rousseau later put it, was to "find a form of association that defends and protects the person and goods of each associate with all the common force, and by means of which each one, uniting with all, nevertheless obeys only himself and remains as free as before."[42] For Rousseau, natural man was free because he obeyed only the impulse of his own will; civil man might become free by uniting his will with the general will and (in some sense) obeying only himself. Natural man was equal because he never entered into relationships admitting of comparison; civil man might become equal by being equally subject to the general will.

---

[38] Ibid., 91.   [39] Masters, Introduction to Rousseau, *First and Second Discourses*, 3.
[40] Jean-Jacques Rousseau, *The Social Contract* 1.1.
[41] Rousseau, *Second Discourse*, 160.   [42] Rousseau, *The Social Contract*, 1.6.

But what of the individual who refuses to unite his voice with the general will? That man "will be forced to be free" by the whole society, Rousseau conceded, which meant in practice that society had to force each man to see himself as part of the whole.[43] But how will such a transformation in society take place? How will civilization's solitary individuals be transformed into public-spirited citizens ruling together as part of one general will? That transformation, Rousseau suggested, would require a godlike legislator who destroys traditional Christianity while uniting church and state together in a "purely civil profession of faith."[44] It is easy, in light of subsequent history, including the French Revolution and the horrors of the twentieth century, to find in Rousseau the basic recipe for revolutions that begin with lip service to freedom and equality and end with a dictator who ruthlessly forces men to conform to a pattern of behavior and thought provided – and created – by the state. The quelling of dissent and various efforts to "force men to be free" are rationalized as benevolent exercises designed to give men what they truly desire. As Lewis' Oxford colleague Isaiah Berlin noted, the "Jacobins, Robespierre, Hitler, Mussolini, and the Communists all use this very same method of argument, of saying men do not know what they truly want – and therefore by wanting it for them, by wanting it on their behalf, we are giving them what in some occult sense, without knowing it themselves, they themselves 'really' want."[45]

The paradoxical Rousseauian idea of forced conformity in the name of freedom is what Lewis identified as the "deep hatred of personal freedom hidden in the heart" of the modern Enlightenment project.[46] From Rousseau, he traced the ascent of the modern totalitarian impulse to George Wilhelm Frederick Hegel, the early nineteenth-century Prussian philosopher and theologian who tried to reconcile the apparent contradiction bubbling to the surface in Rousseau. In the name of freedom, the individual is forced to submit to the general will. The key to reconciling the apparent contradiction, according to Hegel, was to take a long view of history and its ultimate purposes. Hegel appropriated the general framework of salvation history found in Christian traditions and applied it to secular world events. History, Hegel taught, was "the progress of the

---

[43] Ibid., 1.7.   [44] Ibid., 4.8.
[45] Isaiah Berlin, *Freedom and Its Betrayal*, ed. Henry Hardy (Princeton University Press, 2002), 47.
[46] Lewis, *Screwtape Letters*, 196. "Even in England we were pretty successful," Screwtape continues. "I heard the other day that in that country a man could not, without a permit, cut down his own tree with his own axe, make it into planks with his own saw, and use the planks to build a tool-shed in his own garden" (ibid.).

consciousness of freedom."[47] The march of History – with a capital H – culminates in the creation of the modern bureaucratic state, which reconciles the apparent tension between law and freedom. "The State," Hegel declared, "is the Divine Idea as it exists on Earth."[48] There are many nuances in Hegel's philosophy of history and his theory of the state, but Hegel's writings provided philosophical cover for totalitarian statists on the Left and Right. True freedom, they insist with one voice, is found only in the arms of the state. From Hegel's vantage point in the nineteenth century, the creation of the modern state was the end toward which History inexorably marched.

HISTORY RESUMED

Hegel's view, no doubt, would have looked different had he lived to see the devastation his own state would endure in World War I. Horrific fighting on the continent killed or wounded some 30 million European men, including a young C.S. Lewis, who was first bedridden with trench fever and then injured during the war.[49] The senseless destruction of the war crushed the hope many had placed in the forward march of History. Far from a rational dialectic, the history of mankind seemed, to borrow a line from Macbeth, to be a "tale told by an idiot, full of sound and fury, signifying nothing." Soon after the war, Albert Einstein's general theory of relativity, confirmed by photographs of a solar eclipse taken in May 1919, destroyed the confidence men had placed even in the order and simplicity of the physical world. Space and time, Einstein proved, were relative rather than fixed and absolute. Einstein's unsettling discovery soon filtered into popular discussions of ethics and politics, already affected by the devastation of the Great War. "At the beginning of the 1920s," Paul Johnson notes, "the belief began to circulate, for the first time at a popular level, that there were no longer any absolutes: of time and space, of good and evil, of knowledge, above all of value."[50] In the

---

[47] G.F.W. Hegel, *Philosophy of History*, trans. Sibree (New York: American Dome Library Co., 1902), 64. Lewis had a long-standing interest in Hegel, evidenced by his including "Hegelania" as a distinct territory in his first book after his conversion. See C.S. Lewis, *The Pilgrim's Regress: Wade Annotated Edition*, ed. David C. Downing (Grand Rapids, MI: Wm. B. Eerdmans, 2014), 218–219.

[48] Hegel, *Philosophy of History*, 87.

[49] See Chapter 1, section on "The Political and Apolitical C.S. Lewis."

[50] Paul Johnson, *Modern Times: The World from the Twenties to the Eighties* (New York: HarperCollins, 1983), 4.

Western world God was dead, as Nietzsche declared. But also dead was the entire Enlightenment project of uncovering universal principles of justice through the exercise of reason unaided, or unburdened, by tradition and theology. Popular thought leaders, in the press and in the academy, now openly proclaimed that no such principles exist.

In 1776 the American founders, under the sway of Newton and Locke, had appealed to natural rights under the laws of nature and nature's God to justify their revolution. But in 1922 the American intellectual historian Carl Becker spoke for many when he insisted that "to ask whether the natural rights philosophy in the Declaration of Independence is true or false is essentially a meaningless question."[51] It was meaningless because the world had no meaning – or at least no meaning apart from the stories we choose to tell about it. And the story being told about the world in the twentieth century was that values are relative, a matter of taste and perspective. Lewis thought and argued that the new moral subjectivism posed an existential threat to democracy and the rule of law. He was not alone. One of Lewis' chief contemporary influences, G.K. Chesterton, for example, maintained that democracy has "no basis except in a dogma about the divine origin of man." "Men will more and more realize that there is no meaning in democracy if there is no meaning in anything," Chesterton warned. "And there is no meaning in anything if there is not a centre of significance and an authority that is the author of our rights."[52] Here, then, was the problem: Modern liberal democracies rest on a theoretical foundation that is undercut by certain popularized versions of physical science. Those popular claims are twofold: (1) the physical world can be exhaustively catalogued and analyzed with reference only to physical matter, and (2) man, as a physical organism, can be quantified without being qualified.

Lewis detected one of the subtle influences of the new outlook in the way modern philologists understood the purpose of language. In the widely read textbook *The Meaning of Meaning* (1923), Cambridge University professors C.K. Ogden and I.A. Richards offered an ambitious new theory of language and symbolism they hoped would serve as an alternative to classical metaphysics. Ogden and Richards argued that words act as symbols to communicate information about an object. They insisted, however, that the words we use to communicate metaphysical

---

[51] Carl Becker, *The Declaration of Independence: A Study in the History of Political Ideas* (New York: Harcourt, Brace, 1922), 277–278.
[52] G.K. Chesterton, *What I Saw in America* (New York: Dodd, Mead, 1922), 308.

ideas – beauty, goodness, and the like – have no referent outside the subjective emotions the words describe. Emotions, which biochemistry explains as material phenomena, were the real referents of such terms as "good" and "beautiful." One particularly telling footnote in a chapter titled "The Meaning of Beauty" repeated Nietzsche's dictum: "Words relating to values are merely banners planted on those spots where a new blessedness was discovered – a new feeling."[53] In other words, the language of values – which the authors lumped into a broader category called "emotive speech" – told us nothing true about the things being described. To call something beautiful is not to make a statement about the thing; rather, it is to make a statement about the feelings the thing provokes in us.

In the late 1930s, Ogden and Richards' book provided the inspiration and framework for an English-language textbook provocatively titled *The Control of Language*. In a foreword to the book, renowned University of Western Australia English professor Walter Murdoch[54] insisted that his own teachers had never taught him "to look language squarely in the face and ask what it is up to, what its purpose was, and how it did its job."[55] According to new theories of language, what descriptors of value "were up to" was communicating the state of our own emotions. "We appear to be saying something very important about something" when we use value-laden or emotive speech, the authors of *The Control of Language* insisted, summarizing a central tenet of Ogden and Richards' work, "and actually we are only saying something about our own feelings."[56]

Lewis was horrified at the prospect of the emotive theory of language being peddled to schoolboys, and he devoted his 1943 Riddell Memorial Lectures at the University of Durham to a trenchant critique of *The Control of Language* (which he referred to publicly only as "The Green Book").[57] In his Riddell Lectures, later published as *The Abolition of Man*, Lewis maintained that the subtle teaching of *The Control of Language*, and other texts like it, would have a pernicious effect on the pupils to whom it was assigned. "The very power of [the authors] depends on the

[53] C.K. Ogden and I.A. Richards, *The Meaning of Meaning: A Study of the Influence of Language upon Thought and the Science of Symbolism*, 3rd ed., rev. (New York: Harcourt, Brace, [1922] 1930), 153, n. 3.

[54] Great uncle to current News Corporation Executive Chairman Rupert Murdoch.

[55] Walter L.F. Murdoch, foreword to Alec King and Martin Ketley, *The Control of Language* (London: Longmans, Green, 1939), vii.

[56] King and Ketley, *The Control of Language*, 20.

[57] Lewis' marked-up copy is on display at the Wade Center at Wheaton.

fact that they are dealing with a boy," Lewis insisted, "a boy who thinks he is 'doing' his 'English prep' and has no notion that ethics, theology, and politics are all at stake."[58] But the stakes were high and they involved what Lewis later called the entire "human tradition of value."[59] What Lewis variously referred to as the doctrine of objective value, the Moral Law, the Natural Law, and, finally, the Tao[60] was the central preoccupation of Western political philosophy for centuries. It was what John Rawls dubbed the West's "dominant tradition," a tradition that was teleological and presumed "that institutions are just to the extent that they effectively promote" the rational good.[61]

Lewis feared the practical consequences of the modern rejection of the dominant tradition, particularly for its effects on politics. "A dogmatic belief in objective value," he warned, "is necessary to the very idea of a rule which is not tyranny or an obedience which is not slavery."[62] Of course, Lewis' contention that any theory of rightful political authority would have to start with an unquestioned belief in objective value was not itself an argument for the objectivity of values. Indeed, as Lewis admitted, simply warning about the practical consequences of value-subjectivism is not the same as refuting value-subjectivism. "The true doctrine might be a doctrine which if we accept we die," he conceded.[63] Yet Lewis was not trying to breathe new life into a noble lie when he appealed to that dominant tradition in Western philosophy. He was, instead, offering a rational defense of the tradition that anticipated many of the arguments the Scottish political philosopher Alasdair MacIntyre would become famous for making. "What the Enlightenment made us for the most part blind to and what we badly need to recover," MacIntyre wrote nearly two decades after Lewis' death, is "a conception of rational enquiry as embodied in a tradition, a conception according to which the standards of rational justification themselves emerge from and are part of a history in which they are vindicated by the way in which they transcend the

---

[58] Lewis, *The Abolition of Man*, 5.   [59] Ibid., 41.

[60] In *Abolition*, Lewis uses "Tao" to refer to the first principles of speculative and practical rationality. Although he does cite some of the teachings of Confucius, Lewis' own intellectual influences were chiefly Plato, Aristotle, Augustine, Aquinas, Milton, Hooker, Johnson, George MacDonald, and others in the Western canon. As Kathryn Lindskoog notes, Lewis' use of "the Tao" does not directly correspond to its meaning among Chinese Confucianists. See Kathryn Kindskoog, *Surprised by C.S. Lewis, George Mac-Donald, and Dante: An Array of Original Discoveries* (Mercer University Press, 2001).

[61] John Rawls, *Collected Papers*, ed. Samuel Freeman (Cambridge, MA: Harvard University Press, 1999), 412.

[62] Lewis, *Abolition of Man*, 73.   [63] Ibid., 27.

limitations of and provide remedies for the defects of their predecessors within the history of that same tradition."[64] Such a critical engagement with the "human tradition of value," Lewis insisted without hyperbole, was the key to saving our civilization and our souls.

ABOLISHING MAN

Contrary to the theory of value put forward in "The Green Book," Lewis insisted, "all teachers and even all men" had for many years "believed the universe to be such that certain emotional reactions on our part could be either congruous or incongruous to it – believed, in fact, that objects did not merely receive, but could merit, our approval or disapproval, our reverence, or our contempt."[65] Yet despite his desire to align himself with "all teachers and even all men" throughout the centuries, Lewis' own thought was undoubtedly shaped by a very specific tradition rooted in the teachings of Plato and Aristotle and "baptized" by later Christian thinkers such as Augustine and Aquinas. In each of the three main arguments he advances in *The Abolition of Man*, Lewis draws heavily from and reiterates points developed within this tradition.

First, Lewis argued that the primary task of early education is to train our emotions to respond correctly to objects in the world. That is to say, we must learn to love what is lovable and to despise what is despicable. Before considering abstract questions of justice and morality, we must be trained and brought up in good habits, learning to love things that are good and beautiful. As Aristotle taught, only those "brought up in fine habits" can "be adequate students of fine and just things, and of political questions generally."[66] Yet according to Augustine, every created thing is good and each good thing "can be loved in the right way or in the wrong way – in the right way, that is, when the proper order is kept, in the wrong way when that order is upset."[67] Virtue is thus a matter of loving, and not merely knowing, what is true and good and beautiful. The fictional

---

[64] Alasdair MacIntyre, *Whose Justice? Which Rationality?* (Notre Dame, IN: Notre Dame University Press, 1988), 7. Given the relationship between Lewis and Anscombe – see our brief discussion of Anscombe's criticism of Lewis' argument against naturalism in Chapter 3 – it is intriguing to note that MacIntyre was himself deeply indebted to Anscombe's seminal essay, "Modern Moral Philosophy" (1958). See Alasdair MacIntyre, *After Virtue: A Study in Moral Theory*, 3rd ed. (Notre Dame, IN: University of Notre Dame Press, 2007 [1981]), 53.

[65] Lewis, *Abolition of Man*, 27–28.   [66] Aristotle, *Nichomachean Ethics* 1095b.

[67] Augustine, *City of God* xv. 22.

Eustace Scrubb in the Chronicles of Narnia series represents someone educated in one of the schools where the ideas of "The Green Book" would predominate; he reacts poorly to everything. The son of "very up-to-date and advanced people," Eustace is not merely ignorant of, but also does not love, what is true and good.[68]

A rightly ordered human soul is one in which reason submits to the authority of God, on the one hand, and our emotions and appetites submit to the authority of reason, on the other. Following Plato, Lewis divides the soul of man into three parts: appetite, emotion, and reason. Our appetite pertains to bodily urges and base desires; emotions pertain to passions such as anger or fear. Neither appetite nor emotion is, in itself, moral or immoral. Each has a proper function. A well-ordered human soul is one in which reason rules the appetites through an alliance with well-trained emotions.[69] A brave man, for example, is one whose emotions ally with his reason to face danger in an appropriate situation, whereas a coward yields to fear precisely when he ought not to. This tripartite model of the soul provides the foundation for Lewis' analysis, and the model presumes that (1) there is a real and objective good and that (2) a proper education begins by training the emotions to respond correctly to the objective world, "welcoming everything good and abhorring everything not good."[70] The fact that people disagree about what is good is no knock against the theory, for it is presumed that a person whose soul is disordered will not correctly perceive the good, since his or her appetite will have usurped the proper place of his or her reason and ruled in its stead.

Still, many people – including the authors of "The Green Book" – have denied that the proper function of reason is to apprehend an objective good at all. Instead, they agree with Hobbes' contention that "whatsoever is the object of any man's appetite or desire, that is it which he for his part calleth good," since there is nothing "simply and absolutely so, nor any rule of good and evil to be taken from the nature of the objects themselves, but from the person of the man."[71] The Hobbesian view upends Plato's vision of a rightly ordered soul and makes appetite the legitimate (or at least unavoidable) ruler of reason, with thoughts serving passions "as scouts and spies" that "find the way to the things desired."[72] David Hume followed Hobbes on this very point, arguing for an instrumentalist conception of reason, such that "reason is, and ought only to be the slave

[68] C.S. Lewis, *Voyage of the Dawn Treader* (New York: HarperCollins, 2008 [1952]), 3.
[69] Plato, *Republic*, 441c–442d .   [70] Plato, *Laws*, 654b.   [71] Hobbes, *Leviathan*, 1.6.
[72] Ibid., 1.8.

of the passions, and can never pretend to any other office than to serve and obey them."[73] On the Hobbesian/Humean model, our end goal or ultimate desire is provided by arational and amoral appetite and emotion, and reason is merely the means by which we scheme to satisfy our desires.

Among other things, this new reductionist psychology upends traditional theories of education, which had presumed that educators were trying to train emotion to aid reason in ruling the appetite. But if the term "good" describes only our own emotions or desires, then the tripartite model of the soul makes no sense. And "when all that says 'it is good' has been debunked," Lewis contended, "what says 'I want' remains."[74] The new man, created by the new education, is a man without properly trained emotions, a man without a chest. This, in Lewis' view, makes him something less than a man, akin to a beast, motivated only by his own base desires and sense of what will give him pleasure. Of course, the new man might have culturally refined tastes and a mild temperament, but that would be only a by-product of his environment. There is no sense in saying any one man is better than another. As one of the new men in *That Hideous Strength* explains, all human desires and motives are "merely animal, subjective epiphenomena."[75] When his environment changes, and he becomes something else, it is useless to talk of values improving or regressing, since values have all been seen through.

In response to this challenge, Lewis' second main point in *The Abolition of Man* was simply that moral values are basic and cannot be debunked in this way. The classical authorities Lewis drew from all insisted that practical morality involved moving from foundational moral axioms to specific applications of those axioms in concrete cases. In other words, the axioms of practical reason are the premises of a moral argument rather than its conclusion, things that are "so obviously reasonable that they neither demand nor admit of proof."[76] But what if someone does not see the axioms? How, then, can an argument commence? This is the problem Lewis was dealing with. No argument against moral nihilism is possible if the interlocutor does not "see" basic moral principles. It is like arguing about geometry with a man who does not assent to the validity of the law of noncontradiction or who denies that parallel lines do not touch. A denial of the premises leaves nothing more to be said. The difficulty is that in order to see the premises, one needs to be educated in

---

[73] David Hume, *A Treatise of Human Nature* (New York: Penguin, 1969 [1739]), 462.
[74] Lewis, *Abolition of Man*, 65.   [75] Lewis, *That Hideous Strength*, 293.
[76] Lewis, *Abolition of Man*, 40.

virtue from an early age. Only experience rooted in a proper education allows one to apprehend the first principles, since, as Aristotle maintained, "vice corrupts principle" and mars one's moral vision.[77]

This explains, in part, why Lewis spent his prestigious Riddell Memorial Lectures criticizing the pedagogy of an upper-school English-language textbook. "The authors themselves," Lewis declared, "hardly know what they are doing to the boy [who imbibes their subtle teaching about value], and he cannot know what is being done to him."[78] Yet what the authors were doing, Lewis thought, was robbing the pupil of his inheritance in the human tradition of value, dividing him from the moral traditions of his ancestors and presenting him with something altogether new and sinister. The moral philosophy undergirding "The Green Book," when thought through, requires that we "scrap traditional morals as a mere error" and then "put ourselves in a position where we can find no ground for any value judgements at all."[79]

But can there be any argument against a man who denies the validity of the first principles of traditional morality? What more can be said? Lewis addressed the problem in a twofold response. First, those who set out to debunk traditional morality are usually half-hearted in their skepticism. They wish either to dispense with some values while retaining others or to elevate one traditional value – duty to family or country or compassion for the poor – to a preeminent place in the hierarchy of values. This is a very different thing from debunking value altogether. If the innovator believes his own morality to be something more than arbitrary sentiment, then the project of moral innovation cannot rest on the shifting sands of moral subjectivism. "Only by such shreds of the *Tao* as he has inherited is he even able to attack it," Lewis pointed out. He is engaged in a self-refuting project.

Still, the committed nihilist who dispenses with pretensions to value altogether provides a very different challenge to the Tao. We may, of course, question whether true nihilism or moral ignorance is possible.[80]

---

[77] Aristotle, *Ethics* 1151a. As Aristotle maintained, "Reason does not teach the principles in mathematics or in actions; [with actions] it is virtue, either natural or habituated, that teaches correct belief about the principle. The sort of person [with this virtue] is temperate, and the contrary sort is intemperate" (1151a). An intemperate person is one who desires the wrong thing, because he or she does not understand the proper end of his or her action.

[78] Lewis, *Abolition of Man*, 5.   [79] Ibid., 46.

[80] See, e.g., J. Budziszewski's *What We Can't Not Know: A Guide*, rev. ed. (Ignatius Press, 2011).

But suppose a man's conscience is so marred by intellectual vice that he truly does not see – and adamantly denies the existence of – first moral principles. Towards the Tao that man "may be hostile," Lewis maintained, "but he cannot be critical: he does not know what is being discussed."[81] It is like trying to have a rational discussion with a madman. He is, as Aristotle said, a man without premises.[82]

Lewis often treated the man ignorant of the first principles of reason as a hypothetical possibility but an empirical rarity. In the formulation of Richard Hooker, who offered what Lewis considered to be the highest and most beautiful expression of the natural-law tradition,[83] the "first principles of the Law of Nature are easy; hard it were to find men ignorant of them."[84] In his BBC broadcast talks, Lewis raised the possibility that you might find "an odd individual here and there who did not know" the law of nature, "just as you find a few people who are colourblind or have no ear for a tune."[85] Lewis' comparison of color-blindness to moral ignorance should not be read as a denial that the first principles of reason are both true for all and, at some level, known by all.[86] There was no person simply ignorant of the law of nature. Yet Lewis did consider it a possibility that a person's moral knowledge could be effaced by inordinate passions or evil habits.[87] In the Chronicles of Narnia series, some of the "talking animals"– animals, that is, that have the ability to reason – become so corrupt on the inside that they turn into irrational beasts. "Wouldn't it be dreadful," Lucy asks in *Prince Caspian*, "if some day in our world, at home, men started going wild inside, like the animals here, and still looked like men, so that you'd never know which were which?" Lewis never suggested that men could be born without chests, as a man might be born color-blind, but he did fear the possibility that propaganda and conditioning actually could create a race of sub-men whose perception of the first principles of reason had been destroyed.

Lewis' third and final point was about the practical consequences of the authors' subtle teaching in "The Green Book." If we persist down the road of moral subjectivism, he insisted, we will lose our civilization and our souls. Why? The answer is because the moral cornerstones of goodness and duty will have been destroyed. If man, in his conquest of nature,

---

[81] Lewis, *Abolition of Man*, 47.
[82] See Lewis' appeal to Aristotle on this point in Lewis, "The Poison of Subjectivism," 106.
[83] C.S. Lewis, *English Literature*, 462–463.
[84] Hooker, *Laws of Ecclesiastical Polity*, book I, ch. 12, sec. 2.
[85] Lewis, *Mere Christianity* (New York: HarperCollins, 2009 [1952]), 5.
[86] See Aquinas, *S.T.* I–II Q. 94, A. 4.   [87] See ibid.

marches on to conquer human moral nature, then all will be lost. At the moment of his final triumph, man will discover that he is motivated – and can only be motivated – by the arbitrary epiphenomena of material nature. Morality will have been simply an illusion. The grand paradox is that nature regains the upper hand over man at the very moment of nature's seeming defeat. Man, who strove to put nature under his control, finally submits to nature's power. The practical consequences are far-reaching. Education and propaganda become one and the same. So, too, do legitimate rule and tyranny. Duty and goodness cease to exist, and man becomes whatever his appetites and passions make of him.

According to the new outlook, whatever man wants is necessarily arbitrary, and the motivations for his actions are simply supplied by material nature. Man's power to mold himself and conquer nature is therefore illusory. In reality, environment shapes man, and this means that some humans (motivated by their own environment) will decide what to make of the rest of humanity. "The final stage," Lewis predicted, "is come when Man by eugenics, by pre-natal conditioning, and by an education and propaganda based on a perfect applied psychology, has obtained full control of himself."[88] The dire aspect of this scenario is not that some men will try to influence others, for that has always been part of education and child-rearing. Indeed, Lewis presumed, with Aristotle, that only one brought up in fine habits could see the first principles of practical reason. The real danger was in the novelty of the modern situation. The "manmoulders of the new age," Lewis predicted, "will be armed with the powers of an omnicompetent state and an irresistible scientific technique: we shall get at last a race of conditioners who really can cut out all posterity in what shape they please."[89] In the process of deciding what to make of us, the conditioners will be motivated only by their own arbitrary wishes, only "by the *sic volo, sic jubeo.*"[90]

The dystopian future Lewis envisioned in *The Abolition of Man* plays out in *That Hideous Strength*, the plot of which involves a scientific social planning agency called the National Institutes for Coordinated

---

[88] Lewis, *Abolition of Man*, 59.   [89] Ibid., 60.

[90] The Latin phrase, which roughly means "This I want, this I command," is an allusion to Juvenal's Satire VI and Luther's famous allusion to Juvenal in his open letter on translating Scripture. See Martin Luther, "Open Letter on Translating" (September 8, 1530), trans. Gary Mann from "Sendbrief von Dolmetschen," in *Dr. Martin Luther's Werke* (Weimar: Hermann Boehlaus Nachfolger, 1909), Band 30, Teil II, pp. 632–646. Published online at the Christian Classics Ethereal Library www.ccel.org/ccel/luther/translat ing.ii.html.

Experiments, or N.I.C.E. N.I.C.E.'s mission is to overcome and subdue nature with science, and the point of the novel, Lewis insists in the book's foreword, is identical with that of *The Abolition of Man*. The political implications are manifest, and one quote in particular opens a window through which we get a glimpse of Lewis as a political theorist. Of the Deputy Director of N.I.C.E., Lewis narrates: "he had passed from Hegel into Hume, thence through Pragmatism, and thence through Logical Positivism, and out at last into the complete void."[91] The ideas of the sixteenth century, Lewis warned, pass in modern times from Hegel into nothing and culminate finally in a world of posthumanity.

---

[91] Lewis, *That Hideous Strength*, 353. Chronologically, David Hume (1711–1776) predates G.W.F. Hegel (1770–1831).

5

Lewis' Lockean Liberalism

The *state of nature* has a law of nature to govern it, which obliges every one: and reason, which is that law, teaches all mankind, who will but consult it, that being all *equal and independent*, no one ought to harm another in his life, health, liberty, or possessions: for men being all the workmanship of one omnipotent, and infinitely wise maker; all the servants of one sovereign master, sent into the world by his order, and about his business[.]

    – John Locke, *Second Treatise of Government* (1690)

In 1959 many of the world's leading evolutionary biologists, including the famed scientist and secular humanist Sir Julian Huxley, attended a centennial celebration of Charles Darwin's *On the Origin of Species* at the University of Chicago. Huxley was an archetype of the modern man against whom Lewis set his sights in *The Abolition of Man*: a champion of the modern project to reshape human nature through eugenics, social planning, and the ideological construction of a new morality. "Many people," Huxley wrote years earlier,

assert that this abandonment of the god hypothesis means the abandonment of all religion and all moral sanctions. This is simply not true. But it does mean, once our relief at jettisoning an outdated piece of ideological furniture is over, that we must construct something to take its place.[1]

The rendering of God and the moral law as two bits of threadbare "ideological furniture," and the project to construct something new to replace traditional morality, horrified Lewis. He warned that these

---

[1] Julian Huxley, "The New Divinity," in *Essays of a Humanist* (London: Chatto & Windus, 1964), 222.

83

philosophical trends would come to be accepted under the claimed authority of scientists speaking outside of their areas of expertise.[2]

Dan Tucker, a local Chicago newspaperman, attended the conference and reported that he heard in many of the "learned speeches, and particularly [Huxley's,] ... such precise and detailed illustrations of what Lewis wrote about in 'The Abolition of Man' that they really were a bit frightening."[3] After writing an editorial piece critical of the conference, Tucker sent a press clipping to Lewis. In a handwritten letter dated December 8, 1959, Lewis responded to Tucker, connecting the themes in *Abolition* directly to modern political trends. Echoing an argument he made elsewhere, Lewis wrote that in "every age those who wish to be our masters, if they have any sense, secure our obedience by offering deliverance from our dominant fear."[4] In an age in which the fear is wizardry, the medicine man becomes the master. When the world fears hellfire, clerics rule the day. "In England," Lewis concludes, "the omni-competent Welfare State has triumphed because it promised to free us from the fear of poverty."[5] What Lewis dubbed "scientocracy" – a form of government in which the claimed power to rule is premised on technological or scientific prowess divorced from traditional moral norms – was, he insisted, the gravest threat to freedom in the modern world.[6]

Lewis' prescient argument in *The Abolition of Man* earned his book the number 7 spot on *National Review* magazine's list of 100 greatest books of the twentieth century.[7] The editors of *National Review*, like countless others, consider the work a classic defense of freedom in the face of totalitarian opposition. Yet if Lewis was correct about the unhealthy assumptions embedded in modern thought, and about the

---

[2] "Now I dread specialists in power because they are specialists speaking outside their special subjects," Lewis wrote. "Let scientists tell us about sciences. But government involves questions about the good of man, and justice, and what things are worth having at what price; and on these a scientific training gives a man's opinion no added value." See C.S. Lewis, "Is Progress Possible?," in Walter Hooper, ed., *God in the Dock: Essays on Theology and Ethics* (Grand Rapids, MI: William B. Eerdmans, 1970), 315.

[3] Lewis, "Letter to Tucker," in The Collected Letters of C.S. Lewis, *vol. 3: Narnia, Cambridge, and Joy 1950–1963* (New York: Harper Collins, 2007), 1104 n. 246.

[4] Lewis, "Letter to Tucker," 1104.   [5] Ibid.

[6] Lewis uses the term "scientocracy" in the letter to Tucker above. Also, see generally John G. West, ed., *The Magician's Twin: C.S. Lewis on Science, Scientism, and Society* (Discovery Institute Press, 2012).

[7] *National Review*, "The Non-Fiction 100" (May 3, 1999). Published online at www.national review.com/articles/215718/non-fiction-100.

dire practical necessity of returning to a "crude and nursery-like belief in objective values,"[8] it is perhaps puzzling that Lewis did *not* favor a return to an ancient or medieval approach to politics. He was, and remained, a classical liberal committed to the key conceptions of that tradition.[9] Yet Lewis was also steeped in the classics of Western antiquity, and he heaped no lavish praise on modern democracy and maintained no optimism about the fate of modern society. In his 1959 letter to Tucker, Lewis confessed that he was at his "wit's end" with regard to the problems of modern governance and he shared his own cynical reservations about the false promises of democracy.[10] In practice, democracy "neither allows the ordinary man to control legislation nor qualifies him to do so."[11] What is more, Lewis noted, the "real questions are settled in secret and the newspapers keep us occupied with largely imaginary issues. And this is all the easier because democracy always in the end destroys education."[12]

What, then, is the solution? Beyond the restoration of liberal education, Lewis' suggestions were few and cursory.[13] "Only a power higher than man's can really find a way out," he feared.[14] It is, however, significant that Lewis did not propose returning to an ancient or medieval approach to politics, especially given his critical approach to modern thought. "Every age has its own outlook," Lewis noted in his essay on the importance of reading books outside of one's own time. "It is specially good at seeing certain truths and specially liable to make certain mistakes." The only way to palliate the intellectual diseases of one's own age, Lewis argued, is to "keep the clean sea breeze of the centuries blowing through our minds." And he insisted this can be done "only by reading old books," a practice he championed in his personal life as well as his professional work.[15] We have already mentioned how exceptionally situated Lewis was to comment on the ancients and the moderns, and his

---

[8] Lewis, "The Poison of Subjectivism," in Walter Hooper, ed., *The Seeing Eye: And Other Selected Essays from Christian Reflections* (New York: Ballantine Books, 1967), 81.

[9] Lewis, "Is Progress Possible?," in Walter Hooper, ed., *God in the Dock* (Grand Rapids, MI: Wm. B. Eerdmans, 1970), 314.

[10] Lewis, "Letter to Tucker," 1105.

[11] Ibid. See the full quotation in Chapter 1, n. 16.   [12] Ibid., 1104–1105.

[13] See C.S. Lewis, "Democratic Education," in Walter Hooper, ed., *Present Concerns* (New York: Harcourt, 1986), 32–36, and "Screwtape Proposes a Toast," in *The Saturday Evening Post* (December 19, 1959). We will discuss one of Lewis' suggestions – the idea of a Christian veto party – in the conclusion of the next chapter.

[14] Lewis, "Letter to Tucker," 1105.

[15] Lewis, "On the Reading of Old Books," in Hooper, *God in the Dock*, 202.

characterization of himself as a dinosaur who knew the classical thinkers almost first-hand.[16] Lewis' debt to just Plato and Aristotle is immeasurable,[17] let alone the countless other figures – major and minor – that populated the literary and historical universe Lewis inhabited.[18]

Against the democratic ethos of modern times, we might expect, then, for Lewis to harken back to a more hierarchical conception of the universe, and thus a more aristocratic orientation to politics. In a qualified defense of John Milton, Lewis described in detail what this hierarchical conception of the universe meant. In a chapter titled "Hierarchy" in *A Preface to Paradise Lost*, Lewis jousted with modern critics who found in Milton a "disquieting contrast between republicanism for the earth and royalism for Heaven," and who even suggested that Milton was secretly joining the devil's side in rebelling against God's tyrannical rule.[19]

How can Milton really favor a monarchical deity while favoring republican politics for mere human beings? The question, Lewis warned, imports modern sensibilities and anachronistically imbues Milton with an egalitarian ethos he would have found quite puzzling. On the contrary, Lewis argued, Milton's central thought "belongs to the ancient orthodox tradition of European ethics from Aristotle to Johnson ... " The central idea is that hierarchy is built into the very fabric of reality:

According to this conception, degrees of value are objectively present in the universe. Everything except God has some natural superior; everything except unformed matter has some natural inferior. The goodness, happiness, and dignity of every being consists in obeying its natural superior and ruling its natural inferiors. When it fails in either part of this twofold task we have disease or monstrosity in the scheme of things until the peccant being is either destroyed or corrected. One or the other it will certainly be; for by stepping out of its place in the system ... it has made the very nature of things its enemy. It cannot succeed.[20]

---

[16] See Chapter 1, section on "The Apolitical and Political C.S. Lewis."

[17] As illustrated in the previous chapter.

[18] One need only leaf through Lewis' *English Literature in the Sixteenth Century* (Oxford: Oxford University Press, 1954) to grasp just how vast and comprehensive Lewis' mastery was. As Jacobs writes, "Only a man very secure in the depths of his learning – and Lewis read *every single sixteenth-century book* in Duke Humfrey's Library, the oldest part of Oxford's great Bodleian Library, in preparation for writing this history – can risk such an exhibition of panache: he obviously knows too much to be accused of frivolity" (emphasis in original). See Alan Jacobs, *The Narnian: The Life and Imagination of C.S. Lewis* (San Francisco, CA: Harper, 2005), 184–185.

[19] C.S. Lewis, *A Preface to Paradise Lost* (Oxford: Oxford University Press, 1961), 73–81.

[20] Ibid., 73–74.

Lewis found the hierarchical conception operative not only in the realm of politics as described by Aristotle, but also throughout the plays of Shakespeare and the works of Dante and Montaigne.[21]

Aristotle taught us, Lewis noted in his commentary on Milton, that the justice or injustice of any political rule depends *not* on the existence of a social contract but on the nature of the parties involved. If the ruling party is a natural superior, then the rule is just. If the party claiming a right to rule is an inferior, or even an equal, then the result is tyranny. The supposed tension between obedience to God as monarch and resistance to Charles II is chimerical on this reading. We must first ask whether Charles II is our natural superior. If he is not, "rebellion against him would be no departure from the hierarchical principle, but an assertion of it; we should obey God and disobey Charles for one and the same reason – just as even a modern man might obey the law and refuse to obey a gangster for one and the same reason."[22]

Here we find the reason why, despite his obvious and ardent admiration of Aristotle, Lewis did not endorse a hierarchical ordering of political life. Of course, Lewis did not reject hierarchy simply – far from it. Indeed, he often lamented the leveling effects of democracy in every arena outside politics. "Ethical, intellectual, or aesthetic democracy is death," he warned.[23] Hierarchy had its proper place in modern life, but that place was not in the political realm. In another passage that jars the modern ear, Lewis agreed with Aristotle that some men were fit to be slaves; Lewis denounced actual slavery only because he thought no men were fit to be masters.[24] Similarly, Lewis pronounced himself to be a democrat because he believed in the "Fall of Man" – not because most men were "so wise and good that everyone deserved a share in the government."[25] While Lewis vehemently rejected the modern route to pragmatism, positivism,

---

[21] Addressing moderns who find the gender hierarchy of *The Taming of the Shrew* jarring, Lewis writes that Katherine's subordination is "very startling to a modern audience; but those who cannot face such startling should not read old books." Lewis likens Shakespeare's attitude toward hierarchy to Montaigne's maxim that "to obey is the proper office of a rational soul." Lewis is quoting from Michel de Montaigne, *The Complete Works of Michael de Montaigne, Comprising His Essays, Letters, etc.* (New York: Worthington, 1888), 224.

[22] Lewis, *A Preface to Paradise Lost*, 77.

[23] Lewis, "Democratic Education," in *Present Concerns*, 32.

[24] Lewis, "Equality" in *Present Concerns*, 17. See also his reply to critics after "Humanitarian Theory of Punishment," in *God in the Dock*, 295–300. In a note on p. 298, Lewis suggests that *he* might actually be a natural slave.

[25] Lewis, "Equality," in *Present Concerns*, 17.

and the posthuman void that he analyzed in *Abolition* and depicted in *That Hideous Strength*, he also rejected as impractical and untenable any return to the past of the virtuous pagan or the medieval synthesis.

Lewis' positive political thought was heavily indebted to the classical liberal tradition that developed and took its bearings in Britain during the early modern period. In particular, Lewis endorsed a version of John Locke's social contract theory to ground political legitimacy, and he adopted a version of John Stuart Mill's harm principle in his approach to questions about the legislation of morality. Although many of Lewis' best-known works contain withering critiques of modern political thought, Lewis never wrote a treatise on politics or offered a sustained vision of a well-functioning political order.[26] Even so, Lewis did think deeply about politics, and he was well aware of the great conversation about human nature and political order that philosophers had been engaged in across the centuries.

It is, additionally, possible to construct a *framework* for thinking about politics from Lewis' voluminous body of work. The modern elements in Lewis' political thought reflect his attempt to reconcile the hierarchical nature of reality, including the reality of human nature as it was first noted and understood by pagan political philosophers, with the consequences of the fall. When offering provisional answers to perennial political questions, Lewis was also attentive to practical realities, including the reality that a majority of his countrymen were not in any meaningful sense Christian. Perhaps surprisingly, this self-professed "dinosaur" – the last of a dying breed of "Old Western men" who could read and understand ancient texts as a native – was in matters of politics a classical liberal in the mold of John Locke and, to a lesser extent, John Stuart Mill.[27]

LOCKE AND LEWIS

In extant publications, Lewis first mentions Locke in a rather unfavorable light in a letter to his boyhood friend and confidante Arthur Greeves. While finishing a compilation of various philosophers, a twenty-year-old Lewis admits to finding Spencer and William James challenging and not

---

[26] To make this observation is not to slight Lewis; he did not set out to become a political philosopher.

[27] See Lewis' reference to himself as part of a dying breed of old Western men in "De Descriptione Temporum," in *Selected Literary Essays* (Cambridge: Cambridge University Press, 1969).

at all like the "simple minded gentlemen of the Locke or Paley type."[28] By the time Lewis was forty-one, an established scholar, dedicated Christian, and member of the now-celebrated literary association called the Inklings, he had adjusted his assessment. Writing to his brother Warnie on New Year's Eve of 1939, Lewis noted he was reading Locke's *Treatises* and was struck by Locke's objection to Filmer in the *First Treatise* that a hereditary line from Adam to the present day would undermine every established monarchy except one. Lewis concluded about the treatises, "It is a very richly and racily written book like all Locke, and I'm enjoying it."[29]

It is not hard to decipher what might have led one Oxford man to revise his judgment of another. In October 1923, before an unemployed Lewis had secured his fellowship at Magdalen, he visited the new Master of University College, Michael Sadler, who had been reading some of Lewis' work and acting as a reference to possibly introduce him to a career in journalism. Sadler, on learning of Lewis' private tutoring with W.T. Kirkpatrick, exclaimed, "Oh, then you are the Lockian private pupil! Now that's very interesting."[30] Sadler advised Lewis to read Locke's *On Education* and Rousseau's *Emile* so as to reflect on his own experience. Lewis, although having already read Locke's *Education*, left Sadler and immediately picked up Locke from the library.[31] The episode, combined with Lewis' writing an essay on Locke in the months to follow, sheds some potential biographical light on how the mature Lewis came to a more appreciative view of Locke.[32] Perhaps unsurprisingly, then, we find many Lockean elements in Lewis' political thought.

Locke set out to construct a theoretical conception of politics that might avoid civil strife and bloodshed while neither privileging peace over justice nor embracing the amorality of Hobbes's statist solution. Locke's project was to limit government to the protection of individual natural

---

[28] Lewis, *Collected Letters*, vol. 1, p. 440. For brief references to Locke, see also *English Literature*, 435, and *The Abolition of Man* (New York: HarperCollins, 2001 [1944]), 73. Despite Locke's aversion to poetry and call for children to wear leaky shoes to build character dealing with cold feet in his *Thoughts on Education*, Lewis describes Locke in a footnote in *Abolition* as "one of our most sensible writers on education."

[29] Lewis, *Collected Letters*, vol. 2, p. 314.

[30] Lewis, *All My Road before Me: The Diary of C.S. Lewis* (San Diego: Harcourt Brace Jovanovich, 1991), 274.

[31] Ibid.

[32] Ibid., 323, 327–328. Lewis mentions working on a Locke essay on May 15 and June 4–5, which indicates it was a substantive project.

rights, and Locke explicitly tied the substance and source of those rights to the classical natural-law tradition as it found expression in the writings of Richard Hooker.[33] Nevertheless, Locke departed from the classical tradition by deemphasizing government's perfecting role. As Ellis Sandoz puts it, Locke "lowered his sights a bit by largely (but not entirely) abandoning the political goals of inculcating virtue and righteousness in citizens or subjects. He modified in the process the social contract theory whereby more modest goals become central."[34] Against the backdrop of the twentieth-century totalitarian turn in Western civilization, Lewis found much to praise in Locke's formula. Lewis warned across his letters and writings that "where benevolent planning, armed with political and economic power, can become wicked is when it tramples people's rights for the sake of their good."[35] By lowering the aim of government and limiting its perfecting role, Locke's theory addressed Lewis' main fear about the trajectory of modern government: that it will increasingly concentrate and deploy technological power to trample private rights under the paternalistic theory that government ought to "do us good or make us good."[36]

Locke's description of government's modest goal of protecting rights thus coincides with Lewis' description of the limited end of government as promoting "the ordinary happiness of humans in this life."[37] This is but one of several major points of commonality we see between the two figures. Both thinkers believed God to be the ground and author of human nature (and thus morality) and that God had made morality accessible via

---

[33] We leave aside for the moment several debates this description might broach, such as how sincere Locke's invocation of Hooker is. More important for the gist of this chapter is Lewis' affinity for Hooker as another linkage between Locke and Lewis. As we have noted, Hooker comes in for some very high praise in Lewis, *English Literature in the Sixteenth Century*, 49, where Lewis describes Hooker's articulation of natural law as the tradition's "fullest and most beautiful expression." Lewis' very high praise of Hooker in this instance and in his fuller treatment of Hooker elsewhere in the book (441–463), and Locke's extensive drawing on Hooker in the *Second Treatise*, offers additional linkages that hint toward Lewis' positive reception of Locke.

[34] Ellis Sandoz, *A Government of Laws: Political Theory, Religion, and the American Founding* (Baton Rouge: Louisiana State University Press, 1990), 19. Although Locke lowered his sights for the government's explicit role for inculcating virtue, his *Thoughts on Education* is all about inculcating virtue. Locke's view of the state is that of a minimalist, so it's a mistake to equate a lesser role for government inculcation of virtue with a diminished appreciation for the task of educating for virtue simply.

[35] Lewis, *Collected Letters*, vol. 3, pp. 91–92.

[36] Lewis, "Is Progress Possible?," in *God in the Dock*, 314.

[37] C.S. Lewis, *Mere Christianity* (HarperCollins, 2009), 199.

both direct revelation and natural reason.[38] Because each thinker believed natural law to be accessible to human beings as such, neither thought Christianity introduced a new morality. Since Christians do not have a monopoly on moral truth, and given the fall of man, both thinkers detested theocracy and feared the abuses that would accompany governments that understood their primary role to be producing virtuous or pious citizens. Given this fear – despite believing in a hierarchical universe – Locke and Lewis have a very limited view of government's role and warrant. Finally, Locke proposed and Lewis accepted a version of social contract theory to explain the grounds of legitimate government.[39]

GOD AS ANCHOR

Lewis, as we have noted, believed God to be the author of an objective morality that should govern human behavior. "God made us: invented us as a man invents an engine. A car is made to run on petrol, and it would not run on anything else. Now God designed the human machine to run on Himself."[40] While Lewis' rhetorical strategy in the opening of *Mere Christianity* and his appendix and overall argument in *Abolition* presuppose that human beings can access morality even apart from acknowledging its source, Lewis' natural-law theory and his political thought rely on God as the ontological source of all morality.[41] Another way to say this is that when it comes to moral inquiry, epistemology and ontology are distinct. One can recognize and practice elements of the natural law without acknowledging its ultimate source.

There is agreement here with Locke, for Locke's natural-law theory differed from other early modern theories in that Locke described

---

[38] Of course, some Locke scholars find the theistic elements of Locke's work disingenuous and esoterically subversive, in which case they would say that Lewis' view aligns with Locke's exoteric teaching. But our point here is to present Locke as Lewis read him, rather than to engage debates in the fractured world of Locke scholarship.

[39] Perhaps a bit tongue-in-cheek, Lewis described a rough summary of "the classical political theory" of England to be that "you promised not to stab your daughter's murderer on the understanding that the State would catch him and hang him." Despite his casual description of the theory, the essay in which it appears is a straightforward application of Lockean social contract theory to the criminal justice system in England. See "Delinquents in the Snow," in *God in the Dock*, 306–310.

[40] Lewis, *Mere Christianity*, 50. Locke has similar language regarding God's role as creator in the *First Treatise*, section 53.

[41] See Jeremy Waldron, *God, Locke, and Equality: Christian Foundations in Locke's Political Thought* (Cambridge: Cambridge University Press, 2002).

humanity's rights as "inalienable" as opposed to "absolute." Locke posited God as the source and ultimate owner of all property, and as such, there is always a transcendent higher law whereby a government may be judged.[42] The law of nature, while lacking an earthly enforcer, is still operable and knowable in the state of nature. Natural rights might be violated, but they cannot be alienated. Hobbes, by positing that man had absolute rights over himself, allowed that man could give over his rights to the state, allowing the state absolute power unanswerable to a higher standard. On the contrary, argued Locke, a real standard remains applicable in and out of the state of nature. God has authored this higher standard, and both Locke and Lewis identified the law of nature with reason itself.

REVELATION AND THE LAW OF NATURE

Lewis could incorporate his belief in natural law with a robust commitment to God's revelation in Scripture in part because he believed Scripture acts as a source of political ends, but not necessarily political means. This idea is important for two reasons. The first is that given the scarcity of specific and concrete political content in the New Testament, Christians should not expect to learn how to govern society from the Bible:

Christianity has not, and does not profess to have, a detailed political programme for applying "Do as you would be done by" to a particular society at a particular moment. It could not have. It is meant for all men at all times and the particular programme which suited one place or time would not suit another. And, anyhow, this is not how Christianity works. When it tells you to feed the hungry it does not give you lessons in cookery. When it tells you to read the Scriptures it does not give you lessons in Hebrew and Greek, or even in English grammar. It was never intended to replace or supersede the ordinary human arts and sciences: it is rather a director which will set them all to the right jobs, and a source of energy which will give them all new life, if only they will put themselves at its disposal.[43]

Politics is among the "ordinary human arts and sciences," and thus is a craft or techne that can be learned by those inside and outside the church.

The second reason Christians should realize that Christianity is a source of ends and not means is it counters the notion that only Christianity can provide a common morality for any given society. An explicitly and

---

[42] John Locke, "Second Treatise: Section 6," in *Two Treatises of Government* (Cambridge: Cambridge University Press, 1988).

[43] Lewis, *Mere Christianity*, 79.

exclusively Christian conception of morality or politics goes against the very promise of Lewis' natural-law theory. Lewis believed that God had imprinted His moral law on every human heart, whether or not that person had come to faith in Jesus Christ. As such, any attempt to ground a nation's laws exclusively on Christianity is folly at best and an invitation to tyranny at worst. It is folly because Christians will inevitably disagree about the relative virtues and merits of various economic and political systems. When a Christian citizen enters the political fray to advocate a particular social and economic system as the best means to accomplish a morally permissible end (e.g., taking care of widows and orphans), he or she does *not* have the authority to represent his or her prudential judgment as required by Christianity. "By the natural light, He has shown us what means are lawful," Lewis insisted. To "find out which one is efficacious He has given us brains. The rest He has left to us."[44]

The attempt to equate Christianity with a new moral or political program presupposes that Christianity offers a unique morality that replaces (rather than, perhaps, develops and refines) an already existing natural morality. Lewis strongly denied that this is true:

The first thing to get clear about Christian morality between man and man is that in this department Christ did not come to preach any brand new morality. The Golden Rule of the New Testament ... is a summing up of what everyone, at bottom, had always known to be right. Really great moral teachers never do introduce new moralities: it is quacks and cranks who do that.[45]

Locke took a similar view, as expressed in his *Reasonableness of Christianity* and *Letter Concerning Toleration*. In *Reasonableness* Locke argued for a minimalist view of what is required for salvation, interpreting several passages of Scripture so as to confirm Scripture's emphasis on Jesus' role as King and Messiah. Belief in Jesus' kingship is what Locke is trying to establish, and in doing so he understands Jesus to be a King enforcing an already existing moral law.

If Jesus is King and Messiah, and if salvation requires obedience to the King's laws, it follows that obedient subjects must follow the law. Happily, according to Locke, making this obedience possible is exactly what Jesus came to do. In an extensive argument, Locke offers scriptural support for his contention that Jesus is *the* great moral teacher, come to

[44] Lewis, "Meditation on the Third Commandment," in *God in the Dock*, 199.
[45] Lewis, *Mere Christianity*, 78.

call us back to the moral law we have rejected. As he concludes these passages, Locke writes:

Thus we see our Saviour not only confirmed the moral law, and, clearing it from the corrupt glosses of the Scribes and Pharisees, showed the strictness as well as obligation of its injunctions; but moreover ... [he] requires the obedience of his disciples to several of the commands he afresh lays upon them; with the enforcement of unspeakable rewards and punishments in another world, according to their obedience or disobedience ... There is not, I think, any of the duties of morality, which he has not, somewhere or other, by himself and his apostles, inculcated over and over again to his followers in express terms.

The message of Christianity presupposes a moral law everyone has broken and knows he has broken.

Although Christianity presupposes a universally binding (and knowable) morality, it does not propose a universal form of government. This point is hammered home in a few passages in Locke's *Letter*, perhaps most explicitly when he deals with the Mosaic law:

There are, indeed, many cities and kingdoms that have embraced the faith of Christ, but they have retained their ancient forms of government; with which the law of Christ hath not at all meddled. He, indeed, hath taught men how, by faith and good works, they may attain eternal life. But he instituted no commonwealth. He prescribed unto his followers no new and peculiar form of government ...[46]

Locke and Lewis share an understanding both that God authors human nature and morality *and* that Christianity assumes such a common morality in preaching a message of repentance. Both see an overlap between the Mosaic law and the natural law.[47] For Locke and Lewis, God's authorship of the law of nature makes community possible among Christians and pagans alike. Nevertheless, each insists the fall is so significant that a corrupt human nature, armed with presumptuous and unfounded authority, presents humanity with the perpetual danger of an overreaching and tyrannical state that springs forth from the imprudent concentration of power. Christians, of course, are not free of this temptation to concentrate power and are in fact particularly tempted to concentrate and abuse political power in the name of Christianity.

---

[46] John Locke, *A Letter Concerning Toleration* (Indianapolis, IN: Hackett, 1983), 44.

[47] See, e.g., C.S. Lewis, "The Poison of Subjectivism," in *The Seeing Eye*, 271, and John Locke, *The Works of John Locke in Nine Volumes*, 12th ed. (London: Rivington, 1824), vol. 6, "The Reasonableness of Christianity," 13.

THE DANGERS OF OVERBEARING GOVERNMENT

Lewis' belief in the universality of the natural law and his belief in humanity's fallen nature prompted his stout rejection of any society run by the church or ostensibly governed by strictly Christian principles. "On those who add 'Thus said the Lord' to their merely human utterances," Lewis warned, "descends the doom of a conscience which seems clearer and clearer the more it is loaded with sin."[48] In his reply to Professor Haldane, Lewis explained his dislike of theocracy:

I believe that no man or group of men is good enough to be trusted with uncontrolled power over others. And the higher the pretensions of such power, the more dangerous I think it both to the rulers and to the subjects. Hence, Theocracy is the worst of all governments ... the inquisitor who mistakes his own cruelty and lust of power and fear for the voice of Heaven will torment us infinitely because he torments us with the approval of his own conscience and his better impulses appear to him as temptations.[49]

Lewis' opposition to a Christian-only vision of morality sets him against the church–state framework of the "late medieval pseudo-Crusader, of the Covenanters, of the Orangemen," as well as (we would add) some American Christians who link God and country in a way that would surely draw Lewis' ire. Because Lewis believed Scripture revealed ends and not means, he did not claim any one particular political system or party as God's prescribed ideal.[50]

As dangerous as theocracy could be, however, Lewis was not so short-sighted as to think religion was the primary pretext for totalizing government aspirations. At the particular time in which he wrote, Lewis thought the greatest threat to Western civilization *and* Christianity was not theocracy (which holds almost no purchase in the modern West) or nationalistic fascism (which had been largely defeated in the late war), but scientific technocracy.[51] As Lewis confessed:

---

[48] Lewis, "Meditation on the Third Commandment," in *God in the Dock*, 198.

[49] Lewis, "A Reply to Professor Haldane," in *Of Other Worlds: Essays and Stories* (New York: Harcourt Brace Jovanovich, 1975), 81.

[50] It is telling that despite Lewis' affinity for democracy, Narnian politics are decidedly monarchical.

[51] Lewis, "Is Progress Possible?," 314–315. "Again, the new oligarchy must more and more base its claim to plan us on its claim to knowledge. If we are to be mothered, mother must know best. This means they must increasingly rely on the advice of scientists, till in the end the politicians proper become merely the scientists' puppets. Technocracy is the form to which a planned society must tend. Now I dread specialists in power because they are specialists speaking outside their special subjects. Let scientists tell us about sciences. But

I dread government in the name of science. That is how most tyrannies come in. In every age the men who want us under their thumb, if they have any sense, will put forward the particular pretension which the hopes and fears of that age render most potent. They "cash in." It has been magic, it has been Christianity. Now it will certainly be science.[52]

Although Locke did not see science as a chief political danger in eighteenth-century England, the tyrannical misuse of authority by powerful governments was for Locke a pressing concern. The entirety of the *First Treatise* is devoted to combating a dangerous and false religious conception of political authority, and the *Second* is Locke's positive answer to the question of what conception can work without the liabilities of Robert Filmer's divine-right-of-kings theory.[53] Though not mentioned by name, Locke surely had Hobbes in mind as well in his rejection of absolute monarchy in section 93 of the *Second Treatise*. Accepting the argument for absolute monarchy, Locke maintained, "is to think, that men are so foolish, that they take care to avoid what mischiefs may be done them by polecats, or foxes; but are content, nay think it safety, to be devoured by lions."[54]

In his *Letter*, Locke places the blame for religious conflict, persecution, and tumult squarely on the government's refusal to tolerate religious differences. Although members of various religious sects have earned blame for their actions and seditious behavior, their misbehavior was, Locke maintained, a direct result of the government's entirely avoidable intolerance. The violence and dangers of these factions, though real, were provoked by the *political* choices of the magistrate. Locke's closing pages assert, and reassert, that the violence and discord resulting from the improper mixing of religion and politics stems from the political sphere, and thus the solution had to be political as well. These sects would not be accused of sedition and rebellion "if the Law of Toleration were once so settled, that all Churches were obliged to lay down Toleration as the Foundation of their own liberty ..." As a result, "these Causes of Discontents and Animosities being once removed, there would remain nothing in

---

government involves questions about the good for man, and justice, and what things are worth having at what price; and on these a scientific training gives a man's opinion no added value. Let the doctor tell me I shall die unless I do so-and-so; but whether life is worth having on those terms is no more a question for him than for any other man."

[52] Lewis, "Letter to Tucker," 315.

[53] See Robert Filmer, *Patriarcha, or The Natural Power of Kings* (London: Richard Chiswell, 1680).

[54] Locke, "Second Treatise: Section 93," in *Two Treatises of Government*.

these Assemblies that were not more peaceable, and less apt to produce Disturbance of State, than in any other Meetings whatsoever."[55] Of course, neither Lewis nor Locke thought religious groups were blameless in fomenting conflict or social strain, and, as we have seen, Lewis was particularly wary of Christians equating their own politics with God's will and thus blasphemously breaking the third commandment in a dangerous and public way. Nevertheless, both Lewis and Locke criticized governments for exceeding their proper warrant and inflaming otherwise manageable and minor tensions in the body politic.

THE SOCIAL CONTRACT

Locke's *Letter on Toleration*, like Lewis' various writings about politics and ethics, emerged against the backdrop of world-historical events. Locke and Lewis each argued for a discrete application of universal principles to address practical political questions rooted in the challenges of a particular time and place. Lewis, an educated and interested observer of politics, and a fierce advocate for a practical renaissance of natural-law philosophy in contemporary culture and education, nevertheless did not see himself as an innovative, original or even classical natural-law theorist. Indeed, on the latter point, Lewis adamantly insisted that he was *not* "trying to reintroduce in its full Stoical or medieval rigour the doctrine of Natural Law."[56] What, then, was Lewis doing with all of his talk about the Tao and the law of human nature? If he did not advocate a return to an ancient or medieval doctrine of natural law, eschewed a return to monarchy or aristocracy, and rejected any attempt to reintegrate church and state, to what political doctrine did Lewis subscribe?

Although Lewis never systematically described his political philosophy, he did have a political system of choice, and his thinking, as we have noted, was heavily influenced by a strong belief in the fallen nature of humanity. Lewis was a partisan of classical liberal democracy, not because it allowed for maximum political participation for all of a nation's citizens, but because it curtailed the likelihood of political tyranny. He was a democrat because he believed human nature had been corrupted, which contrasted sharply with the claims of other democrats,

[55] Locke, *A Letter Concerning Toleration*, 51.
[56] Lewis, "On Ethics," in *Christian Reflections*, 55. The context of this quotation is an affirmation from Lewis that his point in "On Ethics" is negative; namely, one cannot choose from a number of moral systems using moral criteria.

such as Rousseau, who believed humanity to be "so wise and good that everyone deserved a share in the government."[57]

Lewis warned that believing in democracy for such a reason was dangerous because human beings are in fact neither wise nor good:

> The danger of defending democracy on those grounds is that they're not true. And whenever their weakness is exposed, the people who prefer tyranny make capital out of the exposure. I find that they're not true without looking further than myself. I don't deserve a share in governing a hen-roost, much less a nation. Nor do most people – all the people who believe advertisements, and think in catch-words and spread rumours.
>
> The real reason for democracy is just the reverse. Mankind is so fallen that no man can be trusted with unchecked power over his fellows.[58]

One of Lewis' political principles was a belief in government's duty to restrain wrongdoing as could be understood given the law of nature.[59] And it is in describing this restraining and punitive duty that we see Lewis' closest endorsement of Locke's theory, by substance if not by name.

Contrary to the classical tradition of Aristotle and Aquinas, but in line with Lockean social contract theory, Lewis held that men enter into a social contract for the "mutual preservation" of their property. Because the law of nature remains in force whether people are in the state of nature or political society, citizens have the right to revolt and produce a new government if the existing one consistently violates their natural rights. Lewis worried about just this possibility in England. In his short essay "Delinquents in the Snow," Lewis complained about how the legal process failed to deal properly with hooligans who had been caught stealing and vandalizing his home. In his view, the presiding judge was far too lenient on the young criminals, and Lewis worried what such laxity might mean for England's political future. Describing how the social contract should work in theory, he warned of the consequences that would occur if the system broke down in practice. "According to the classical political theory of this country," Lewis summarized, "we

---

[57] Lewis, "Equality," in *Present Concerns*, 17. In "On the Transmission of Christianity," in *God in the Dock*, 118, Lewis referred to Rousseau as the "father of the totalitarians."

[58] Ibid.

[59] Lewis' endorsement of this restraining duty, and his perennial concern about government overreach, echo a formulation of James Madison's in *Federalist* 51: "In framing a government which is to be administered by men over men, the great difficulty lies in this: you must first enable the government to control the governed; and in the next place oblige it to control itself."

surrendered our right of self-protection to the State on the condition that the State would protect us."[60]

A dilemma arises when the state does not live up to its end of the contract. The state's promise of protection is what morally grounds our obligation to civil obedience, according to Lewis. On the classical Lockean theory, the government's protection of natural rights, including the right to property, is what explains why it is right to pay taxes and wrong to exercise vigilante justice. Yet at present, Lewis observed,

> the State protects us less because it is unwilling to protect us against criminals at home and manifestly grows less and less able to protect us against foreign enemies. At the same time it demands from us more and more. We seldom had fewer rights and liberties nor more burdens: and we get less security in return. While our obligations increase their moral ground is taken away.[61]

Lewis drew the same conclusion from this state of affairs that Locke did. Those citizens who have entered into the social contract have the right to revolt, and will so revolt when the state breaches their trust and no longer carries out its function.[62] "When the State cannot or will not protect," Lewis warned in Lockean overtones, "'nature' is come again and the right of self-protection reverts to the individual."[63]

LIMITED ROLE OF GOVERNMENT

Lewis was obviously concerned about the abuses of an overly ambitious government. What *positive* role did he envision for government? After all, human depravity gives both the rationale for government as well as reason to fear its excesses. As James Madison claimed in a famous passage from *Federalist* no. 51, no government would be necessary if men were angels and no limitations on government power would be necessary if angels governed men. The reality, however, is that government is necessary; yet there are clear dangers with investing men with untrammeled

---

[60] Lewis, "Delinquents in the Snow," in *God in the Dock*, 308. Lewis goes on to quote Samuel Johnson's anecdote about killing the murderer of one's daughter if he is acquitted, noting that this would mean a return to the "state of nature."

[61] Ibid. For Lewis' description of this same concern as expressed in a dream, see Lewis, "A Dream," in *Present Concerns*, 37–40. The "morally grounds" language here in "Delinquents," as well as Lewis' belief in the Tao in or out of society, tells us that he is thinking here more of Locke than of Hobbes.

[62] Though as Locke notes in the *Second Treatise*, chapter 18, sections 208–209, they will not revolt unless the tyranny is widespread and grave.

[63] Lewis, "Delinquents in the Snow," 308.

power. Although Lewis strongly preferred a very limited government, he
wrestled with the tension between his desire for a limited government
(which both protects and respects a robust private sphere) and his
acknowledgment that we have massive social needs that only government
can address.[64] This tension reveals a difference between Lewis' normative
view of what politics should be and his realistic view of what politics is,
given infinite need and finite resources. Government must exist, Lewis
acknowledged, but he always insisted that government exists for the good
of individuals, and this characterization of government as instrumental to
individual goods represents an additional modern and Lockean element in
Lewis' political thought. Consider two quotes by Lewis about the ultimate
purpose of government:

As long as we are thinking of natural values we must say that the sun looks down
on nothing half so good as a household laughing together over a meal, or two
friends talking over a pint of beer, or a man alone reading a book that interests
him; and that all economies, politics, laws, armies, and institutions, save insofar as
they prolong and multiply such scenes, are a mere ploughing the sand and sowing
the ocean, a meaningless vanity and vexation of the spirit. Collective activities are,
of course, necessary, but this is the end to which they are necessary.[65]

. . . it is easy to think the State has a lot of different objects – military, political,
economic, and what not. But in a way things are much simpler than that. The
State exists simply to promote and to protect the ordinary happiness of human
beings in this life . . .[66]

In each formulation, Lewis insists that the state exists *for* individuals.
Arguably, the way Lewis chooses to represent the relationship between
the individual and the state in these passages represents a break from the
classical Aristotelian and Thomistic natural-law tradition, which maintains that the political community fosters a truly common good that is not
simply reducible to private, individual goods.[67] For Lewis, however,

---

[64] We will consider Lewis' view of morals legislation in more detail in the next chapter.

[65] Lewis, "Membership," in *The Weight of Glory* (New York: Macmillan, 1980), 121.
Lewis' excerpt from "The Weight of Glory," in the tenth footnote of the first chapter, is
instrumental here. Lewis' Christian worldview emphasizes the individual over the nation
because individuals are eternal and nations are mortal. "There are no ordinary people.
You have never talked to a mere mortal. *Nations, cultures, arts, civilisations – these are
mortal, and their life is to ours as the life of a gnat.* But it is immortals whom we joke
with, marry, snub, and exploit – immortal horrors or everlasting splendours."

[66] Lewis, *Mere Christianity*, 169.

[67] For an extensive treatment of the political common good in the classical tradition, see
Matthew D. Wright, "A Vindication of Politics: Political Association and Human Flourishing," dissertation, University of Texas, 2011.

political activity – voting, organizing, lobbying, soldiering – is only a means to genuine aspects of human flourishing, not an intrinsic part of that flourishing in itself.

This latter, technical point seems to mark Lewis off as uniquely modern, and Lockean, in his political orientation. Yet Lewis does acknowledge that collective activities are necessary, and at times he recognizes the appeal of developing technocratic government solutions to address our collective social problems. The temptation to invest government with more power, he noted, always works on a real need that has been neglected.[68] Lewis' constant fear, which he often voiced, was that legitimate human problems that require social coordination and collective activity will give rise to solutions – the N.I.C.E. perhaps – that are far worse than the original crisis. "We have on the one hand a desperate need; hunger, sickness, and the dread of war," Lewis noted. "We have, on the other, the conception of something that might meet it: omnicompetent global technocracy."[69]

The temptation to use a real need as a pretext to accumulate and concentrate power is not a new one, but the difference in the mid-twentieth century, Lewis warned, was that "success" looked more and more like a legitimate possibility. Lewis contrasted the dilemmas of past societies with the unprecedented opportunities offered by science and extensive government bureaucracy:

In the ancient world individuals have sold themselves as slaves, in order to eat. So in society. Here is a witch-doctor who can save us from the sorcerers – a war-lord who can save us from the barbarians – a Church that can save us from Hell. Give them what they ask, give ourselves to them bound and blindfold, if only they will. Perhaps the terrible bargain will be made again. We cannot blame men for making it. We can hardly wish them not to. Yet we can hardly bear that they should.

The question about progress has become the question whether we can discover any way of submitting to the worldwide paternalism of a technocracy without losing all personal privacy and independence. *Is there any possibility of getting the super Welfare State's honey and avoiding the sting?*[70]

Whether we can get the welfare state's honey without the sting was perhaps *the* most pressing practical political question for Lewis, and the stakes were (and are) enormous. While acknowledging the great needs for which technology promises answers, Lewis endorsed simple goods that he

---

[68] Lewis, "Equality," in *Present Concerns*, 18.
[69] Lewis, "Is Progress Possible?," in *God in the Dock*, 315–316.
[70] Ibid. (emphasis added).

feared were endangered by a know-it-all state: "To live one's life in his
own way, to call his house his castle, to enjoy the fruits of his own labour,
to educate his children as his conscience directs, to save for their prosper-
ity after his death."[71] He was skeptical that the modern state can deliver a
painless cure. Repeating his argument in *Abolition*, Lewis predicted
soberly that "some men will take charge of the destiny of others. They
will be simply men; none perfect; some greedy, cruel and dishonest." He
then asked rhetorically, and with an allusion to Lord Acton's famous
aphorism that absolute power corrupts absolutely, whether "we discovered some new reason why, this time, power should not corrupt as it
has done before?"[72]

Lewis' political thought is so imbued with concerns about governmen-
tal overreach that even a positive portrayal slips back into warnings about
the dangers of abuse. While this theme consistently shows up in Lewis'
formal and personal writings, nevertheless we can glean from Lewis'
various treatments of politics that his ideal government was meant to
protect negative rather than positive freedoms. Lewis' political vision, and
his endorsement of social contract theory generally, has much in common
with Locke's political philosophy, including Locke's view of the government's chief end or purpose as the protection of property.

But is there a difference here between Locke's view of the end of
government and Lewis' view? On the one hand, Lewis stated, "The State
exists simply to promote and to protect the ordinary happiness of
human beings in this life."[73] Locke, on the other hand, wrote, "The
great and *chief end*, therefore, of men's uniting into commonwealths,
and putting themselves under government, *is the preservation of their
property*."[74] A modern understanding of property may mislead one into
thinking that Locke viewed the protection of material goods as the
highest purpose of the state. On the contrary, Locke's understanding
of "property" cannot be reduced to a crass materialism that a contemporary understanding of government's purpose might encourage. Persons, Locke writes, are willing to enter into the social contract "for the
mutual preservation of their lives, liberties, and estates, which I call by
the general name, property."[75]

---

[71] Ibid.   [72] Ibid. Lewis explicitly cites Lord Action in "Membership," 168.
[73] Lewis, *Mere Christianity*, 169.
[74] Locke, "Second Treatise: Section 124," in *Two Treatises of Government* (emphasis in
original).
[75] Ibid., section 123.

Lewis' view of politics thus clearly shares some strong affinities with Locke's thought. Both Locke and Lewis believed that the end of government was the protection of individuals and their property, broadly understood. Both claimed that God is the ultimate source of property, and as such, God is the ontological source of genuine morality, though people could still access that morality without acknowledging God as its source or agreeing on how to best relate to God. Lewis followed Locke's understanding of the social contract, including Locke's belief that the law of nature provided a higher standard by which government should be judged. Lewis also agreed that when a government ceases to live up to that higher standard (and by extension it breaches the social contract), the people reclaim rights once given up, and they have moral justification for revolution. Both thinkers were much more concerned about the threat government authority posed to the liberty of citizens than they were about the threat that freedom posed to social security.[76] Yet on some matters Lewis differed significantly from Locke, and some of these differences stemmed from the fundamental changes between Locke's predominantly Christian England and Lewis' essentially post-Christian England. What help, then, is Lewis' thought with regard to the question of what it means to be a Christian citizen in a religiously diverse and morally pluralistic modern democratic society? For American evangelicals in particular, who laud Lewis' work, the Oxford don's reflections on this vexed issue are at once instructive and challenging.

---

[76] Lewis was not doctrinaire about his opposition to the welfare state, but he did insist that it came with a cost and a danger. In a very interesting letter to a woman who apparently had a very bad experience with the American health care system, Lewis commented: "What you have gone through begins to reconcile me to our Welfare State of which I have said so many hard things. 'National Health Service' with free treatment for all has its drawbacks – one being that Doctors are incessantly pestered by people who have nothing wrong with them. But it is better than leaving people to sink or swim on their own resources." See Lewis, *Collected Letters*, vol. 3, p. 1064.

6

Screwtape is in the Details

Politics in the Post-Christian West

In short, we do not get good laws to restrain bad men. We get good men to restrain us from bad laws.

– G.K. Chesterton, *All Things Considered* (1908)

"Speaking not only for myself but for all other Old Western men whom you may meet," Lewis concluded his inaugural address at Cambridge University, "I would say, use your specimens while you can. There are not going to be many more dinosaurs."[1] Cambridge had plucked Lewis away from Oxford by offering him a chair in medieval and Renaissance literature, and Lewis' title for his first address was "De Descriptione Temporum," a "description of the times." In the address Lewis turned his observant eye to a watershed difference between a previous age of Austen, Milton, and Shakespeare and the modern age of machines, Darwin, and progress. As one steeped in the ancients but living among the moderns, Lewis offered himself as a specimen of the Old Western Man, someone who could speak to both sides of the divide. This offering of himself was unusual for Lewis, who often argued for the priority of what an author wrote *about* as opposed to what we might glean from attending to the author himself.[2] Yet Lewis used the occasion of his personal change in circumstances (moving from Oxford to Cambridge) to underscore the tectonic shifts that had transformed Western society in the twentieth century.

---

[1] C.S. Lewis, *De Descriptione Temporum: An Inaugural Lecture* (Cambridge University Press, 1955).

[2] See, for example, Lewis, "The Personal Heresy in Criticism," discussed in Chapter 4, section on "The Early Modern Turn."

The themes of change and time were of particular interest to Lewis, and his grappling with the nexus between Christian faith and an ever-changing Western culture remains relevant and insightful half a century after his death. As we have seen in previous chapters, Lewis defended the enduring truth and relevance of natural law, or the Tao, a body of "primary moral principles on which all others depend" and which has an inherent reasonableness that "shines by its own light."[3] There is no guarantee, however, that men and women will apprehend the good of these moral principles nor wisely apply them to particular historical moments and places. Times change, even if axiomatic moral principles do not, and thus Lewis' insights about the changes in Western culture remain pertinent for students of politics generally, and scholars and practitioners working in the natural-law tradition in particular. How do adherents of an unchanging moral law engage a religiously and morally pluralistic democratic society?

On first glance Lewis seems an unlikely guide to such a question, and his readers are wise to distinguish between Lewis' direct and fully articulated thought and his more speculative musings, and even his letters. Though connected, determining what Lewis thought about political life and Christian citizenship is a distinguishable task from drawing on Lewis for how *we* should now think about such matters. Lewis did not devote any full-length work to how his Christian natural-law theory might be applied to particular problems in a pluralistic society. Nevertheless, despite his professed antipathy toward the practical details of political life, Lewis did address many specific political issues and described what a Christian society might look like. From these specific issues and general statements we can glean a Lewisian approach to Christian political life in a post-Christian culture.

CONVERTED PAGANS AND APOSTATE PURITANS

How then did Lewis understand what was distinct about modern times? While he attended to changes in literature in his Cambridge address and educational pedagogy and philosophy in *Abolition*, Lewis' most straightforward account of the changes in the modern mind are found in his essay "Modern Man and His Categories of Thought." Though primarily concerned with implications for Christian apologetics, Lewis' observations

---

[3] Lewis, *Miracles: A Preliminary Study*, rev. ed. (New York: HarperCollins, 1996 [1947]), 34–35.

pertain to the culture broadly speaking, and thus to political thinking as well. "In the last hundred years," Lewis wrote, "the public mind has been radically altered." Lewis proposed that six changes have contributed to this radical break: (1) an educational revolution, (2) the emancipation of women, (3) the advance of historical developmentalism or what he called "Evolutionism," (4) the rise of Proletarianism or democratic egalitarianism, (5) an emphasis on practical knowledge over wisdom, and (6) an increasing skepticism toward reason. With the possible exception of Lewis' thoughts on the emancipation of women,[4] these descriptions provide a good synopsis of Lewis' views on modernity.[5]

Lewis described the educational revolution for the upper classes as a shift away from the "ancients." No longer schooled in the thought of Plato or Aristotle, or even Virgil or Horace, the educated classes had a diminished set of values with which to compete with the values of "modern industrial civilization." The result Lewis described as an isolated "Provincialism," which cuts off each succeeding generation from the wisdom and folly of its forebears, leading to a myopic intellectual vision and a dearth of standards by which to judge contemporary thought.[6] What follows is what Lewis referred to – borrowing from his friend Owen Barfield – as chronological snobbery. Such a development bodes ill for moral education, as it breeds contempt among the young for the wisdom of their elders, and thus undercuts their ability to distinguish genuine and time-tested wisdom from passing fads and trivialities.

The second and related change in how the modern man thinks is what Lewis called "Developmentalism" or "Historicism."[7] This idea, related to

---

[4] Lewis' observation on how the emancipation of women has changed modernity is probably one he would have repudiated later in his life. In this article, written in 1946, Lewis argued that the presence of women among men would impair the masculine mind's "disinterested concern with truth for truth's own sake" because the men would be more interested in impressing the fairer sex. Given Joy Davidman Gresham's collaboration with Lewis on several works, including *Till We Have Faces*, not to mention his debate experience with Elizabeth Anscombe two years later, it seems likely that Lewis would have at least tempered this view. See also Lewis' discussion of friendship between a man and woman in *The Four Loves* (Orlando, FL: Harcourt, 1988 [1960]), particularly pp. 72–73.

[5] Lewis, "Modern Man and His Categories of Thought," in Walter Hooper, ed., *Present Concerns: A Compelling Collection of Timely, Journalistic Essays* (Orlando, FL: Harcourt, 1986), 61–66.

[6] For Lewis' antidote to this condition, see his "On the Reading of Old Books," in Walter Hooper, ed., *God in the Dock* (Grand Rapids, MI: Wm. B. Eerdmans, 1970), 200–207.

[7] See Lewis' essay "Historicism," in Walter Hooper, ed., *The Seeing Eye: And Other Selected Essays from Christian Reflections* (New York: Ballantine Books, 1967), 100–113.

Lewis' treatment of epochal change in the Cambridge address, pertains to the modern faith in progress. Modern men and women are influenced by their experience with ever-improving machines and their sense of ever-increasing human accomplishment.[8] The modern default expectation of reality is that "almost nothing can be turned into almost anything": order from chaos, life from nonlife, reason from instinct, civilization out of savagery, and virtue from animalism. The problem with this way of looking at the world is not the judgment that progress in various human endeavors is desirable, but rather that there is a natural and inevitable stream of progress that we must discern and join. History with a capital "H" is now the source of wisdom and value, and prophecy about its future direction reveals humanity's sacred duty.

Lewis sharply contrasted this modern faith in progress with Christian teaching, for Developmentalism rejects both the goodness of God's original creation and the fall that has corrupted it. The differences between the two approaches as applied to politics are profound. For the Christian natural-law theorist, the very standards of what counts as progress are inextricably bound up in the Tao, which itself is rooted in God's character, proclaimed by divine revelation, and discoverable by natural reason. Contrary to the progressive view, Lewis noted that Christianity holds that "the Best creates the good and the good is corrupted by sin, [but that] for Developmentalism the very standard of good is itself in a state of flux."[9]

"Proletarianism" was Lewis' term for what resulted from a particular form of democratic thinking that flatters the "people" without reservation. Having accepted the Lockean principle that government legitimacy requires the consent of the governed, democratic citizens have conflated their authority with political infallibility. As a result the Proletariat "are self-satisfied to a degree perhaps beyond the self-satisfaction of any recorded aristocracy. They are convinced that whatever may be wrong with the world it cannot be themselves."[10] Lewis noted that for apologetic and evangelistic efforts this shift in class self-satisfaction puts God "in the dock."[11] Whereas early Christians, Jews, and pagans alike assumed there was something amiss with them, modern men and women do not share a

---

[8] Lewis, "Modern Man and His Categories of Thought," 63–64.   [9] Ibid.

[10] Ibid. This is not to say that Lewis never worried about the complacency of the rich and powerful. His concern was how man's categories of thought have changed, and arguably the rich and powerful have always been party to the vices of complacency and indifference.

[11] See "God in the Dock," in *God in the Dock*, 240–244.

sense of sin and therefore do not recognize their need for salvation.[12] How to proclaim the good news changes when the target audience does not believe in the bad news. Moreover, the test God now needs to pass – what gets him out of the dock – is not whether Christian revelation about him is true, but whether belief in God is helpful or therapeutic for the individual.

The political implications of this shift follow the religious implications. Democratic societies unwilling to entertain the possibility that the people may be badly mistaken about particular policies or moral views will foster a politics of flattery and obfuscation, encouraging politicians to avoid unpopular but necessary stands in order to stay in office. In addition, like the modern view of religion, politics becomes primarily about what the government can do for me or my particular interest group. Ascertaining the truth about whether a particular tax policy promotes the *common* good for the nation becomes wholly secondary to whether I personally benefit from the policy.

This shift in religious and political thinking from "Is it true and good in itself?" to "What's in it for me?" illustrates another change: an emphasis on practicality. Whereas a pragmatic approach to religion downplays the question of truth, a purely pragmatic approach to politics leads to a political conversation almost exclusively concerned with technocratic means rather than principled ends for human beings individually and in community. "Ends" are assumed to be common but in fact are expressed with elastic words or phrases that obscure rough edges: national interest, economic growth, or American (or British) values. The difficulty and controversy that accompany conflicting political ends are precisely what Rawls famously tried to avoid by making his political theory "political" rather than "metaphysical."[13] If Lewis is right about the reality of the natural law, however, burying our deep disagreements about the ends of politics is quixotic. Nevertheless, in such a society, the Christian political thinker has to first make the case that a democratic debate or discussion about genuine ends and goods is necessary (and desirable) before he or she can move to advocating any particular conception of those ends and goods.[14]

---

[12] As evidence of the ancient pagan sense of guilt, Lewis pointed to "the fact that both Epicureanism and the Mystery Religions both claimed, though in different ways, to assuage it [i.e., guilt]." Thus the Gospel "promised healing to those who knew they were sick." See ibid., 244.

[13] See *Political Liberalism* (New York: Columbia University Press, 1993) and *Justice as Fairness: A Restatement* (Cambridge, MA: Harvard University Press, 2001).

[14] This is, of course, similar to how the Christian apologist must first make the case that there is "bad news" about the human condition before any articulation of the "good news" can be comprehensible.

Finally, Lewis anticipated the advent of modern skepticism by observing that modern man has a general and unalarmed belief that reason is not a valid means of proving anything. Irrational causes, rooted in subconscious desires or economic interests (or, we would now add, racial and gender identities), are the real origin of thoughts. Lewis wrote of modern man, exaggerating only a bit, "He accepts without dismay the conclusion that all our thoughts are invalid."[15] This shift fits in nicely with Lewis' criticism of emotivism in *Abolition*, and the fallout for political discourse is significant. If we believe the positions held by our fellow citizens are grounded entirely in subrational and often intractable characteristics, then attempting to persuade them with reason and evidence is hopeless. In a talk to the Oxford Socratic Club, reprinted in a 1944 issue of the *Socratic Digest*, Lewis insisted that the *ad hominem* fallacy is *the* intellectual error of the twentieth century. He dubbed the fallacy "Bulverism," after a fictional character who mastered how to explain *why* people are wrong without first demonstrating that they *are* wrong.[16]

Lewis believed that it was important to take into account the particularities of modernity for the purpose of apologetics, and this careful consideration applies also in the realms of politics and ethics. Even more critical than these six changes, and indeed encompassing many of them, is the secularization of the West. Despite the lingering formal ties between some churches and states, including Lewis' own Church of England, the age of Christendom had passed. He referred to himself in his autobiography as "a converted Pagan living among apostate Puritans."[17] As we will see in examining Lewis' views on morals legislation, he urged the Church to recognize that most people in England were not Christians.

---

[15] Lewis, "Modern Man and His Categories of Thought," 66. See also Lewis' essay "Bulverism," in *God in the Dock*, 271–277.

[16] See "Bulverism," 271–277.

[17] Lewis, *Surprised by Joy: The Shape of My Early Life* (London: Harcourt, 1955), 39. In *Mere Christianity* (New York: HarperCollins, 2009 [1952]), he described the Christian as living in "Enemy-occupied territory," called by God to "take part in a great campaign of sabotage" (p. 51). In the most important sense this is Lewis' description of earth after the fall; it is the "silent planet" in Lewis' Space Trilogy, because it is "bent," cut off from God's oversight through delegated angelic authorities. Thus even the most virtuous and Christian-friendly society would be enemy territory. But even within this understanding of the corrupted nature of the world there are societies that reflect God's goodness in better and worse ways. See, generally, Lewis, *Out of the Silent Planet* (New York: Scribner, 2003 [1938]).

What practical role, then, did Lewis envision for natural-law philosophy in the affairs of post-Christian Western democracies? In Lewis' view, such societies are cut off from an appreciation of the past, committed to the utopian ideal of unlimited progress, self-satisfied, concerned with technos rather than telos, and skeptical about reason. In addition to these characteristics, one must also consider the religious, racial, moral, and cultural pluralism that increasingly characterizes Western societies. In the last pages of *Abolition* Lewis admitted that he was at a loss regarding how the doctrine of objective value can be reconnected to the pursuit of knowledge. While trying to articulate a role for scientific inquiry that did not descend into materialistic reductionism, he asked, "Is it, then, possible to imagine a new Natural Philosophy, continually conscious that the 'natural object' produced by analysis and abstraction is not reality but only a view, and always correcting the abstraction? I hardly know what I am asking for."[18] It is also not entirely clear what Lewis was asking for in regard to the social role of Christian natural-law philosophy in a secular and pluralistic society that had ceased believing in the inherent rationality of basic moral norms.

We are reminded of an emeritus law professor who sat through a seminar on Lewis' political thought and then remarked that it was great fun but terribly unsatisfying to revel in Lewis' wit without wrestling with the "so what?" questions. How should Christians arrive at sound positions on controversial political issues? Should Christians attempt to organize politically? How far should Christians go in making the requirements of the positive law line up with the requirements of the moral law? Although Lewis claimed to care little for practical politics, he thought deeply about the proper relationship between Christianity and public life, and he ventured answers to many of these thorny questions in essays, articles, and private letters.

THE PRACTICAL PROBLEM OF CHRISTIAN POLITICS

Christian communities in the first centuries had no political power and little prospect of gaining control of the Roman Empire's key political institutions. Still, as N.T. Wright notes, it is clear "that the kingdom of God was itself, and remained [to early Christians], a thoroughly political concept; that Jesus' death was a thoroughly political event; that the

---

[18] Lewis, *The Abolition of Man* (New York: HarperCollins, 2001 [1944]), 89.

existence and growth of the early church was a matter of community-building, in conflict, often enough, with other communities."[19] The challenge of pluralism has thus confronted Christianity since its inception. Christians reading Lewis in twentieth-century England or America, however, differed from their ancient forebears in that they were citizens or subjects of representative governments who (theoretically) shared in responsibility for the exercise of secular political power. Despite the profoundly different political situations of first-century Christians and Christians in the modern West, Lewis often treated the question of Christian politics in a way that nonetheless echoed St. Paul's advice to early church in Rome. "If it is possible," Paul admonished, "as far as it depends on you, live at peace with everyone."[20] The practical challenge for Christians, wrote Lewis along similar lines, lies in discovering how to "live as innocently as we can with unbelieving fellow-subjects under unbelieving rulers who will never be perfectly wise and good and who will sometimes be very wicked and very foolish."[21]

Living as innocently as possible in a fallen world might be the extent of Christian political thought if Christians were completely powerless or came to believe, as some Christians do, that wielding coercive force is a betrayal of the gospel.[22] If Lewis thought that quietism or political non-involvement was a legitimate option for Christians living with and under the authority of unbelieving neighbors, then thinking about practical political problems would be merely academic. Although Lewis' political temperament at times places him within the "just leave me alone" brand of conservatism, he nevertheless did believe in a positive political role for the ordinary citizen, if only to serve as a check on the overly ambitious schemes of planners and optimists.[23] To what degree, though, should Christian citizens who have a share in political power endeavor to impose a Christian vision for the political community? Lewis' treatment of this

---

[19] N.T. Wright "Paul and Caesar: A New Reading of Romans," http://ntwrightpage.com/Wright_Paul_Caesar_Romans.htm.

[20] Romans 12:17–18 (NIV).

[21] Lewis, "The Humanitarian Theory of Punishment," in *God in the Dock*, 292–293.

[22] This is not to conflate pacifism with passivism. Obviously Lewis did not live to encounter the works of John Howard Yoder or Stanley Hauerwas.

[23] See "Democratic Education," in *Present Concerns*. Lewis' "belief" is not a terribly hopeful one, however, as he evidences near-despair in some of his correspondence about the prospects of democracy preserving the common good. See his letter to Dan Tucker, December 8, 1959: "I am, you see, at my wit's end on such matters" (Lewis, *Collected Letters*, vol. 3, p. 1105). One begins to wonder about his professed indifference to politics.

vexed question comes out particularly in his discussion of homosexuality, religious education in schools, and divorce law. And it is on these practical questions that Lewis parts ways with many traditionalists and evangelicals.

Lewis' views on homosexuality are never treated in a systematic manner, though we learn from occasional references in his works and letters what he thought about it. He certainly regarded homosexual behavior as sinful.[24] But though he considered it a sin, he did not seem to consider it a very serious one.[25] In describing the prevalence of sodomy in the schools he attended as a youth, Lewis admitted that homosexuality was a carnal vice. Yet he viewed spiritual sins such as cruelty and pride as being much more deadly.[26] Lewis wrote that the real reason homosexuality was despised was not because of Christian morality but because "it is, by adult standards, the most disreputable and unmentionable, and happens also to be a crime in English law. The World may lead you only to Hell; but sodomy may lead you to jail and create a scandal, and lose you your job."[27]

In two of his letters Lewis made his position more clear with regard to the legality of homosexuality and morals legislation in general. In a letter responding to an acquaintance at Magdalene College, Lewis wrote,

---

[24] See, e.g., Lewis' letter to Sheldon Vanauken on May 14, 1954, in *Letters*, vol. 3, pp. 471–474. In the letter, Lewis writes that he takes "it for certain that the *physical* satisfaction of homosexual desires is sin."

[25] No doubt Lewis' attitude toward homosexuality was strongly influenced by his close and enduring friendship with Arthur Greeves, a childhood friend whom later biographers have identified as homosexual. See, e.g., A.N. Wilson, *C.S. Lewis: A Biography* (New York: W.W. Norton, 1990), 44, and McGrath, C.S. Lewis – *A Life: Eccentric Genius, Reluctant Prophet* (Carol Stream, IL: Tyndale House, 2013), 72. For the collected correspondence between Lewis and Greeves, see Walter Hooper, ed., *They Stand Together: The Letters of C.S. Lewis to Arthur Greeves*, 1914–1963 (New York: Macmillan, 1979).

[26] Warnie Lewis, C.S. Lewis' brother, disputed Lewis' description of how rampant homosexuality was in Wyvern, the school they both attended. Whether Lewis exaggerated, although interesting from a biographical perspective, does not diminish what his description reveals about his views on homosexuality. See also Lewis' ranking of pederasty as a much lesser sin than spying or snitching; *Letters*, vol. 3, p. 678.

[27] Lewis, *Surprised by Joy*, 61. Lewis goes so far as to claim in a subsequent paragraph that among the cold, cruel world of his school, the sodomy performed by older boys on younger boys was actually a "foothold or cranny left for certain good things." This "good thing" apparently is thinking of someone other than oneself, as it is the only thing Lewis mentions. It is difficult to understand how Lewis can so cleanly separate the spiritual vices of cruelty and pride from the act of sodomy. For a young boy entering the public school, we cannot imagine a much crueler initiation than sexual abuse.

"I quite agree with you about Homosexuals: to make the thing criminal cures nothing and only creates a blackmailer's paradise. Anyway, what business is it of the State's?"[28] In an earlier letter addressing homosexuality, Lewis further expounded on the relationship between sin and the positive law. Writing to a Mrs. Edward Allen, Lewis responded:

> I quite agree that no *sin*, simply as such, should be made a *crime*. Who the deuce are our rulers to enforce their opinion of sin on us? – a lot of professional politicians, often venal time-servers, whose opinion on a moral problem in one's life we [should] attach very little value to. Of course many acts which are sins against God are also injuries to our fellow-citizens, and must on that account, but only on that account, be made crimes. But of all the sins in the world I [should] have thought homosexuality was the one that least concerns the State. We hear too much of the State. Government is at its best a necessary evil. Let's keep it in its place.[29]

Although Lewis' comments come across as uniquely modern, and perhaps libertarian, the argument that sin, as such, should *not* be made illegal on that account falls well within the classical natural-law tradition. "Human law is framed for the mass of men, the majority of whom are not virtuous," Thomas Aquinas noted in his *Summa Theologiae*. "Therefore human law does not prohibit every vice from which virtuous men abstain, but only the more serious ones from which the majority can abstain, and especially those that harm others and which must be prohibited for human society to survive, such as homicide, theft, and the like."[30] Homosexuality, Lewis indicated, was of all sins the "one that least concerns the State," presumably because Lewis considered homosexuality to occasion little social harm.

This limited view of the state also crops up in his thoughts on the place of religion in public education. In a preface written by Lewis to the 1946 book *How Heathen Is Britain?*, Lewis describes cultural education as much more organic than programmatic.[31] A Christian generation filled with Christian teachers cannot help but pass on Christianity to its children almost irrespective of the particular curricula or formal pedagogy chosen by educational boards or committees. By the same reasoning, a

---

[28] Lewis, *Letters*, vol. 3, p. 1154. For Lewis' more pastoral thoughts on the plight of the Christian with same-sex attraction, see his letter to Sheldon Vanauken, ibid., pp. 471–472.

[29] C.S. Lewis to Mrs. Edward A. Allen (February 1, 1958), in Warren Lewis, ed., *Letters of C.S. Lewis*, rev. ed. (Orlando, FL: Harcourt, 2003 [1966]), 473.

[30] *S.T.* I–II, Q. 96, A. 2.

[31] Lewis, "On the Transmission of Christianity," in *God in the Dock*, 114–119.

post-Christian generation *cannot* pass on Christian thinking even with explicitly Christian content. Concerning the cultural transmission of values and virtues, personnel is policy. Lewis spoke of the increasing secularization of society as the "decline of religion," and he argued that if the current generation knew little of Christianity it was because most members of the previous generation were not Christians.[32] We cannot blame eunuchs for being childless, Lewis suggested. Nor can we blame modern British teachers for not teaching Christianity. Given this understanding of how education works, Lewis found unrealistic the notion that a programmatic injection of Christian teaching and influence in public schools could reinvigorate the church, the state, and public morality. Such a view – popular in some quarters then and now – supposes that the lack of government-supported Christian education is a cause, rather than an effect, of an increasingly post-Christian society.

Lewis had no objection to Christian schools in principle, and he encouraged private Christian schools wherever possible. Nor did he share an American-style opposition to public religious education based on a separation between religion and society or church and state. He did, however, oppose the imposition of Christian education on a secular or pluralistic society as both imprudent and counterproductive. By mandating a Christian curriculum to be taught by largely non-Christian or nominally Christian teachers, "we should only be making masters hypocrites and hardening thereby the pupils' hearts."[33] "Rebaptizing" the English schools with the force of law would not work. Rather than attempt to transform society through the levers of local and national education policy, Lewis concluded that Christians would do better to work on the small and individual scale by creating private, independent, and genuinely Christian schools; raising Christian children in Christian families; and evangelizing to adult neighbors and teens.[34] Whereas with regard to homosexuality Lewis doubted the efficacy of the state's power to punish or restrict undesirable behavior, with respect to education he doubted the state's ability to promote or inculcate true religion and positive moral character through the levers of public education absent an already-existing religious and moral culture.

---

[32] Ibid., 118.   [33] Ibid.

[34] Which isn't to say Lewis thought religious education was by any means foolproof: "[B]ut remember how much religious education has exactly the opposite effect to that wh. was intended, how many hard atheists come from pious homes." *Letters*, vol. 3, p. 507.

Finally, Lewis' views on marriage and divorce bring into focus his thinking about Christian mores and morals legislation in a secular society. By some measures, Lewis took a very strict view of marriage and divorce. In *Mere Christianity* Lewis acknowledged that while churches differed on the question of whether divorce was ever permissible, they all think of divorce "as something like cutting up a living body, as a kind of surgical operation. Some of them think the operation so violent that it cannot be done at all; others admit it as a desperate remedy in extreme cases."[35] In a letter written before he married divorcée Joy Davidman Gresham, Lewis told an inquiring friend that he believed that even the innocent party should not remarry after a divorce.[36]

Despite these views, Lewis did not believe it falls within the state's purview to protect or promote the Christian ideal of marriage. In *Mere Christianity* he distinguished between the Christian and secular views of marriage:

I should like to distinguish two things which are very often confused. The Christian conception of marriage is one: the other is the quite different question – how far Christians, if they are voters or members of Parliament, ought to try to force their views of marriage on the rest of the community by embodying them in the divorce laws. A great many people seem to think that if you are a Christian yourself you should try to make divorce difficult for everyone. I do not think that. At least I know I should be very angry if the Mohammedans tried to prevent the rest of us from drinking wine. *My own view is that the Churches should frankly recognise that the majority of the British people are not Christians and, therefore, cannot be expected to live Christian lives.*[37]

The practical upshot of this view, Lewis went on to argue, was that there should be legal marriage recognized by the government and applicable and available to all, and a Christian version of marriage that is clearly distinguishable from the legal version.[38] Lewis did not here exclude Christian-specific morals legislation in principle, even as his prudential assessment of Britain's populace excluded it in practice for the foreseeable future.

Lewis' views on these three controversial issues – homosexuality, religion in public schools, and marriage and divorce – offer some striking insights into his political thought and raise questions for the practical

---

[35] Lewis, *Mere Christianity*, 96.   [36] *Letters*, vol. 3, p. 189.

[37] Lewis, *Mere Christianity*, 101–102 (emphasis added). Tolkien was none too pleased about this passage. See www.christianitytoday.com/ct/2012/december-web-only/why-cs-lewis-was-wrong-on-marriage-jrr-tolkien-was-right.html.

[38] Lewis, *Mere Christianity*, 112.

application of his Christian natural-law theory to particular social issues. In the letter to Mrs. Allen about homosexuality, Lewis wrote that only sins that injured fellow citizens should be subject to legal sanction. He warned that an infusion of Christian teaching into public school curricula would do more harm than good. In his writings on marriage, Lewis argued that churches should recognize the pervasive secularity of the culture and refrain from imposing their particular Christian ideals on an unbelieving public. The strength of Lewis' commitment to a transcendent moral reality might be rivaled only by his distrust of government's ability to determine, enforce, and encourage that same morality. Yet this distrust of government must be tempered by some rule or principle that does ground laws that regulate our moral behavior, or else we undercut the very purpose of protecting life and property that Lewis identified in the previous chapter. We find that principle in Lewis' letter to Mrs. Allen. Sins can be treated as crimes only to the extent to which they injure our fellow citizens. We thus appear to have uncovered another dynamic at work in Lewis' approach to politics. While Lewis' approach was Lockean at its core, the practical application of Lewis' political thought was strongly tempered by his adherence to the "harm principle." Although not absent from the classical natural-law tradition, as we note above, the "harm principle" does find a distinct and full expression in the liberal political theory of John Stuart Mill.

TELEOLOGY, PERFECTIONISM, AND THE HARM PRINCIPLE

John Stuart Mill's exposition of the harm principle is found in the first chapter of his classic work, *On Liberty*. In this essay Mill articulates a principle that purports to solve a perennial problem for government: By what right should a government restrict any one individual member within the range of its authority? Or, as Mill described it, how should we determine "the nature and limits of the power which can be legitimately exercised by society over the individual"?[39] Mill understood himself to be opposing the standard teleological response to this question. He wrote, "The ancient commonwealths thought themselves entitled to practice, and the ancient philosophers countenanced, the regulation of every part of private conduct by public authority, on the ground that the State had a deep interest in the whole bodily and mental discipline of every one

---

[39] John Stuart Mill, *On Liberty and the Subjection of Women*, ed. Alan Ryan (New York: Penguin Classics, 2006 [1859]), 7.

of its citizens."[40] In other words, classical governments[41] had been teleo-logical because they relied on an achievable ideal of the good life for human beings, and perfectionist because governments should help citizens realize that good life. The goal of government policy, to borrow from the title of Robert George's book, is to make men moral.[42]

While Mill acknowledged that such an outlook might have been appropriate for small city-states, larger cities and nations committed to individual rights and liberties required a new formulation of the relation-ship between the one and the many. For Mill there is only one principle that can govern the individual in "compulsion and control," whether through "physical force" or "moral coercion":

That principle is, that the sole end for which mankind are warranted, individually or collectively, in interfering with the liberty of action of any of their number, is self-protection. That the only purpose for which power can be rightfully exercised over any member of a civilized community, against his will, is to prevent harm to others. His own good, either physical or moral, is not a sufficient warrant. He cannot rightfully be compelled to do or forbear because it will be better for him to do so, because it will make him happier, because in the opinions of others, to do so would be wise or even right.

The only part of the conduct of any one, for which he is amenable to society, is that which concerns others. In the part which merely concerns himself, his inde-pendence is, of right, absolute. Over himself, over his own body and mind, the individual is sovereign.[43]

This formulation of course raises a number of questions, including what it means to "harm" someone else. Mill attempted to answer this question, and ground his understanding of liberty, not by appealing to abstract rights but by relying on utility. After qualifying his position, he wrote, "I regard utility as the ultimate appeal on all ethical questions; but it must be utility in the largest sense, grounded on the permanent interests of man as a progressive being."[44] This does not answer the question of what

---

[40] Ibid., 19.

[41] There is some infelicity of translation when trying to render in English what Aristotle meant by *polis*. See Harry Jaffa, "Aristotle," in Leo Strauss and Joseph Crospey, eds., *History of Political Philosophy*, 2nd ed. (Chicago, IL: University of Chicago Press, 1972), 64–129.

[42] Robert P. George, *Making Men Moral: Civil Liberties and Public Morality* (Oxford University Press, 1995).

[43] John Stuart Mill, *On Liberty*, 16. We see here the distinction between Mill's principle and older accounts that take harm into account but more as a prudential limit on govern-ment's perfecting reach than a substantive principle.

[44] Ibid., 17.

constitutes "harm"; it merely pushes the question further back by asking what the permanent interests of man as a progressive being are and who decides them. Answering this question – how to determine harm to one's neighbor and humanity's permanent interests – is the key to understanding the relationship between Lewis' political thought and Mill's harm principle.

It is clear that Lewis' positions on the legality of marriage and divorce, homosexuality, and religious education illustrate what looks very much like a commitment to Mill's harm principle.[45] In his letter concerning homosexuality, Lewis wrote that the state should not criminalize sinful acts just because they are sinful. In a clear paraphrase of Mill, he went on to write that "many acts which are sins against God are also injuries to our fellow-citizens, and must on that account, *but only on that account*, be made crimes."[46] Christians should not insist that the state enforce their understandings of education and marriage because (given Lewis' view of marriage and education) this would interfere with or harm the liberty and interests of their nonbelieving neighbors.

As Mill's quotation on the ancients makes plain, his understanding of politics and liberty is incommensurable with the Aristotelian understanding of teleology and human flourishing. Yet Lewis' understanding of teleology and natural law is deeply indebted to Aristotle. Indeed, while Lewis did rely on a version of the harm principle, Aristotle's thought bears considerably more weight than does Mill's, or perhaps anyone else's, including Aquinas, Hooker, or Locke.[47] Moreover, as Gilbert Meilander observed, the consequences of actions, though important for Lewis, do not reveal the "goodness" or "badness" of the action itself. The morality of any action depends on its adherence to the Tao. As Lewis noted in a comment on Shakespeare's *King Lear*:

---

[45] This despite Adam Barkman's conclusion drawn from Lewis' marginalia of Mill's work that Mill was wrong "about nearly everything." Barkman, *C.S. Lewis and Philosophy as a Way of Life* (Allentown, PA: Zossima Press, 2009), 447.

[46] Lewis, *Letters*, 473 (emphasis added).

[47] Lewis responded to a letter inquiring about his reliance on Thomas Aquinas by pointing back to Aristotle (*Letters*, vol. 3, p. 980): "You will find people who say I am much influenced by Thomism. I do (now) *use* the *Summa* a good deal, mainly as a sort of dictionary of medieval belief. But the appearance of influence is really due to the fact that I am often (especially on ethics) following Aristotle where Aquinas is also following Aristotle; Aquinas and I were, in fact, at the same school – I don't say in the same class! And I had read *Ethics* long before I ever looked at the *Summa*."

In King Lear (III:vii) there is a man who is such a minor character that Shake-speare has not given him even a name: he is merely "First Servant." All the characters around him – Regan, Cornwall, and Edmund – have fine long-term plans. They think they know how the story is going to end, and they are quite wrong. The servant has no such delusions. He has no notion how the play is going to go. But he understands the present scene. He sees an abomination (the blinding of Old Gloucester) taking place. He will not stand it. His sword is out and pointed at his master's breast in a moment: Then Regan stabs him dead from behind. This is his whole part: eight lines all told. But if it were real life and not a play, that is the part it would be best to have acted.[48]

For Lewis the rightness of an action depends on its conformity to the moral law, consequences be damned. What keeps Lewis from being a deontolo-gist committed only to the law as such is his teleological understanding of the law as meant to help human beings become a certain sort of creature. This view could not be further from a utilitarian ethic – whether Mill's or another's – in which the principle that guides all moral calculations is a particular calculus of pleasure.[49] Pleasure, although important in Lewis' view of the world,[50] can be a derivative, but not an overriding determinant, of moral action. The propriety of pleasure is determined by its relationship to the moral law.[51]

How, then, can we understand Lewis' appropriation of Mill's harm principle given his rejection of consequentialism in general and a pleasure principle in particular? The answer may lie in the difference between harm as a subsidiary principle and as an overriding one. It is possible to take harm and consequences into account without embracing full-blown con-sequentialism or utilitarianism. Lewis subscribed to the harm principle not because he thought it would allow each individual and society as a whole the maximum amount of pleasure possible, nor because he believed the individual is sovereign over his or her own body and mind. Instead, Lewis subscribed to Mill's harm principle because it offered one method

[48] Lewis, "The World's Last Night," in C.S. Lewis, *The World's Last Night and Other Essays* (San Diego, CA: Harcourt Brace, 1987), 104–105. This is also cited in Gilbert Meilander, *The Taste for the Other: The Social and Ethical Thought of C.S. Lewis* (Grand Rapids, MI: Wm. B. Eerdmans, 1978), 224.

[49] This is not to tag Mill with a crude pleasure calculus.

[50] See Lewis, *The Screwtape Letters* (New York: Macmillan, 1961), 101–102. "God is a hedonist," says Screwtape. See Lewis affirming this in his own voice; *Letters*, vol. 3, p. 685.

[51] C.S. Lewis, "Christianity and Culture," in *Christian Reflections*, 21. In addition, a recently unearthed letter from Lewis emphasizes the priority of joy over pleasure. "My private table is one second of joy is worth 12 hours of Pleasure." www.theguardian.com/books/2014/dec/09/unseen-cs-lewis-letter-defines-joy-surprised-by-joy.

of protecting the integrity of the Church as well as the more modest good of earthly politics itself. Lewis can be described in some measure as a "liberal perfectionist." As Robert George explains,

Perfectionism holds that one cannot hope to ascertain what it is right (and wrong) for governments to do ... without considering what is for (and against) human well-being (including moral well-being) and fulfillment. Liberal perfectionists join perfectionist critics of liberalism in arguing that anti-perfectionism's ideal of government neutrality about the human good is illusory. They agree that governments must inevitably act on the basis of some controversial conception of the human good; and they see the chief responsibility of governments as choosing wisely among competing conceptions.[52]

As we described in the previous chapter, Lewis' political conception of choice was a version of Lockean republicanism or liberal representative democracy, arising in part from his distrust of government and a strong view of the fall.

Governments do indeed have a positive role to play in human affairs, according to Lewis, but their warrant is limited. When it comes to morals legislation, they should not legislate against sinful actions as such, but only as such behavior might harm others. The limits Lewis endorses with his version of the harm principle achieve two purposes. First, if honored these limits protect the Church from the temptation to engage in the idolatry of theocracy, what Lewis called the worst of all governments. Second, and related, Lewis' conception protects the realm of the political. More specifically, it would protect the common goods of citizens as such from the inevitable bungling and potential tyranny that would result from a government that deliberately engages in soulcraft. The first purpose of limited government is to safeguard the sanctity of the Church. The second purpose is to protect the integrity of the political realm.

Lewis' restrictions on the legislation of sin as such were informed not by a desire for the maximization of a sort of pleasure (Mill), nor in order to protect individual autonomy (say, Rawls), but by his Christian understanding of politics and government. In an insightful essay in which Lewis considered the desirability of a Christian political party, he again reminded his readers that Christianity can be useful in

---

[52] George, *Making Men Moral: Civil Liberties and Public Morality* (New York: Oxford University Press, 1993), 162. George uses perfectionism to mean that governments must admit that there are competing conceptions of the human good, and these conceptions can also be considered as competing teleologies.

articulating ends, but not so much in discovering the best means toward those ends.[53] Lewis called this essay "Meditation on the Third Commandment," because a Christian party runs the grave risk of blaspheming the name of the Lord. Lewis explained:

The danger of mistaking our merely natural, though perhaps legitimate, enthusiasms for holy zeal, is always great ... The demon inherent in every party is at all times ready enough to disguise himself as the Holy Ghost; the formation of a Christian Party means handing over to him the most efficient make-up we can find. And when once the disguise has succeeded, his commands will presently be taken to abrogate all moral laws and to justify whatever the unbelieving allies of the "Christian" Party wish to do.[54]

The danger of such a Christian party is that its members can claim heavenly warrant for hellish behavior, and Lewis bolstered his point with several historical examples drawn from the Catholic Crusaders and the Protestant Orangemen.

Lewis can be described as liberal because of his emphasis on the rights of individuals and families and the limited role he envisions for local and national governments. Yet his liberalism stems from a commitment not to neutrality among competing conceptions of the good nor to the greatest happiness for the greatest number. Lewis was not a utilitarian. He borrows the harm principle from Mill, but only because his understanding of Christianity provides a specific vision of the human good. This vision is that human beings are created to be in relationship with God. Because an excessive and improper involvement of religion with politics threatens the integrity of the Christian church and the well-being of society, Lewis invokes the harm principle to protect society from the dangers of theocracy and to protect the Church from the dangers of blasphemy. Lewis prudentially adopted a utilitarian strategy in order foster a regime most likely to promote and facilitate human flourishing. As such, his commitment to teleology is not necessarily undermined by his use of Mill's harm principle.

Clearly Lewis understood his commitment to a type of democratic social contract to be consistent with natural law or moral objectivity as well as a teleological human nature; but what about perfectionism? How did Lewis conceive of a government's role in making men and women moral? If perfectionism means the willingness of a government to promote and inculcate a conception of the good, as George uses the term,

[53] Lewis, "Meditation on the Third Commandment," in *God in the Dock*, 196–199.
[54] Ibid., 198.

then Lewis can be called a perfectionist. If perfectionism requires a specific theory as to how a government should do this, then Lewis is not a perfectionist. He was entirely skeptical that government can enforce or even inculcate a conception of the good at all. This skepticism raises an enormous problem.

Lewis admitted in his articulation of the harm principle that sins that "injure" fellow citizens can and should be punished. In his seminal essay on criminal justice, "The Humanitarian Theory of Punishment," Lewis argued that government can and must punish wrongdoers. In other words, government has a duty to the protection of "property," broadly understood to include fundamental liberties and social relationships. At the same time, Lewis' responses to the trio of controversial issues – marriage, homosexuality, and religion in the schools – makes clear that for him Christianity alone cannot provide a comprehensive conception of when and how the government may legitimately coerce or punish.

Herein lies the practical problem. It is one thing to write that only sins that injure others should be punished, and quite another to apply this principle to real-life situations. Is the embryo or fetus a human person, and if so does abortion thereby injure another? If pornography stores are found to decrease the property values of a neighborhood, or correlate with higher rates of sexual assault, does this justify the government's regulation of that sin? If sexual orientation is none of the government's business, or even describes a protected class of citizens, do traditional Christians or Muslims have any business complaining about having to cater to or perform at a same-sex marriage ceremony? These hypotheticals require answers on specific moral questions. Arguably Lewis would agree that governments should leave a citizen alone doing such-and-such activity until they cross a specific line. While Lewis offers a great deal of resources for how a Christian might think about morality simply, his writings are much less helpful with regard to political application and conflict. Simply put, Lewis does not help us decide where governments should draw these lines.

Lewis' theory here does not fail in its answer; it hardly acknowledges the question, so our observation that Lewis does not offer specific answers to many complex political questions barely rises to the level of criticism. We do not fault Lewis for failing to make good on claims he never made. He was, after all, primarily concerned with making the case for Christianity and not for any particular political program. To his credit, he did acknowledge that Christians ought to set about trying to answer these difficult questions.[55] In *Mere Christianity* Lewis calls for Christian economists and statesmen to put "do as you be done by" into action. This statement might be hard to reconcile with Lewis' other assertions that the Church needs to realize that most of the British population is not Christian and should not be forced to live according to Christian morality. A possible solution, however, would be for Lewis to claim, as he does in "The Poison of Subjectivism," that "do as you would be done by" is not specific to Christianity but also accessible to nonbelievers through the Tao.[56]

We might wish Lewis had taken up this line of reasoning more directly. Articulating the difference between which duties are Christian-specific and which are applicable to human beings as such seems crucial for Christian citizenship in a pluralistic society. John Locke, for instance, relied on a morally robust law of nature to offer guidance to the magistrate in his dealing with this very question in his *Letter Concerning Toleration*.[57] Still, Lewis does not leave his readers completely bereft of practical political advice. We conclude this chapter with two Lewis-inspired lessons for Christian citizenship in a pluralistic public square. These lessons correspond with two questions. First, how does the Christian go about determining the right position on a contested moral and political question? Second, assuming that Christians can arrive at sound positions about various political issues, should they organize as a Christian political party in order to advocate their views?

DETERMINING GOOD AND EVIL

While Lewis did not construct a full-fledged theory of natural law or politics, he did describe how he determined the morality of a given issue. In 1940 an Oxford pacifist society invited Lewis to address them. The war with Germany was well under way, Warnie Lewis was serving in France, and children from London were being housed at Lewis' home to escape the bombings.[58] As we have noted, Lewis himself had served in the First

---

[55] Lewis, *Mere Christianity*, 79.   [56] Lewis, *Christian Reflections*, 76–77.

[57] See, e.g., Locke's response to the charge that keeping the state out of religion will allow for religious harlotry and killing of infants for religious reasons. Things that are "not lawful in the ordinary course of life, nor in any private house" do not therefore become lawful in "the Worship of God." John Locke, *Letter Concerning Toleration*, ed. and intro. Mark Goldie (Indianapolis, IN: Liberty Fund, 2010 [1689]), 37.

[58] This happens in *The Lion, the Witch and the Wardrobe* as well. The Pevensie children, Peter, Susan, Edmund, and Lucy, stay at a professor's country house to avoid the London raids.

World War, leading a small group of men as a second lieutenant and receiving wounds for which he was eventually sent home. In the essay "Why I Am Not a Pacifist," Lewis not only described his defense of Christian soldiering, but more importantly for our purposes he offered a method of moral reasoning that can be applied to any moral question. In responding to the particular question about pacifism, Lewis recognized the priority of a more general question: "How do we decide what is good or evil?"[59] The remainder of his essay considers that general question by outlining a response to the specific question of whether Christians can participate in war.

Many people believe we decide what is moral by listening to our consciences. Lewis agreed, though he qualified two different meanings of the word "conscience." Conscience can mean "the pressure a man feels upon his will to do what he thinks is right," or it can mean "his judgment as to what the content of right and wrong are."[60] Conscience in the first sense is always to be obeyed, but conscience in the second sense is teachable. With regard to its grasp on moral truth, it can be mistaken, it can improve, and it can deteriorate. Lewis was particularly interested in how mistaken consciences in the second sense can be corrected.

He likened conscience to the faculty of reason and argued that the reasoning process consists of three parts: facts, intuitions, and proofs. The facts are the basic agreed-on empirical realities (i.e., pacifism deals with war and killing), and these facts come from first-hand experience or reliable authority. Intuition refers to "the direct, simple act of the mind perceiving self-evident truth, as when we see that if A and B both equal C, then they equal each other."[61] The third part is reasoning, or proofs. Lewis called this part the "art or skill of arranging the facts so as to yield a series of such intuitions which linked together produce a proof of the truth or falsehood of the proposition we are considering."[62]

Lewis wrote that conscience also consists of these three parts. When we reason we consider whether a proposition is true or false, but when we reason with our consciences we want to know whether an action is right or wrong. Without using the explicit terminology, Lewis here is appealing

[59] Lewis, "Why I Am Not a Pacifist," in Walter Hooper, ed., *The Weight of Glory: And Other Addresses* (New York: HarperCollins, 2001 [1949]), 33.
[60] Ibid., 33.   [61] Ibid., 34.   [62] Ibid.

to the distinction between theoretical and practical reason. Our reasoning power, however, is still vulnerable to the noetic effects of sin:

The main difference between Reason and Conscience is an alarming one. It is thus: that while the unarguable intuitions on which all depend are liable to be corrupted by passion when we are considering truth and falsehood, they are much more liable, they are almost certain to be corrupted when we are considering good and evil. For then we are concerned with some action to be here and now done or left undone by ourselves. And we should not be considering this action at all unless we had some wish either to do it or not to do it, so that in this sphere we are bribed from the very beginning.[63]

How can we avoid letting our own self-interest corrupt our reasoning? Lewis recommended relying on authority to remedy this tendency to stack the deck in favor of our preexisting desires. He observed that it is rarely a question of *whether* to rely on authority, but more often a question of what authority and how conscious that reliance is. "Each man's experience is so limited," he wrote, "that [reliance on authority] is the more usual; of every hundred facts upon which to reason, ninety-nine depend on authority."[64]

This authority can be divided into four categories: special or general, and human or divine. Special human authority refers to the particular society in which someone lives. General human authority takes into account thinkers and philosophers from all of human history. Special divine authority proceeds from a deity, or a religious tradition. Hence when Lewis consulted special human authority he consulted the history of England, and with general authority he cited Plato, Aristotle, Zarathustra, Cicero, Montaigne, and a host of others. Not surprisingly, Lewis identified Christianity as his divine authority.[65]

Lewis' method required a number of steps. First, one must establish what the facts are in a particular case. Second, one must consider what Lewis called the basic intuitions of morality, namely, what is good and what is evil. These intuitions must be nearly universally held. Third, one

---

[63] Ibid., 36.

[64] Ibid., 34. Lewis made a stronger statement a few paragraphs later: "[F]ew of us have followed the reasoning on which even ten percent of the truths we believe are based. We accept them on authority from the experts and are wise to do so, for though we are thereby sometimes deceived, yet we should have to live like savages if we did not."

[65] While Lewis distinguishes between special and general human authority, he draws only from special divine authority and not from general divine authority. It's not clear what that would look like, though perhaps it might resemble something like Lewis' compilation of various religious statements about aspects of the Tao in the appendix of the *Abolition of Man.*

must consider the facts and moral intuitions so that one can determine the morality (or immorality) of a given act. Finally, in order to guard against one's own untrustworthy motives, one should consider authority to weigh how others have reasoned about the issue in question. For the Christian, divine authority, by which Lewis meant both Scripture and Church tradition, outweighs special and general human authority.

The particular case Lewis addressed in this essay was whether a Christian should obey his government's call to fight in a war. While he has been criticized for oversimplifying the issues, this specific test case offers an example of Lewis' method in action.[66] As far as the facts go, Lewis mentioned two. The first is that everyone agrees that war is disagreeable. The other fact was that there is no way of testing the "main contention urged by pacifists" that "wars always do more harm than good."[67] The only other details that Lewis mentions are matters of definition, that is, that war is about killing, involves nation-states, and so on.

Natural-law theory comes into play most prominently in Lewis' consideration of intuitions. With regard to intuition Lewis is searching for a basic moral principle with which "no good man has ever disputed"; he is "in search of a platitude." According to Lewis' own method, he should attempt to reason to a conclusion once he has identified the relevant facts and the particular moral intuition. Lewis first identified his basic moral intuition, then made a qualification, and finally applied it to the issue of pacifism. He claimed as his basic moral intuition the knowledge that "love is good and hatred bad, or that helping is good and harming bad." Before applying what sounds like an incredibly simple moral principle to pacifism, he qualified it:

We have next to consider whether reasoning leads us from this intuition to the Pacifist conclusion or not. And the first thing I notice is that intuition can lead to no action until it is limited in some way or other. You cannot do simply good to

---

[66] In an entry on this article in the *C.S. Lewis Readers' Encyclopedia*, Marvin D. Hinten of Bowling Green State University briefly argues that Lewis did not display his finest reasoning in this article. See Hinten, "Why I Am Not a Pacifist," in Jeffrey D. Schultz and John G. West Jr., eds., *The C.S. Lewis Readers' Encyclopedia* (Grand Rapids, MI: Zondervan Publishing House, 1998), 425–426. See also Stanley Hauerwas, *War and the American Difference: Theological Reflections on Violence and National Identity* (Grand Rapids, MI: Baker Academic, 2011), 71–82.

[67] Lewis, "Why I Am Not a Pacifist," 39. Hinten and Hauerwas criticize this point, noting that most pacifists do not rely on this claim.

simply Man; you must do this or that good to this or that man. And if you do this good, you can't at the same time do that; and if you do it to these men, you can't also do it to those.[68]

Lewis elaborated on what the Tao means for the intuition that helping is good and harming bad (the law of beneficence):

Hence from the outset the law of beneficence involves not doing some good to some men at some times. Hence those rules which so far as I know have never been doubted, as that we should help one we have promised to help rather than another, or a benefactor rather than one who has no special claim on us, or a compatriot more than a stranger, or a kinsman rather than a mere compatriot.[69]

Finally, Lewis applied his line of reasoning to pacifism:

this in fact most often means helping A at the expense of B, who drowns while you pull A on board. And sooner or later, it involves helping A by actually doing some degree of violence to B. But when B is up to mischief against A, you must either do nothing (which disobeys the intuition) or you must help one against the other. And certainly no one's conscience tells him to help B, the guilty. It remains, therefore, to help A.[70]

The next step in Lewis' method is to consider special and general human authority, and divine authority. Lewis quickly concluded that the great thinkers of England and the world were nearly unanimous in their approval of the just war.[71] In considering divine authority Lewis consulted the Thirty-nine Articles of the Anglican Church in addition to his interpretation of Scripture. Lewis concluded that neither Church tradition nor the Bible itself offers substantial backing to the pacifist position. He summarized his conclusion in the final paragraph:

---

[68] Ibid., 41.   [69] Ibid., 41–42.

[70] Ibid., 42. Lewis continued in his argument, "If the argument is not to end in an anti-Pacifist conclusion, one or other of two stopping places must be selected. You must either say that violence to B is lawful only if it stops short of killing, or else that killing of individuals is indeed lawful, but the mass killing of a war is not." As far as the first stopping point, Lewis agreed that it is better if possible to avoid killing individuals, though he did not completely rule out the death penalty. He strongly disagreed with the second stopping point (the mass killing of war) because he did not see another way for aggressive nations to be stopped. The mass killings of a war are sometimes a necessary price to pay for Lewis because death suffered or inflicted is not the ultimate evil. He wrote that there are much worse things, such as "the suppression of a higher religion by a lower," or even "a higher secular culture by a lower."

[71] Ibid., 45–47. Again, Hinten attacks this claim, arguing that Lewis ignored early church fathers such as Origen and Tertullian and theologians from peace churches such as George Fox and Menno Simons.

This, then, is why I am not a Pacifist. If I tried to become one, I should find a very doubtful factual basis, an obscure train of reasoning, a weight of authority both human and Divine against me, and strong grounds for suspecting that my wishes had directed my decision. As I have said, moral decisions do not admit of mathematical certainty. It may be, after all, that Pacifism is right. But it seems to me very long odds, longer odds than I would care to take with the voice of almost all humanity against me.[72]

This brief outline of Lewis' argument does not do justice to Lewis' full argument in the essay, and indeed this was not its purpose. Whether Lewis' argument against pacifism succeeds is tangential to whether the method he used to arrive at his conclusion is helpful.

Unfortunately, Lewis' exposition of his method can accomplish only so much. Even a cursory examination reveals that Lewis' method invites some difficult questions. One such question is how the method can handle issues that do not attract such (putative) universal acclaim as does just-war theory.[73] Nevertheless, Lewis' conscience-and-authority method does offer a model that can be criticized and improved on. It raises an additional question, however, that pertains to the Christian once the train of moral reasoning has run its course and a position is adopted. How might Christians go about promoting their views about contested moral issues in a pluralistic society?

THE CHRISTIAN VETO SUGGESTION

Earlier in this chapter we quoted Lewis' "Meditation on the Third Commandment" to illustrate his reasons for opposing a formal Christian political party.[74] Such religiously affiliated parties are not uncommon in European parliamentary politics, though Lewis' concern was that a Christian party was particularly susceptible to blasphemy.[75] Lewis' argument on that score, however, was not entirely negative.

The essay includes Lewis' most practical political advice in the most conventional sense, and as with much of his political thought, he borrows the idea from a more overtly political thinker, Jacques

---

[72] Ibid., 53.

[73] We agree with Hinten that just war is not as universally praised as Lewis would have us believe, but the point remains. Lewis did not hint at how his method would have handled issues that even he believed were controversial, e.g., homosexuality or divorce.

[74] See the section above on "Teleology, Perfection, and the Harm Principle."

[75] See, e.g., Bryan McGraw's treatment of Christian parties in Europe in *Faith in Politics: Religion and Liberal Democracy* (Cambridge University Press, 2010), 33–64.

Maritain. Lewis opens the essay by noticing that the notion of explicitly Christian parties has become increasingly popular even though "the printer's ink is hardly dry" on Maritain's 1940 *Scholasticism and Politics*.[76] Lewis' meditation clearly follows chapter 8 of Maritain's work, "Catholic Action and Political Action," in which Maritain distinguishes three layers of Catholic activity: the first concerns the ongoing and strictly spiritual ministries of the Catholic Church *as* the Catholic Church (the spiritual); the second is the actions of Catholic citizens in the earthly realm regarding mundane matters affecting everyone in society (the temporal); and the third layer consists of those issues in which the formal Church is somehow engaged with a temporal matter insofar as Catholic teaching directly speaks to a political matter.[77]

The second layer is what Maritain refers to as the political, and for reasons that Lewis shared, Maritain is wary of a Catholic party operating in the name of the Church in partisan politics. Yet Maritain did offer a suggestion as to what Catholics might do as a voting bloc that would avoid the dangers of a Christian party while still practicing faithful Christian citizenship. "M. Maritain has hinted," Lewis writes, "at the only way in which Christianity (as opposed to schismatics blasphemously claiming to represent it) can influence politics."

What was Maritain's hint? Faithful Catholic citizenship can be found, Maritain writes, "not by taking sides for a certain political idea of the political common good, judged more favourable to religion, nor by making Catholics, as such, enter upon the service of historical forces and temporal interests linked to this idea . . .":

it is rather by laying *every political camp whatsoever* under the necessity of respecting these rights and values, if it does not wish to be fought by the Catholic masses. Such procedure raises above the diversity of political ideas concerning the political common good, – political ideas to which a Christian may legitimately adhere, – the idea of religious and spiritual values to be served, and thus maintains

---

[76] Jacques Maritain, *Scholasticism and Politics*, trans. Mortimer Adler (New York: Macmillan, 1940). We could add Lewis' reading of this book, and writing on it, to the wealth of evidence we alluded to in the first chapter regarding Lewis' supposed lack of interest in political matters.

[77] The Catholic Church has often taken actions that appear to outsiders as politically motivated, but from an internal Catholic perspective merely affirm and apply the Church's teaching to Catholics who happen to be politicians. See, e.g., the case of Archbishop Rummel's excommunication of three Catholic segregationist politicians in 1962 Louisiana. www.nola.com/175years/index.ssf/2011/11/1953_archbishop_called_for_an.html

under the only ascendant of the things of God, even in political matters, the efforts of Catholics in so far as they are Catholics.[78]

Maritain's chapter is one heavily conceptual offering in a book that contains several vigorously argued and in-depth chapters, and so Lewis is right to refer to Maritain's Christian veto option as a "hint." Nevertheless, it is a hint that Lewis endorsed and briefly expanded on in his "Third Commandment" essay.

The brevity of Lewis' treatment should not diminish the strength of the endorsement. Lewis as a "mere" Christian broadens Maritain's idea to include not just Roman Catholics but Christians generally, an "interdenominational Christian Voters' Society" that "might draw up a list of assurances about ends and means which every member was expected to exact from any political party as the price of his support."[79] Drawing up this list of assurances would have been quite the ecumenical challenge in Lewis' day, to put it mildly, and surely the challenge would be even greater in ours. Nevertheless, Lewis did describe this possibility as the "only way" Christians *as* Christians might engage politically in a healthy way, and his "Why I Am Not a Pacifist" address illustrates one approach to moral discernment that Christians might draw from in articulating such a "list of assurances."

The strongest evidence for Lewis' endorsement of this essentially negative or withholding religio-political stratagem is that in a weekly Anglican newspaper Lewis wrote of this proposed Christian Voters' Society that he (Lewis) was "prepared in principle, for membership and obedience *to be obligatory on Christians.*"[80] Coming from a figure who emphasized the importance of what all Christians held in common as opposed to tertiary matters, as well as a thinker who disdained party politics and was suspicious of collective schemes and external meddling, this is a remarkable statement. Given Lewis' disposition and political views, his endorsement of this notion as a matter of Christian obligation is indeed radical.

We might wish that Lewis had considered just how this idea would play out, but then again it does not surprise us that Lewis would return to first things even in an essay mainly about politics and idolatry. For after briefly endorsing Maritain's suggestion, Lewis noted in a concluding line that there was yet another way to influence society. Ultimately, the best way of being salt and light in the culture is to share the Gospel. After all, "He

---

[78] Maritain, *Scholasticism and Politics*, 211–212 (emphasis in original).
[79] Lewis, "Meditation on the Third Commandment," 199.
[80] Ibid., 199 (emphasis added).

who converts his neighbor has performed the most practical Christian-political act of all." This is not to say that Lewis would encourage evangelization merely for the sake of politics. Rather, Lewis's final encouragement to his audience is that while political schemes and practices have their place, the truly Christian witness in the political world will be found in the sort of people Christians are called to be: fallen, redeemed, loved, and loving God and neighbor as themselves. This prioritization of the personal over the programmatic echoes his thought about British education and the futility of trying to rescue Christian morality by equipping unbelieving teachers with Christian doctrine and pedagogy.[81]

Lewis recognized that in articulating the basics of mere Christianity and defending the enduring truths of the natural law he did not thereby solve the tangible problems of discernment and application. He addresses this gap between theory and practice in his conclusion to "On Ethics":

In thus recalling men to traditional morality I am not of course maintaining that it will provide an answer to every particular moral problem with which we may be confronted ... Who could ever have supposed that by accepting a moral code we should be delivered from all questions of casuistry? Obviously it is moral codes that create problems of casuistry, just as the rules of chess create chess problems. The man without a moral code, like the animal, is free from moral problems. The man who has not learned to count is free from mathematical problems. A man asleep is free from all problems. Within the framework of general human ethics problems will, of course, arise and will sometimes be solved wrongly. This possibility of error is simply the symptom that we are awake, not asleep, that we are men, not beasts or gods.[82]

For all the many gifts Lewis had and all the genres his work fits into, he did not undertake the role of politician or political strategist. His most valuable work for those citizens in the Christian tradition is found in laying out the framework, setting up the chess pieces in such a way as to connect Christian faith and doctrine with the categories of thinking necessary to engage the modern world. It is up to others, he might say, to actually move the pieces.

[81] Lewis, "On the Transmission of Christianity," in *God in the Dock*, 118.
[82] Lewis, "On Ethics," in *Christian Reflections*, 56.

7

Conclusion: Politics in the Shadowlands

For that which cannot be shaken shall remain. That which is immortal in God shall remain in man. The death that is in them shall be consumed. It is the law of Nature – that is, the law of God – that all that is destructible shall be destroyed.

          – George MacDonald, *Unspoken Sermons* (1867)

C.S. Lewis was, on the surface, an apolitical man. Lewis' academic work focused primarily on English literature and literary criticism, but in his own day (as in ours) he was known outside the academy as "one of the most influential spokesmen for Christianity in the English-speaking world." "With erudition, good humor, and skill," a 1947 cover story for *Time* magazine proclaimed, "Lewis is writing about religion for a generation of religion-hungry readers brought up on a diet of 'scientific' jargon and Freudian clichés."[1] By the late 1940s, his popular novels and religious writings had sold in the millions, and sales continue apace today. Lewis' commitment to Christian apologetics, which he embraced as a religious duty, made him wary of partisan political entanglements, and he was careful never to support or become involved with "anything that had a directly political implication."[2]

Lewis was largely successful at distancing himself from the partisan controversies of his own time. We noted earlier his refusal of Winston

---

[1] "Don v. Devil," *Time* (1947) 40(10): 67–73.

[2] Lewis, quoted in William Griffin, *Clive Staples Lewis: A Dramatic Life* (San Francisco, CA: Harper and Row, 1986), 235. We were alerted to this quote reading John G. West's essay, "Finding the Permanent in the Political: C.S. Lewis as a Political Thinker" (July 15, 1995), *The Independent Institute*, www.independent.org/newsroom/article.asp?id=1566.

Churchill's offer to make him an honorary Commander of the British Empire. "There are always ... knaves who say, and fools who believe," Lewis explained in his letter to the Prime Minister's office, "that my religious writings are all covert anti-Leftist propaganda, and my appearance on the Honours List wd. of course strengthen their hands."[3] Despite the distance he kept from practical politics, however, Lewis did have much to say about the underlying principles of a just political order. All of his writings – fiction and nonfiction alike – are saturated with the enduring themes of Western political philosophy, and he was as insightful as any twentieth-century dystopian novelist or political theorist at diagnosing the ills of modern government.

Those ills, as Lewis saw them, are straightforwardly laid out in *The Abolition of Man*, a book Lewis' literary executor, Walter Hooper, described as "an all but indispensable introduction to the entire corpus of Lewisiana."[4] The book is, in many ways, a primer for everything else Lewis wrote. In *Abolition*, Lewis paints, with broad strokes, a picture of the modern crisis in ethical and political thought. As Leon Kass recounted in his 2009 National Endowment for the Humanities Lecture, Lewis' overarching argument in *Abolition* is that "the dehumanization threatened by the mastery of nature has, at its deepest cause, less the emerging biotechnologies that might directly denature bodies and flatten souls, more the underlying value-neutral, soulless and heartless accounts that science proffers of living nature and of man."[5] Kass sees his own work in bioethics as an extension of Lewis' project to defend an older and richer philosophical anthropology. In addition to Kass, Lewis' work on this score has had a profound impact on a number of serious scholars and noted public

[3] C.S. Lewis, Letter to the Prime Minister's Secretary (December 4, 1951), in Walter Hooper, ed., *Collected Letters of C.S. Lewis*, 3 vols. (New York: HarperCollins, 2004), vol. 3, p. 147 Lewis, *Collected Letters*, vol. 3, p. 147. Lewis may have had critics such as George Orwell in mind. Orwell accused Lewis of hiding his anti-left agenda in his broadcast talks. George Orwell, "As I Please," *Tribune*, October 27, 1944, from Adam Barkman, *C.S. Lewis and Philosophy as a Way of Life* (Allentown, PA: Zossima Press, 2009), 452.

[4] Walter Hooper, note 1 to "On Ethics," in *Christian Reflections*, ed. Walter Hooper (Grand Rapids, MI: Eerdmans, 1996), 47. Cited by Michael Travers in Bruce L. Edwards, ed., *C.S. Lewis: Life, Works, and Legacy*, vol. 3 (Westport, CT: Praeger, 2007), 108 n. 10.

[5] Leon Kass, "Looking for an Honest Man: Reflections of an Unlicensed Humanist," 2009 Jefferson Lecture for the National Endowment for the Humanities. Transcript available at www.neh.gov/about/awards/jefferson-lecture/leon-kass-lecture.

intellectuals, including Richard John Neuhaus,[6] Jean Bethke Elshtain,[7] John Finnis,[8] Alvin Plantinga,[9] and Joseph Ratzinger.[10]

"There are simply those who can stop reading Lewis, and those who can't," the late Fr. Neuhaus once wrote in the pages of *First Things*. "After a while, some of the latter find that they are thought to be Lewis scholars."[11] We never could quite give up on reading Lewis, but we do not claim on that account to be Lewis scholars. Each of us was, however, introduced to the world of political and social philosophy by reading Lewis, and we have brought some of Lewis' insights to bear in our own work on American politics. It is odd, at first glance, that reading Lewis – a high-brow, Irish-born, apolitical Oxford University don – would put us on separate paths to careers studying American politics and political thought. Yet in addition to the fact that Lewis married an American and adopted two American boys, there is a straightforward conceptual connection between Lewis and the United States. In a 1958 essay for *The Observer*, Lewis described the three "juristic key-conceptions" of the political theory under assault in modern times to be "natural law, the value of the individual, [and] the rights of man."[12] These three key-conceptions, bound up as they are with the American political tradition, have motivated our teaching and occupied our attention in various ways over our careers.

As Ayn Rand once noted, after reading the *Abolition of Man*, Lewis was a "pick pocket of concepts."[13] Lewis no doubt would have been

---

[6] Richard John Neuhaus, "C.S. Lewis in the Public Square," *First Things* 88 (1998): 30–35.

[7] See Jean Bethke Elshtain, "The Abolition of Man: C.S. Lewis' Prescience Concerning Things to Come," in David Baggett, Gary R. Habermas, and Jerry L. Walls, eds., *C.S. Lewis as Philosopher: Truth, Beauty, and Goodness* (Downer's Grover, IL: Intervarsity Press, 2008), 85–95.

[8] See John Finnis, "C.S. Lewis and Test Tube Babies" (1984), in *Collected Essays: Human Rights and the Common Good*, vol. 3 (Oxford University Press, 2011), pp. 273–281.

[9] Plantinga, as we discuss in detail in Chapter 2, has developed and extended Lewis' argument from reason in several scholarly works. See, e.g., Alvin Plantinga, *Where the Conflict Really Lies: Science, Religion, and Naturalism* (Oxford University Press, 2011), 310 n. 4, where he credits Lewis for putting forward one of the first ancestors of Plantinga's own argument against naturalism based on its failure to adequately account for the existence and reliability of reason.

[10] Cardinal Joseph Ratzinger, Fisher Lecture (January 1988) at the Catholic Chaplaincy at Cambridge University. Reprinted as "Consumer Materialism and Christian Hope" in *Teachers of the Faith: Speeches and Lectures by Catholic Bishops* (London: Catholic Bishops' Conference of England and Wales, 2002), 78–94.

[11] Neuhaus, "C.S. Lewis and the Public Square."

[12] C.S. Lewis, "Is Progress Possible?," in Walter Hooper, ed., *God in the Dock* (Grand Rapids, MI: Wm. B. Eerdmans, 1970), 314.

[13] Robert Mayhew, ed., *Ayn Rand's Marginalia: Her Critical Comments on the Writings of over 20 Authors* (Second Renaissance Press, 1995), 90–94.

amused by Rand's unflattering epithet, since his goal never was to say something new. Instead, he took it as his task to rationally defend moral principles, ancient wisdom, and what he insisted on calling "mere" Christianity. Lewis brought to this task a deep knowledge of religion, philosophy, history, and literature. As we have noted, his first lectureship was in philosophy, and Lewis retained a deep interest in philosophy throughout his career. After eventually landing a permanent position lecturing on English literature, Lewis acknowledged that it would comfort him all his life

to know that the scientist and the materialist have not the last word: that Darwin and Spencer undermining ancestral beliefs stand themselves on a foundation of sand; of gigantic assumptions and irreconcilable contradictions an inch below the surface. It leaves the whole thing rich in possibilities: and if it dashes the shallow optimism it does the same for the shallow pessimisms. But having once seen all this "darkness," a darkness full of promise, it is perhaps best to shut the trap door and come back to ordinary life: unless you are one of the really great who can see into it a little way – and I was not.[14]

Lewis was the first to concede that he was not among the great philosophers. But he did have a philosophical mind, and he brought illuminating insights from his study of philosophy with him when he returned to "ordinary life."

In his academic work, as well as in his popular writings, Lewis paid close attention to ideas. In approaching his scholarship on English literature, Lewis always took particular interest in the *ideas* the author was communicating. Similarly, our goal when embarking on this project was not to write yet another biography of Lewis; rather, we wanted to understand and recover the political ideas he communicated. Many of the philosophical insights that the mature Lewis brought to ordinary life have manifest political implications, and each of the chapters in this book tackles a different aspect of Lewis' political thought. In each chapter, we have tried to illumine and unpack a distinct argument that Lewis made about politics or natural law. Lewis, of course, did not claim to be original, and the case for studying Lewis' political thought does not rest on demonstrating its originality. Lewis was uniquely gifted at distilling ancient wisdom into clear, cogent, lucid prose. If only for his ability to synthesize and present a corpus of knowledge in a compelling way, Lewis' writings are worthy of our continued study.

---

[14] Lewis, *Collected Letters*, vol. 1, p. 649.

The major contribution of Lewis' writings was not primarily in groundbreaking substance but in presentation. Lewis offered the postmodern world a vision of reality that could make sense of our lived moral experiences, and he put forth a powerful defense of natural law as a necessary basis for "the very idea of a rule which is not tyranny or an obedience which is not slavery."[15] In Chapter 2, we describe how Lewis' understanding of natural law was rooted in a Christian framework that understands all of nature – including human nature – to have been *created*. Lewis' adherence to the Christian doctrine of creation puts him at odds, for obvious reasons, with atheistic materialism and atheistic rationalism. Lewis, however, thought that the divine creation of reality was more consistent with the existence and reliability of reason than either materialism or rationalism. We therefore reconstruct Lewis' argument for the compatibility of the natural-law tradition with core biblical doctrines and use this chapter to put Lewis in conversation with secular political theorists who claim the idea of creation is fundamentally incompatible with natural law.

Political theorists are not alone in arguing that natural law is incompatible with Christianity; some Christian theologians agree. Karl Barth, the leading academic Protestant theologian of the twentieth century, was very critical of natural-law philosophy. In Chapter 3, we therefore recreate the dispute between Lewis and Barth regarding the appropriate place and role of natural-law philosophy in modern politics and Christian theology. Provocatively, Lewis claimed that Karl Barth's rejection of the natural-law tradition made his theology indistinguishable from devil worship because it led to the worship of power divorced from an eternal and unchanging goodness. But if not theological voluntarism, then what? The introductory chapters thus clear the ground for a consideration of Lewis' own understanding of the history of natural-law philosophy, its theoretical merit, and its application in modern times.

In Chapter 4, we turn to Lewis' grappling with two different questions: (1) How is it that we came to a point at which the natural law is no longer part of mainstream political and moral thought in Western society? (2) What are the consequences of the widespread rejection of the natural-law tradition in our cultural and educational institutions? Lewis answers the first question largely in his treatment of modern philosophical trends in his magnum opus *English Literature in the Sixteenth Century*. In

---

[15] Lewis, *The Abolition of Man* (New York: HarperCollins, 2001 [1944]), 73.

particular, Lewis thought the sundering of classical metaphysics in the early modern period led to an understanding of political sovereignty that was unlimited or unbounded by traditional moral constraints. In works such as *The Abolition of Man*, Lewis then offered a dire warning of a future in which men become enslaved entirely to their passions and appetites because they no longer believe in a model of the universe that can make sense of the rightful rule of reason.

Finally, Chapters 5 and 6 look at some of the concrete details and practical applications of Lewis' political thought. Surprisingly – given Lewis' debt to ancient and medieval thinkers such as Aristotle and Aquinas – he does not advocate a return to a classical, aristocratic conception of political order. Instead, Lewis was committed to classical liberalism in the tradition of John Locke and John Stuart Mill. He described himself as a democrat and believed in the wisdom of limited government, equality under the law, and a robust private sphere. As we detail, however, the application of these broad principles to concrete political questions is difficult and requires prudence and attention to historical and cultural context. In several of his nonfiction essays, Lewis tackled thorny public policy issues involving public regulation of sexual vice, the distinction between civil and religious marriage, and public religious education in ways that may leave many of Lewis' devoted readers unsatisfied.

The enduring value of Lewis' writings on politics and natural law is not that he offered easy solutions to complex political questions. Rather, through both rational argument and imaginative fiction, Lewis defended a compelling account of reality that could make sense of and account for the existence of reason, the freedom of the individual, and a kind of political rule that is not tyranny. The Christian natural-law tradition provided the necessary foundation for this vision of reality. That vision, as it relates to politics, is on display most clearly in Lewis' frequent warning that the modern project of wholesale moral innovation must fail. In *The Abolition of Man* Lewis critiqued those who would jettison the moral precepts of the Tao in favor of a new conception of morality. The moral innovator often attempts to derive all of morality in terms of some overriding principle already contained within traditional morality, such as duty to posterity. Yet, as Lewis masterfully demonstrates, it is only "by such shreds of the *Tao* as he has inherited is he enabled even to attack it."[16] In the process of innovation, the person who isolates duty to

---

[16] Ibid., 41.

one's own as an overriding principle runs roughshod over other principles of the Tao and becomes, in the end, a "Jingoist, a Racialist, an extreme nationalist" – or worse.

Lewis does more than describe this process of dehumanization in abstraction; he personifies his argument in the characters who inhabit his Space Trilogy and the Chronicles of Narnia. In the first two books of Lewis' Space Trilogy, the nameless innovator of *The Abolition of Man* assumes a real personality as the physicist Weston in *Out of the Silent Planet* and *Perelandra*. The first book in the trilogy, *Out of the Silent Planet*, tells the story of two evil scientists, Weston and Devine, and a noble philologist, Ransom, who travel to the planet of Malacandra. As Gilbert Meilander points out, Weston is motivated by a desire to see the human race continue indefinitely.[17] He is Lewis' innovator, who takes the legitimate value of human posterity and warps it beyond recognition by subjugating all other values to it. For the sake of the propagation of the species, Weston is willing to kidnap, murder, lie, and even offer human sacrifice.[18]

In a climactic confrontation between Weston and the benevolent powerful being that rules Malacandra, Weston makes clear his willingness to commit injustice in pursuit of one overarching good. Speaking to Oyarsa, the ruler of Malacandra, Weston defends his intention to conquer Malacandra for the human race:

To you I seem a vulgar robber, but I bear on my shoulders the destiny of the human race. Your tribal life with its stone-age weapons and bee-hive huts, its primitive oracles and elementary social structure, has nothing to compare with our civilization – with our science, medicine and law, our armies, our architecture, our commerce, and our transport system which is rapidly annihilating space and time. Our right to supersede you is the right of the higher over the lower ...

Life is greater than any system of morality; her claims are absolute. It is not by tribal taboos and copy-book maxims that she has pursued her relentless march from the amoeba to man and from man to civilization.[19]

During this conversation, Oyarsa concludes that Weston has been corrupted by the "evil one," but not completely. Weston still hangs on to one shred of the Tao, the special duty to protect the future generations of one's kindred.

---

[17] Meilander, *The Taste for the Other: The Social and Ethical Thought of C.S. Lewis* (Grand Rapids, MI: Wm. B. Eerdmans, 1978), 195–196.

[18] Ibid., 218–219.

[19] Lewis, *Out of the Silent Planet* (New York: Scribner, 2003 [1938]), 135–136.

Lewis used the character of Oyarsa in *Out of the Silent Planet* to express the same inconsistency of the moral innovator in *The Abolition of Man*:

I see now how the lord of the silent world [Satan] has bent you. There are laws all hnau [rational creatures] know, of pity and straight dealing and shame and the like, and one of these is the love of kindred. He has taught you to break all of them except this one, which is not one of the greatest laws; this one he has bent till it becomes folly and has set it up, thus bent, to be a little blind Oyarsa in your brain. And now you can do nothing but obey it, though if we ask you why it is a law you give no other reason for it than for all the other and greater laws which it drives you to disobey.[20]

In this dialogue Lewis reveals that part of what it means to be rational is to live under moral law, but that one can err not only by rejecting the moral law but also by perverting it. Weston's character, though confronted with these truths, still clings to his absolute principle of protecting human posterity and neglects the other principles of the Tao.

The story of Weston's ultimate destiny is told in the trilogy's second book, *Perelandra*. The sequel consists of another interplanetary adventure in which Ransom and Weston find themselves on the virgin planet of Perelandra. Weston discards his former allegiance to the principle of posterity and exchanges it for an all-encompassing faith in spirituality. As he grows dissatisfied with the spread of mere *biological* human life, Weston commits himself to an infinite perpetuation of a sort of *spiritual* humanity, though not any sort of spirituality recognizable by Christianity. Weston insists:

The majestic spectacle of this blind, inarticulate purposiveness thrusting its way upward and ever upward in an endless unity of differentiated achievements towards an ever-increasing complexity of organization, towards spontaneity and spirituality, swept away all my old conception of a duty to Man as such. Man in himself is nothing. The forward movement of Life – the growing spirituality – is everything ... To spread spirituality, not to spread the human race, is henceforth my mission.[21]

Weston describes his work as being motivated first for his own career, then for science, then humanity, and finally for "Spirit itself."[22] What happens to Weston throughout the remainder of the book depicts what happens, ultimately, to those who break with the moral law. The Spirit of

[20] Ibid., 138–139.   [21] Lewis, *Perelandra* (New York: Scribner, 2003 [1944]), 91.
[22] Ibid., 91.

the "Unman," Satan himself, possesses Weston and leads him to an ignominious death.

The third book of Lewis' trilogy takes place in England and introduces a number of insidious characters that form the National Institute of Coordinated Experiments (N.I.C.E.) in an attempt to create a scientific technocracy that will control the entire country.[23] One of the most vivid of these characters is Professor Frost, an ardent materialist and technocrat and a human embodiment of Lewis' completely amoral conditioner in the last chapter of *The Abolition of Man*. Unlike Weston, Frost does not bother with trying to build a new morality around some "new" innovative moral principle. He is first and foremost an objective man, claiming to see human nature and himself as though it and he were nothing but natural objects to be studied with complete detachment.

The last third of *That Hideous Strength* describes a psychological confrontation between Frost and another university professor, the sociologist Mark Studdock. Professor Frost initiates Studdock's training in objectivity by threatening him with a false murder charge if he resists the N.I.C.E.'s operations and promising him unlimited power and influence if he goes along. During the interrogation, Frost describes his own commitment to objectivity. "Before going on," Frost says, "I must ask you to be strictly objective. Resentment and fear are both chemical phenomena. Our reactions to one another are chemical phenomena. Social relations are chemical relations. You must observe these feelings in yourself in an objective manner. Do not let them distract your attention from the facts."[24]

In the course of the conversation Frost discloses that one of the main experiments of the N.I.C.E. is to establish contact with "macrobes," powerful spiritual beings such as Oyarsa from *Out of the Silent Planet*. When Mark asks if these beings are friendly, Frost again displays a complete materialist objectivity:

If you reflect for a moment, said Frost, you will see that your question has no meaning except on the level of the crudest popular thought. Friendship is a

---

[23] Lewis, *That Hideous Strength: A Modern Fairy-Tale for Grown Ups* (New York: Scribner, 2003 [1945]), 23. "The N.I.C.E. was the first-fruits of that constructive fusion between the state and the laboratory on which so many thoughtful people base their hopes of a better world. It was to be free from almost all the tiresome restraints – 'red tape' was the word its supporters used – which have hitherto hampered research in this country." The N.I.C.E. does actually exist in the United Kingdom, though its mission is a good deal more benevolent than Lewis' version. www.nice.org.uk/.

[24] Lewis, *That Hideous Strength*, 255.

chemical phenomenon; so is hatred. Both of them presuppose organisms of our own type. The first step towards intercourse with the macrobes is the realisation that one must go outside the whole world of our subjective emotions. It is only as you begin to do so, that you discover how much of what you mistook for your thought was merely a by-product of your blood and nervous tissues.[25]

Frost's ultimate aim for the future of humanity is the reduction of civilization to a technocracy of the special objective few who understand that all of reality can be reduced to material processes.

In vivid imagery, Lewis describes through the character of Frost what he meant in *The Abolition of Man* when he warned about a world of post-humanity. For years, Lewis narrates, Frost had "theoretically believed that all which appears in the mind as motive or intention [was] merely a by-product of what the body [was] doing." But as time passed the theoretical became the actual, and Frost's mind became a "mere spectator," unable to challenge the purposes of his body. In the end Frost immolates himself in an attempt to escape the illusion of consciousness, only to find that "death itself might not after all cure the illusion of being a soul – nay, might prove the entry into a world where that illusion raged infinite and unchecked."[26] Here we see an illustration of Lewis' argument in *The Abolition of Man* that a man freed from all morality is a slave to physical impulses.[27]

In addition to showcasing the devastating effects of a Tao-less society, Lewis used the characters of Frost and Studdock to illustrate the process by which man comes to experience the reality of the Tao. Shortly before he committed suicide, Frost attempted one final time to break Studdock's resistance to the N.I.C.E. by taking him into "the Objective Room." The objective room was "the first step towards what Frost called objectivity – the process whereby all specifically human reactions were killed in a man ..." The room, Lewis tells us, was "ill-proportioned," with the ceiling too high and the walls too close together, somewhat like a coffin. Strange pictures hung on the walls:

There was a portrait of a young woman who held her mouth wide open to reveal the fact that the inside of it was thickly overgrown with hair ... There was a giant mantis playing a fiddle while being eaten by another mantis, and a man with corkscrews instead of arms bathing in a flat, sadly coloured sea beneath a summer sunset.[28]

---

[25] Ibid., 258.   [26] Ibid., 358.   [27] Lewis, *Abolition of Man*, 77–79.
[28] Lewis, *That Hideous Strength*, 298.

The room teased the mind by seeming to have a discernible pattern, but the closer Mark examined any aspect of the room the less ordered and more surreal it seemed.

Lewis describes a change that began to occur in Studdock's mind as he sat in the Objective Room:

> the built and painted perversity of this room had the effect of making him aware, as he had never been aware before, of this room's opposite. As the desert first teaches men to love water, or as absence first reveals affection, there rose up against this background of the sour and the crooked some kind of vision of the sweet and straight. Something else – something he vaguely called the "Normal" – apparently existed.

Mark Studdock – a man with a thoroughly modern education, an agnostic and religious skeptic – experiences moral reality as he sits in the Objective Room. "He was not thinking in moral terms at all," Lewis writes of that moment, "or else (what is much the same thing) he was having his first deeply moral experience. He was choosing a side: the Normal."[29]

Frost later tested Studdock's newfound adherence to the normal by another visit to the Objective Room. This time the center of the room is occupied by a life-sized crucifix, painstakingly detailed and life-like. Frost commands Studdock to walk on the crucifix, trampling it underneath while performing other obscenities on it. This scene depicts the first inkling that Mark has of the relation between his newly discovered notion of normalcy and Christianity. While not a Christian, Studdock is uncomfortable with Frost's commands, even though disobeying them would likely result in his death. Here Lewis' account of the conversation between Frost and Studdock is worth quoting at length:

> "Pray make haste," said Frost.
>
> The quiet urgency of the voice, and the fact that he had so often obeyed it before, almost conquered him. He was on the verge of obeying, and getting the whole silly business over, when the defencelessness of the figure deterred him. The feeling was a very illogical one. Not because its hands were nailed and helpless, but because they were only made of wood and therefore even more helpless, because the thing, for all its realism, was inanimate and could not in any way hit back, he paused ...
>
> "What are you waiting for, Mr. Studdock?" said Frost.
>
> Mark was well aware of the rising danger. Obviously, if he disobeyed, his last chance of getting out of Belbury alive might be gone. Even of getting out of this

---

[29] Ibid., 299.

room. The smothering sensation once again attacked him. He was himself, he felt, as helpless as the wooden Christ. As he thought this, he found himself looking at the crucifix in a new way – neither as a piece of wood nor a monument of superstition but as a bit of history. Christianity was nonsense, but one did not doubt that the man lived and had been executed thus by the Belbury of those days. And that, as he suddenly saw, explained why this image, though not itself an image of the Straight or Normal, was yet in opposition to crooked Belbury. It was a picture of what happened when the Straight met the Crooked, a picture of what the Crooked did to the Straight – what it would do to him if he remained straight. It was, in a more emphatic sense than he had yet understood, a *cross*.[30]

For the first time in the narrative, Studdock identifies a standard of sorts by which he can order his behavior and attitudes toward the events around him.

No longer afraid of dying for his newfound allegiance to his idea of the normal, Mark turns to Frost and, answering Frost's demand that he walk on the crucifix, said, "It's all bloody nonsense, and I'm damned if I do any such thing."[31] Lewis did not neatly resolve Mark's conversion to a standard of the straight and normal by including a conversion to Christianity. But he did demonstrate in a powerful fictional form his belief that standards of morality and the good are built into the universe. Mark's reaction to the sourness and crookedness of the Objective Room acted as a catalyst in awakening within him a sense of the sweet, straight, and good.

Lewis' depictions of moral innovators and social conditioners in the Space Trilogy are just two of many examples of his attempt to "steal past those watchful dragons" of modern thought by communicating truth in fiction. Lewis often wrote penetrating stories that found wide readership far beyond the small audience for his nonfiction works. The late evangelical writer and apologist Francis Schaeffer noted that secular critics such as B.F. Skinner often responded to Lewis precisely because he was so successful at imbedding his arguments in good literature:

Twice Skinner specifically attacked C.S. Lewis. Why? Because he is a Christian and writes in the tradition of the literatures of freedom and dignity. You will notice that [Skinner] does not attack the evangelical church, probably because he doesn't think it's a threat to him. Unhappily, he is largely right about this. Many of us are too sleepy to be a threat in the battle of tomorrow. But he understands that a man like C.S. Lewis, *who writes literature that stirs men*, is indeed a threat.[32]

---

[30] Ibid., 336.   [31] Ibid., 337.

[32] Francis Schaeffer, *Back to Freedom and Dignity*, vol. 1, book 4 of *The Complete Works of Francis A. Schaeffer* (Westchester, IL: Crossway, 1982), 382–383. Quoted in Scott

Lewis' fiction is a threat to an atheistic and materialistic worldview such as Skinner's because it provides a means by which belief in Christianity and the moral law can be transmitted to a skeptical culture.

There is, however, no obvious or straightforward way to apply Lewis' natural-law ethic to complex political problems in modern pluralistic society. Significantly, Lewis' primary solution for the ethical and moral problems he identified was not a specific political program but instead a commitment to a broadly Aristotelian moral education. However, the moral education Lewis envisioned could not be taught as biology or sociology could in a classroom. Moral education, instead, requires the young to be surrounded by mentors and family members who model the moral precepts. The Tao is passed on through initiation, as "grown birds deal with young birds when they teach them to fly," and as "men transmitting manhood to men."[33]

Lewis' Chronicles of Narnia series is his contribution to the moral education of the young. Like many of Lewis' other works, the Narnia stories contain numerous examples of characters performing moral deeds and obeying the precepts of the Tao. Alongside the positive examples are warnings about those who transgress the moral law. Sometimes transgressors are redeemed, such as Edmund in *The Lion, the Witch and the Wardrobe*, and sometimes they destroy themselves, as do Frost and Weston. Gilbert Meilander nicely summarizes how Lewis' fiction transmits moral education:

[Lewis' stories] serve to enhance moral education, to build character. They teach, albeit indirectly, and provide us with exemplars from whom we learn proper emotional responses. We can think once more of one of the principles of the *Tao*, the law of magnanimity, willingness to expend oneself in a good cause. This is, after all, what the Roman father was appealing to when he tried to teach his son that it was a sweet and seemly thing to die for one's country. It is, Lewis thinks, a message best communicated indirectly: through the father's own example, and also through the stories read to his son. The father's message may well be communicated through a story like *The Last Battle*. There, in a passage cited at the outset of the chapter, Roonwit the Centaur, while dying, sends a message to King Tirian telling him "to remember that all worlds draw to an end and that noble death is a treasure which no one is too poor to buy" ... To overlook the function of the Chronicles of Narnia in communicating images of proper emotional responses is to miss their connection to Lewis' moral thought.[34]

Burson and Jeffrey L. Walls, *C.S. Lewis and Francis Schaeffer: Lessons for a New Century from the Most Influential Apologists of Our Time* (Downers Grove, IL: Intervarsity Press, 1998), 216 (emphasis added).

[33] Lewis, *Abolition of Man*, 32–33.   [34] Meilander, *Taste for the Other*, 213.

The fictional legacy Lewis left behind offers us one of his most potent methods of influencing a culture resistant to the claims of Christian revelation and natural-law philosophy. Lewis' positive arguments for the reality of the natural law or the importance of the doctrine of creation may fall on deaf ears. His abstract depiction of the horrors of a Tao-less society may be ignored or even welcomed. His political preference for a form of Lockean liberalism tempered by Mill's harm principle may be rejected or criticized. But his fiction might still subtly communicate for-gotten truths to a new generation. Or it might not do even that, and it is imperative for us – as we search for the "practical take-away" from Lewis' writings about politics and natural law – to remember that Lewis himself did not measure success in terms of societal outcomes.

In the conclusion to the Narnia series, *The Last Battle*, the world of Narnia is destroyed as Narnia's noble inhabitants struggle to remain faithful to Aslan amid the destruction of all they know. Ultimately, the things being destroyed in Narnia were of only secondary importance. As Lewis insisted:

For it is part of our spiritual law never to put survival first: not even the survival of our species. We must resolutely train ourselves to feel that the survival of Man on this Earth, much more of our own nation or culture or class, is not worth having unless it can be had by honourable and merciful means. The sacrifice is not so great as it seems. Nothing is more likely to destroy a species or a nation than a determination to survive at all costs. Those who care for something else more than civilization are the only people by whom civilization is at all likely to be preserved. *Those who want Heaven most have served Earth best. Those who love Man less than God do most for Man.*[35]

At the end of the day, we must understand Lewis' natural-law theory and political thought within the context of a Christian universe. The practical problems of Christianity and politics are important, and Lewis offered some resources with which to deal with these problems. The theological and ethical questions regarding God's relationship to the good are difficult, and Lewis' thought on the matter can be instructive. Society's resistance to the moral law and rationality is discouraging, and Lewis' vision of moral education under the guise of imaginative fiction can speak to those who will not listen to reason. But Lewis always saw

---

[35] C.S. Lewis, "On Living in an Atomic Age," in Walter Hooper, ed., *Present Concerns: A Compelling Collection of Timely, Journalistic Essays* (Orlando, FL: Harcourt, 1986), 79–80 (emphasis added).

the ultimate value of the natural law to be in *preparatio evangelium*, in preparation for the Gospel.

Lewis was, after all, an apologist whose acknowledged purpose in writing was to "bring about an encounter of the reader with Jesus Christ."[36] This act of bringing individuals within the fold of Christendom, Lewis claimed elsewhere, was in some sense "the most practical Christian-political act of all."[37] Christians living out their faith in obedience to and love for God is, Lewis insisted, the "first thing" that is the key to the moral health and viability of second things, such as cultures, societies, and governments. Lewis' natural-law theory does not resolve the persistent practical problems raised by the interaction of politics and morality, or of cultures and ethics. But part of his answer is an insistence that we will not achieve the perfect answer and that, though culture and politics are important, this life ultimately takes place in the "Shadowlands" and does not compare with the coming reality of heaven.

The ideas Lewis did leave for us – his arguments about the practical importance of natural law, his vision of moral education, and his commitment to individual freedom and the rule of reason – continue to introduce new generations to what Lewis succinctly called the great "human tradition of value."[38] Though Lewis has scores of devoted readers, many of us have only begun to wrestle with Lewis' arguments in a systematic way and to appreciate the depth and clarity of his thought. As Alister McGrath notes, "half a century after his death, the process of receiving and interpreting Lewis has still only begun."[39] We hope this book will contribute in some way to the conversation, still in its beginning stages, about Lewis' surprising legacy in the world of politics and political thought. Yet even more we hope this book will point others to the enduring themes of Lewis' work and the perennial questions he raised about politics and the natural law. These are questions for our age, too – questions we must answer well together, in the face of new challenges, if our families and communities are to flourish in this life, even as we long for the True Narnia.

---

[36] Lewis, "Cross-Examination," in *God in the Dock*, 262. The words are not Lewis', but belong to Mr. Wirt's question. Lewis responded that though this was not his language, it was his purpose.

[37] Lewis, "Meditation on the Third Commandment," in *God in the Dock*, 199.

[38] Lewis, *Abolition of Man*, 41.

[39] Alister McGrath, *The Intellectual World of C.S. Lewis* (Oxford: Wiley-Blackwell, 2013), 5.

Selected Bibliography

Anscombe, G.E.M. *The Collected Philosophical Papers of G.E.M. Anscombe*. 3 vols. Oxford: Blackwell, 1981.

Aquinas, Thomas. *Summa Theologiae*. Trans. Fathers of the English Dominican Province. London: R. & T. Washbourne, 1914–1938.

Aristotle. *The Complete Works of Aristotle: The Revised Oxford Translation*, Ed. Jonathan Barnes. Princeton, N.J.: Princeton University Press, 1984.

Augustine. *City of God*. New York: Penguin Books, 1972.

Bacon, Francis. *Novum organum*, Ed. Thomas Fowler. Oxford: Clarendon Press, 1889.

Valerius Terminus: Of the Interpretation of Nature. The University of Adelaide Library, 2003. http://ebooks.adelaide.edu.au/b/bacon/francis/valerius/.

Baggett, David, Gary R. Habermas, and Jerry L. Walls, eds. *C.S. Lewis as Philosopher: Truth, Beauty, and Goodness*. Downers Grover, IL: Intervarsity Press, 2008.

Balfour, Arthur J. *Theism and Humanism: Being the Gifford Lectures Delivered at the University of Glasgow, 1914*. London: Hodder & Stoughton, 1914.

Ballor, Jordan J. "Natural Law and Protestantism: A Review Essay." *Christian Scholar's Review* (2012) 41(2): 193–209.

Barkman, Adam. *C.S. Lewis and Philosophy as a Way of Life*. Allentown, PA: Zossima Press, 2009.

Barth, Karl. *Church Dogmatics*. New York: Charles Scribner's Sons, 1957.

The Epistle to the Romans, 6th ed. Trans. Edwyn C. Hoskyns. Oxford: Oxford University Press, 1963 [1933].

This Christian Cause. New York: Macmillan, 1941.

Becker, Carl. *The Declaration of Independence: A Study in the History of Political Ideas*. New York: Harcourt, Brace, 1922.

Berlin, Isaiah. *Freedom and Its Betrayal*. Ed. Henry Hardy. Princeton, NJ: Princeton University Press, 2002.

Beversluis, John. *C.S. Lewis and the Search for Rational Religion*. Grand Rapids, MI: Eerdmans, 1985.

Brunner, Emil, and Karl Barth. *Natural Theology*. Trans. Peter Fraenkel. Geoffrey Bles: The Centenary Press, 1946. Reprint. Eugene, OR: Wipf and Stock, 2002.

Budziszewski, J. *The Line Through the Heart: Natural Law as Fact, Theory, and Sign of Contradiction*. Wilmington, DE: ISI Books, 2009.

What We Can't Not Know: A Guide. San Francisco, CA: Ignatius Press, 2011.

Bunce, R.E.R. *Thomas Hobbes*. New York: Continuum, 2009.

Burson, Scott, and Jeffrey L. Walls. *C.S. Lewis and Francis Schaeffer: Lessons for a New Century from the Most Influential Apologists of Our Time*. Downers Grove, IL: Intervarsity Press, 1998.

Busch, Eberhard. *Karl Barth: His Life from Letters and Autobiographical Texts*. Trans. John Bowden. Philadelphia: Fortress Press, 1976.

Calvin, John. *Institutes of the Christian Religion*. Trans. Henry Beveridge. Edinburgh: Calvin Translation Society, 1846.

Chesterton, G.K. *What I Saw in America*. New York: Dodd, Mead, 1922.

Corey, David D. "Socratic Citizenship: Delphic Oracle and Divine Sign." *Review of Politics* (2005) 67(2): 201–228.

Covington, Jesse, Bryan McGraw, and Micah Watson, eds. *Natural Law and Evangelical Political Thought*. Lanham, MD: Lexington Books, 2013.

Darwin, Charles. *The Life and Letters of Charles Darwin Including an Autobiographical Chapter*. Ed. Francis Darwin. 2 vols. London: John Murray, 1887.

On the Origin of Species. New York: D. Appleton, 1864.

Dawkins, Richard. *The Blind Watchmaker: Why the Evidence of Evolution Reveals a Universe without Design*. New York: W.W. Norton, 1996 [1986].

Dostoevsky, Fyodor. *Crime and Punishment*. Ed. George Gibian, trans. Jessie Coulson. New York: W.W. Norton, 1964.

Edwards, Bruce L., ed. *C.S. Lewis: Life, Works, and Legacy*, 4 vols. Westport, CT: Praeger, 2007.

Filmer, Robert. *Patriarcha, or The Natural Power of Kings*. London: Richard Chiswell, 1680.

Finnis, John. "C.S. Lewis and Test Tube Babies" (1984). In *Collected Essays: Human Rights and the Common Good*, vol. 3, pp. 273–281. Oxford: Oxford University Press, 2011.

Foster, M.B. "The Christian Doctrine of Creation and the Rise of Modern Natural Science." *Mind* (1934) 43(172): 446–468.

George, Robert P. *Making Men Moral: Civil Liberties and Public Morality*. New York: Oxford University Press, 1993.

Gilson, Étienne. *From Aristotle to Darwin and Back Again: A Journey in Final Causality, Species, and Evolution*. Notre Dame, IN: University of Notre Dame Press, 1984.

Gorringe, Timothy. *Karl Barth: Against Hegemony*. Oxford: Oxford University Press, 1999.

Grabill, Stephen J. *Rediscovering the Natural Law in Reformed Theological Ethics*. Grand Rapids, MI: William B. Eerdmans, 2006.

Green, Clifford, ed. *Karl Barth: Theologian of Freedom*. Minneapolis, MN: Fortress Press, 1991.

Gresham, Douglas. *Jack's Life: The Life Story of C.S. Lewis.* Nashville, TN: B&H Books, 2005.

Griffin, William. *Clive Staples Lewis: A Dramatic Life.* San Francisco, CA: Harper and Roe, 1986.

Hamilton, Clive. *Spirits in Bondage: A Cycle of Lyrics.* London: William Heinemann, 1919.

Hauerwas, Stanley. *War and the American Difference: Theological Reflections on Violence and National Identity.* Grand Rapids, MI: Baker Academic, 2011.

Hegel, G.F.W. *Philosophy of History.* Translated by John Sibree. New York: American Dome Library Co., 1902.

Hobbes, Thomas. *Leviathan,* Ed. Edwin Curley. Indianapolis, Ind.: Hackett, 1994.

Hooker, Richard. *Of the Laws of Ecclesiastical Polity: Preface, Book 1, Book VIII.* Ed. Stephen McGrade. Cambridge: Cambridge University Press, 1989.

Hooper, Walter, ed. *Collected Letters of C.S. Lewis.* 3 vols. New York: HarperCollins, 2004.

ed. *They Stand Together: The Letters of C.S. Lewis to Arthur Greeves, 1914–1963.* New York: Macmillan, 1979.

Hume, David. *A Treatise of Human Nature.* New York: Penguin, 1969 [1739].

Huxley, Julian. *Essays of a Humanist.* London: Chatto & Windus, 1964.

Jacobs, Alan. *The Narnian: The Life and Imagination of C.S. Lewis.* San Francisco, CA: Harper, 2005.

Joeckel, Samuel. *The C.S. Lewis Phenomenon: Christianity and the Public Sphere.* Macon, GA: Mercer University Press, 2013.

Johnson, Paul. *Modern Times: The World from the Twenties to the Eighties.* New York: HarperCollins, 1983.

Kass, Leon. "Looking for an Honest Man: Reflections of an Unlicensed Humanist." 2009 Jefferson Lecture for the National Endowment for the Humanities. www.neh.gov/about/awards/jefferson-lecture/leon-kass-lecture.

Kilby, Clyde, and Marjorie Lamp Mead, eds. *Brothers and Friends: The Diaries of Major Warren Hamilton Lewis.* New York: Ballantine Books, 1988.

King, Alex, and Martin Ketley. *The Control of Language.* London: Longmans, Green, 1939.

Kreeft, Peter. *C.S. Lewis: A Critical Essay.* Grand Rapids, MI: Eerdmans, 1969.

Lewis, C.S. *A Preface to Paradise Lost.* Oxford: Oxford University Press, 1961.

"A Reply to Professor Haldane" (1946). In *Of Other Worlds: Essays and Stories.* Orlando, FL: Harcourt, 1994 [1966]. Pp. 74–85.

The Abolition of Man. New York: HarperCollins, 2001 [1944].

All My Road before Me: The Diary of C.S. Lewis 1922–27, Ed. Walter Hooper. San Diego, Calif.: Harcourt Brace Jovanovich, 1991.

"Bulverism." *The Socratic Digest* (1944) 2: 16–20. Reprinted in Walter Hooper, ed., *God in the Dock.* Grand Rapids, MI: Wm. B. Eerdmans, 1970. Pp. 271–277.

"Capital Punishment and Death Penalty." *Church Times* (December 1, 1961) 44: 7. Reprinted in Walter Hooper, ed., *God in the Dock.* Grand Rapids, MI: Wm. B. Eerdmans, 1970. Pp. 339–340.

"Christian Hope – Its Meaning for Today." *Religion in Life* (Winter 1952). In C.S. Lewis, *The World's Last Night and Other Essays*. San Diego, CA: Harcourt Brace, 1987 [1960]. Pp. 93–113.

"Christianity and Culture." *Theology* (March 1940) 40: 166–179; "Christianity and Culture" (a letter). *Theology* (June 1940) 40: 475–477; "Peace Proposals for Brother Every and Mr. Bethell." *Theology* (December 1940) 41. Reprinted together as "Christianity and Culture." In Walter Hooper, ed., *The Seeing Eye: And Other Selected Essays from Christian Reflections*. New York: Ballantine Books, 1967. Pp. 15–48.

De Descriptione Temporum: An Inaugural Lecture. London: Cambridge University Press, 1955.

"De Futilitate." Address at Magdalen College during World War II. N.d. In Walter Hooper, ed., *The Seeing Eye: And Other Selected Essays from Christian Reflections*. New York: Ballantine Books, 1967. Pp. 77–98.

"Delinquents in the Snow." *Time and Tide* (December 7, 1957) 38: 1521–1522. Reprinted in Walter Hooper, ed., *God in the Dock*. Grand Rapids, MI: Wm. B. Eerdmans, 1970. Pp. 306–310.

"Democratic Education." *Time and Tide* (April 29, 1944) 24: 369–370. Reprinted in Walter Hooper, ed., *Present Concerns: A Compelling Collection of Timely, Journalistic Essays*. Orlando, FL: Harcourt, 1986. Pp. 32–35.

"Difficulties in Presenting the Christian Faith to Modern Unbelievers." *Lumen Vitae* (September 1948) 3: 421–426. Reprinted in Walter Hooper, ed., *God in the Dock*. Grand Rapids, MI: Wm. B. Eerdmans, 1970. Pp. 240–44.

English Literature in the Sixteenth Century Excluding Drama. Oxford: Oxford University Press, 1954.

"Equality." *The Spectator* (August 27, 1943) 171. Reprinted in Walter Hooper, ed., *Present Concerns: A Compelling Collection of Timely, Journalistic Essays*. Orlando, FL: Harcourt, 1986. Pp. 17–20.

The Four Loves. Orlando, FL: Harcourt, 1988 [1960].

"Funeral of a Great Myth." N.d. In Walter Hooper, ed., *The Seeing Eye: And Other Selected Essays from Christian Reflections*. New York: Ballantine Books, 1967. Pp. 113–130.

"Historicism." *The Month* (October 1950) 4. Reprinted in Walter Hooper, ed., *The Seeing Eye: And Other Selected Essays from Christian Reflections*. New York: Ballantine Books, 1967. Pp. 131–150.

"The Humanitarian Theory of Punishment." *20th Century: An Australian Quarterly Review* (1949) 3(3): 5–12. Reprinted in Walter Hooper, ed., *God in the Dock*. Grand Rapids, MI: Wm. B. Eerdmans, 1970. Pp. 287–300.

"I Was Decided Upon." *Decision* (September 1963) 2: 3; and "Heaven, Earth and Outer Space." *Decision* (October 1963) 2: 4; Interview with Sherwood E. Wirt of the Billy Graham Association. Reprinted together as "Cross-Examination." In Walter Hooper, ed., *God in the Dock*. Grand Rapids, MI: Wm. B. Eerdmans, 1970. Pp. 258–267.

"Is Theology Poetry?" *The Socratic Digest* (1945) 3. Reprinted in Walter Hooper, ed., *The Weight of Glory: And Other Addresses*. New York: HarperCollins, 2001 [1949]. Pp. 116–140.

The Latin Letters of C.S. Lewis. Trans. and ed. Martin Moynihan. South Bend, IN: St. Augustine's Press, 1998.

The Lion, the Witch and the Wardrobe. New York: HarperCollins, 2003 [1950].

The Magician's Nephew. New York: HarperCollins, 2007 [1955].

"Meditation on the Third Commandment." *The Guardian* (January 10, 1941): 18. Reprinted in Walter Hooper, ed., *God in the Dock.* Grand Rapids, MI: Wm. B. Eerdmans, 1970. Pp. 196–199.

"Membership." *Sobornost* (June 1945) 31. Reprinted in Walter Hooper, ed., *The Weight of Glory: And Other Addresses.* New York: HarperCollins, 2001 [1949]. Pp. 158–176.

Mere Christianity. New York: HarperCollins, 2009 [1952].

Miracles: A Preliminary Study, rev. ed. New York: HarperCollins, 1996 [1947].

"Modern Man and His Categories of Thought." October 1946. In Walter Hooper, ed., *Present Concerns: A Compelling Collection of Timely, Journalistic Essays.* Orlando, FL: Harcourt, 1986. Pp. 63–64.

"On Ethics." N.d. In Walter Hooper, ed., *The Seeing Eye: And Other Selected Essays from Christian Reflections.* New York: Ballantine Books, 1967. Pp. 59–76.

"On Living in an Atomic Age." *Informed Reading* (1948) 6: 78–84. Reprinted in Walter Hooper, ed., *Present Concerns: A Compelling Collection of Timely, Journalistic Essays.* Orlando, FL: Harcourt, 1986. Pp. 73–80.

Out of the Silent Planet. New York: Scribner, 2003 [1938].

Perelandra. New York: Scribner, 2003 [1944].

"The Poison of Subjectivism." *Religion in Life* (Summer 1943) 12. Reprinted in Walter Hooper, ed., *The Seeing Eye: And Other Selected Essays from Christian Reflections.* New York: Ballantine Books, 1967. Pp. 99–112.

Preface to B.G. Sandhurst. *How Heathen Is Britain?* Collins Publishers, 1946. Reprinted as "On the Transmission of Christianity" in Walter Hooper, ed., *God in the Dock.* Grand Rapids, MI: Wm. B. Eerdmans, 1970. Pp. 114–119.

Preface to St. Athanasius. *The Incarnation of the Word of God.* Geoffrey Bles, 1944. Reprinted as "On the Reading of Old Books" in Walter Hooper, ed., *God in the Dock.* Grand Rapids, MI: Wm. B. Eerdmans, 1970. Pp. 200–207.

Present Concerns. San Diego, CA: Harcourt Brace Jovanovich, 1986.

The Problem of Pain. New York: HarperCollins, 2009 [1940].

The Screwtape Letters. New York: Macmillan, 1961.

"Screwtape Proposes a Toast." *Saturday Evening Post* (December 19, 1959): 36 and 86–89.

"Sometimes Fairy Stories May Say Best What's to Be Said." *New York Times Book Review* (November 18, 1956). Reprinted in Walter Hooper, ed., *Other Stories and Other Essays on Literature.* New York: Harcourt Brace Jovanovich, 1982.

Studies in Medieval and Renaissance Literature. Cambridge: Cambridge University Press, 1966.

Surprised by Joy: The Shape of My Early Life. London: Harcourt, 1955.

That Hideous Strength: A Modern Fairy-tale for Grown Ups. New York: Scribner, 2003 [1945].

Voyage of the Dawn Treader. New York: HarperCollins, 2008 [1952].

"We Have No Right to Happiness." *Saturday Evening Post* (December 21–28, 1963) 236: 10, 12. Reprinted in Walter Hooper, ed., *God in the Dock*. Grand Rapids, MI: Wm. B. Eerdmans, 1970. Pp. 317–22.

"The Weight of Glory." *Theology* (November 1941) 43. Reprinted in Walter Hooper, ed., *The Weight of Glory: And Other Addresses*. New York: HarperCollins, 2001 [1949], 25–46.

"Why I Am Not a Pacifist." Address at the Oxford Pacifist Society in 1940. In Walter Hooper, ed., *The Weight of Glory: And Other Addresses*. New York: HarperCollins, 2001 [1949]. Pp. 64–90.

"Willing Slaves of the Welfare State." *The Observer* (July 20, 1958): 6. Reprinted as "Is Progress Possible?" in Walter Hooper, ed., *God in the Dock*. Grand Rapids, MI: Wm. B. Eerdmans, 1970. Pp. 311–316.

Lewis, C.S., and E.M.W. Tillyard. *The Personal Heresy: A Criticism*. Oxford: Oxford University Press. 1939.

Lewis, Warren, ed. *Letters of C.S. Lewis*, rev. ed. Orlando, FL: Harcourt, 2003.

——— ed. *The Lewis Papers: Memories of the Lewis Family, 1850–1930*. Unpublished papers of the Lewis family. Wheaton, IL: The Marion E. Wade Center.

Lindskoog, Kathryn. *Surprised by C.S. Lewis, George MacDonald, and Dante: An Array of Original Discoveries*. Macon, GA: Mercer University Press, 2001.

Locke, John. *A Letter Concerning Toleration*. Ed. Mark Goldie. Indianapolis, IN: Liberty Fund, 2010 [1689].

——— "The Reasonableness of Christianity." In *The Works of John Locke in Nine Volumes*, 12th ed. London: Rivington, 1824.

——— *Two Treatises of Government*. Cambridge: Cambridge University Press, 1988 [1689].

MacDonald, George. *George MacDonald: An Anthology*. Ed. C.S. Lewis. New York: Macmillan, 1947.

Machiavelli, Niccolò. *The Prince*. Trans. Harvey C. Mansfield. Chicago, Ill.: University of Chicago Press, 1988.

MacIntyre, Alisdair. *After Virtue: A Study in Moral Theory*, 3rd ed. Notre Dame, IN: University of Notre Dame Press, 2007 [1981].

——— *Whose Justice? Which Rationality?* Notre Dame, IN: University of Notre Dame Press, 1988.

MacSwain, Robert, and Michael Ward, eds. *The Cambridge Companion to C.S. Lewis*. Cambridge: Cambridge University Press, 2010.

Maritain, Jacques. *Scholasticism and Politics*. Trans. Mortimer Adler. New York: Macmillan, 1940.

Martinich, A.P. *The Two Gods of Leviathan: Thomas Hobbes on Religion and Politics*. Cambridge: Cambridge University Press, 2003.

Mayhew, Robert, ed. *Ayn Rand's Marginalia: Her Critical Comments on the Writings of over 20 Authors*. New Milford, CT: Second Renaissance Press, 1995.

McGrath, Alister. *C.S. Lewis – A Life: Eccentric Genius, Reluctant Prophet*. Carol Stream, IL: Tyndale House, 2013.

——— *The Intellectual World of C.S. Lewis*. Oxford: Wiley-Blackwell, 2013.

McGraw, Bryan T. *Faith in Politics: Religion and Liberal Democracy*. New York: Cambridge University Press, 2010.

McNeil, John T. "Natural Law in the Teaching of the Reformers." *Journal of Religion* (1946) 26(3): 168–182.

Meilander, Gilbert. *The Taste for the Other: The Social and Ethical Thought of C.S. Lewis*. Grand Rapids, MI: Wm. B. Eerdmans, 1978.

Mill, John Stuart. *On Liberty and the Subjection of Women*. Ed. Alan Ryan. New York: Penguin Classics, 2006 [1859].

Milton, Philip. "Hobbes, Heresy and Lord Arlington." *History of Political Thought* (1993) 14: 501–546.

Mintz, Samuel I. *The Hunting of Leviathan: Seventeenth-Century Reactions to the Materialism and Moral Philosophy of Thomas Hobbes*. Cambridge: Cambridge University Press, 1962.

Montaigne, Michel de. *The Complete Works of Michel de Montaigne, Comprising His Essays, Letters, Etc*. New York: Worthington, 1888.

Moseley, Carys. *Nations and Nationalism in the Theology of Karl Barth*. Oxford: Oxford University Press, 2013.

Moser, Paul K., and Paul Copan, eds. *The Rationality of Theism*. London: Routledge, 2003.

Nagel, Thomas. *The Last Word*. New York: Oxford University Press, 1997.

Mind and Cosmos: Why the Materialist Neo-Darwinian Conception of Nature Is Almost Certainly False. New York: Oxford University Press, 2012.

Ogden, C.K., and I.A. Richards. *The Meaning of Meaning: A Study of the Influence of Language upon Thought and the Science of Symbolism*, 3rd ed. New York: Harcourt, Brace, 1930 [1922].

Pangle, Thomas. *Political Philosophy and the God of Abraham*. Baltimore, MD: Johns Hopkins University Press, 2003.

Plantinga, Alvin. *Warrant and Proper Function*. New York: Oxford University Press, 1993.

Where the Conflict Really Lies: Science, Religion, and Naturalism. New York: Oxford University Press, 2011.

Plato. *Complete Works*. Ed. John M. Cooper. Indianapolis, Ind.: Hackett, 1997.

Ratzinger, Cardinal Joseph. "Consumer Materialism and Christian Hope." In *Teachers of the Faith: Speeches and Lectures by Catholic Bishops*. London: Catholic Bishops' Conference of England and Wales, 2002.

Rawls, John. *Collected Papers*. Ed. Samuel Freeman. Cambridge, MA: Harvard University Press, 1999.

Justice as Fairness: A Restatement. Cambridge, MA: Harvard University Press, 2001.

Political Liberalism. New York: Columbia University Press, 1993.

Reppert, Victor. *C.S. Lewis' Dangerous Idea: In Defense of the Argument from Reason*. Downers Grove, IL: IVP Academic, 2003.

Rousseau, Jean-Jacques. *The First and Second Discourses*. Ed. Roger D. Masters, trans. Roger D. Masters and Judith R. Masters. Boston: St. Martin's Press, 1964.

The Social Contract and Other Later Political Writings. Ed. Victor Gourevitch. Cambridge: Cambridge University Press, 2003.

Sandoz, Ellis. *A Government of Laws: Political Theory, Religion, and the American Founding*. Baton Rouge: Louisiana State University Press, 1990.

Sayer, George. *Jack: A Life of C.S. Lewis*. Wheaton, IL: Crossway, 2005.

Schultz, Jeffrey D., and John G. West Jr., eds. *The C.S. Lewis Readers' Encyclopedia*. Grand Rapids, MI: Zondervan Publishing House, 1998.

Shields, Jon A. *The Democratic Virtues of the Christian Right*. Princeton, NJ: Princeton University Press, 2009.

Smith, Nicholas D., and Paul D. Woodruff, eds. *Reason and Religion in Socratic Philosophy*. New York: Oxford University Press, 2000.

Strauss, Leo. *Thoughts on Machiavelli*. Chicago, IL: University of Chicago Press, 1978 [1958].

    What Is Political Philosophy? And Other Stories. Chicago, IL: University of Chicago Press, 1988 [1959].

Strauss, Leo, and Joseph Cropsey, eds. *History of Political Philosophy*, 2nd ed. Chicago, IL: University of Chicago Press, 1972.

Tadie, Andrew A., and Michael H. Macdonald, eds. *Permanent Things: Toward the Recovery of a More Human Scale toward the End of the Twentieth Century*. Grand Rapids, MI: Wm. B. Eerdmans, 1996.

von Balthasar, Hans Urs. *The Theology of Karl Barth*. Trans. John Drury. New York: Holt, Rinehart and Winston, 1971.

Waldron, Jeremy. *God, Locke, and Equality: Christian Foundations in Locke's Political Thought*. Cambridge: Cambridge University Press, 2002.

Walsh, Chad. *C.S. Lewis: Apostle to the Skeptics*. New York: Macmillan, 1949.

Webster, John. *Barth's Ethics of Reconciliation*. Cambridge: Cambridge University Press, 1995.

West, John G., ed. *The Magician's Twin: C.S. Lewis on Science, Scientism, and Society*. Seattle: WA: Discovery Institute Press, 2012.

Wilson, A.N. *C.S. Lewis: A Biography*. New York: W.W. Norton, 1990.

Index

CPSIA information can be obtained
at www.ICGtesting.com
Printed in the USA
LVHW010252020222
709936LV00003B/250

9 781107 518971